THE HASMONEANS AND THEIR SUPPORTERS
From Mattathias to the Death of John Hyrcanus I

SOUTH FLORIDA STUDIES IN THE HISTORY OF JUDAISM

Edited by
Jacob Neusner
Ernest S. Frerichs, William Scott Green, James Strange

Number 06
The Hasmoneans and their Supporters
From Mattathias to the Death of John Hyrcanus I

by
Joseph Sievers

THE HASMONEANS AND THEIR SUPPORTERS
From Mattathias to the Death of John Hyrcanus I

by

Joseph Sievers

Scholars Press
Atlanta, Georgia

THE HASMONEANS AND THEIR SUPPORTERS
From Mattathias to the Death of John Hyrcanus I

©1990
Joseph Sievers

Publication of this book was made possible by a grant from the Tisch Family Foundation, New York City. The University of South Florida acknowledges with thanks this important support for its scholarly projects.

Library of Congress Cataloging in Publication Data

Sievers Joseph, 1932-
    The Hasmoneans and their supporters : from Mattathias to the death
    of John Hyrcanus I / by Joseph Sievers.
    p. cm. -- (South Florida Studies in the History of Judaism ; no. 06)
    Includes bibliographical references.
    ISBN 1-55540-449-9 (alk. paper)
    1. Maccabees. 2. Jews--History--168 B.C.-135 A.D. I. Title.
II. Series.
DS121.7.S54 1990
933'.04--dc20   90-8194
                                                      CIP

Printed in the United States of America
on acid-free paper

To the memory of
Elias J. Bickerman (1897-1981)
and
Menahem Stern (1925-1989)

Table of Contents

Preface

One of the results of recent research on the Dead Sea Scrolls and on related documents has been a better appreciation of the vitality and variety of the expressions of Judaism in the second and first centuries. Not only has the image of the Essenes been more clearly defined, but, as a consequence, we have been brought to pay closer attention to the great variety of social, religious, and political groups to be reckoned with in Judea in this period.

This study attempts to trace the development of one recognizable group, the Hasmoneans. From small beginnings in Modein they gradually reached a powerful position in Jerusalem as high priests and leaders of an independent nation. I use the term "Hasmonean" in the sense in which Josephus and the Mishnah already used it, to identify not only the descendants of Simon, but members of the family of Mattathias and their followers in general.

In works about the Hasmonean period many scholars, including Schürer, Abel, and Goldstein, refer to a Maccabean or Hasmonean party. Although Aptowitzer has attempted to define the ideas and positions of this party in his *Parteipolitik der Hasmonäerzeit im rabbinischen und pseudoepigraphischen Schrifttum* (Vienna 1927), his work is so conjectural that few firm conclusions can be drawn from its findings. I have generally avoided the term "party" in reference to the Hasmoneans and their supporters because it is easily misunderstood as referring to a clearly definable political body. We are able to discover sources of support for and of opposition to the Hasmoneans and we are able to trace lines of continuity in outlook and constituencies, but there was of course no political organization that could be called the Hasmonean Party.

Therefore, I have set out to identify the various sources and kinds of support and to define as clearly as possible the different types of relations between, on the one hand, the Hasmonean clan and, on the other hand, *Asidaioi*, Pharisees, peasants, priests, soldiers, groups of Gentiles, etc. Where possible, I have also sought to identify the ideas and goals shared by the Hasmoneans and their supporters. Due to the nature and limitations of our source material, this study must be based to a large extent on inferences from the available data. As in all historical investigations, our conclusions provide at best probabilities, never absolute certainties. Within these limitations, the present study wishes to contribute to a more accurate understanding of the complex political, religious, and social situation in second-century Judea.

The initial results of this investigation were accepted by Columbia University in 1981 as my doctoral dissertation. Since that time, I have had an opportunity to update and extensively revise my earlier work. The literature on Hasmonean history and its various aspects is immense. Therefore I have tried to cite the primary sources as completely as possible and of the secondary literature as much as I found important or useful. In the footnotes I generally follow the style of the *Journal of Biblical Literature* (107 [1988] 583-596), except that for technical reasons I had to use a simplified form of transliteration for Hebrew titles. Unfortunately, Daniel Harrington's *The Maccabean Revolt: Anatomy of a Biblical Revolution* (Wilmington, DE: Glazier, 1988) arrived too late for me to include in this study.

My thanks go to the *Studienstiftung des deutschen Volkes* (Foundation for Higher Learning of West Germany), which supported me, financially and otherwise, from the beginning of my studies in Vienna to the early stages of this project. I would also like to thank Columbia University for granting me a President's Fellowship and a B.Z. Goldberg Felowship.

In the course of my work, I have had the good fortune to be able to avail myself of some of the best libraries in the field: at Columbia University, The Jewish Theological Seminary of America, and Union Theological Seminary in New York City, at the Hebrew University and the École Biblique in Jerusalem, and at the Pontifical Biblical Institute in Rome. To these institutions and to their dedicated staff I wish to express my sincere gratitude. I also wish to thank Professor Neusner for the unexpected offer to publish my work.

Only with the help and encouragement of more than a score of people has this study reached its completion. I wish to thank each one of them, although it is not possible to name them here individually. However, there is one person I must thank in a particular way, Professor Morton Smith. As dissertation adviser and as a friendly critic of the current revised edition, he has enhanced virtually every page of this study. Any remaining deficiencies are of course solely my own responsibility.

Rome, 25 Kislev 5749
4 December, 1988

Introduction

The Sources

First Maccabees

Our most important source for the early history of the Hasmonean family is 1 Macc. It gives a fairly detailed and generally well-informed account of the events leading to the revolt and the Jewish side of the political and military developments from the Hellenistic reforms in Jerusalem to John Hyrcanus' accession to power. Originally it was written in Hebrew, and Jerome found it in that language.[1]

The Hebrew *Vorlage* is recognizable in many places where the Greek is faulty and the text can best be understood by retroversion into Hebrew. Only Greek, Latin, Syriac, and other translations have come down to us.

The unity of 1 Macc has been questioned by a number of scholars,[2] mainly because Josephus in his *Antiquities* did not paraphrase the last three chapters of 1 Macc. But the questions have been answered by Ettelson and Schunck, and thanks to their defense the unity of 1 Macc is now almost universally accepted.[3] However, the work betrays the use of written source material which includes: (a) documents, primarily on foreign relations of the Hasmoneans, probably accessible to the author

---

[1]Jerome, Prologus galeatus, *PL* 28, col. 602-603. Origen gave a Greek transcription of a Hebrew or Aramaic title of the work; Eusebius, *Hist. Eccl.* 6. 25.1. See Abel, *Macc.* pp. IV-V; J.A. Goldstein, "The Hasmoneans: The Dynasty of God's Resisters," *HTR* 68 (1975) 53-58.

[2]Listed by K.D. Schunck, *Die Quellen des I. und II. Makkabäerbuches* (Halle: Niemeyer, 1954), p. 7.

[3]H.W. Ettelson, "The Integrity of I Maccabees," *Transactions of the Connecticut Academy of Arts and Sciences* 27 (1925) 249-384; Schunck, *Quellen*, pp.8-15. See however N. Martola, *Capture and Liberation. A Study in the Composition of the First Book of Maccabees* (Acta Academiae Aboensis, Sec. A, Vol. 63 Nr. 1. Abo: Akademi, 1984). Martola claims a separate author for 1 Macc 8.

in the Jerusalem archives;[4] (b) a Seleucid source from which the author took his information about Seleucid history and his dates according to the Seleucid Macedonian (= Sel. Mac.) era beginning in the autumn of 312 BCE;[5] (c) documents embodying Jewish traditions, derived in large part from sources close to the Hasmonean family and using a Seleucid era similar to or identical with the one used in Babylon, beginning in the spring of 311 BCE (= Sel. Bab.).[6] These source materials, plus traditions preserved orally, were put together by a writer who gave the work - except for the archival documents - a uniform style and a certain cohesiveness.

On the basis of several statements in 1 Macc (especially 5:62; 14:4-15), it has been recognized since Geiger that its author expressed the viewpoint of the Hasmonean dynasty.[7] This is one of the few points on which there is hardly any disagreement among scholars. However, it has often been thought that the author also had to represent the viewpoint of one of the religious sects. Because of the lack of evidence for a belief in an afterlife and because of a certain emphasis on priestly concerns, many scholars have considered 1 Macc the work of a

---

[4]Cf. 1 Macc 14:49; see Bickerman, *Gott* p. 174; Abel, *Macc.* p. XXVII; Schunck, *Quellen* p. 32.

[5]Schunck, *Quellen*, p. 43.

[6]Schunck, *Quellen*, pp. 52-80; Goldstein, *1 Macc.*, pp. 38-48, 100-102. Both Schunck and Goldstein go beyond what is ascertainable in their attempts to pinpoint a variety of extant and hypothetical documents as sources. Goldstein has substantially modified his source analysis in his *2 Macc.*, but even his new version is so hypothetical that it cannot be used. Schunck is almost certainly wrong in insisting that in 1 Macc besides the autumn era of 312 BCE a spring era of the same year was used (*Quellen*, pp. 19-31 and *1. Makkabäerbuch* [JSHRZ 1/4; Gütersloh: Mohn, 1979] p. 291). A spring era of 311 BCE as in Babylon is much more likely and has been advocated, especially on the basis of 1 Macc 10:1, 21 by Bickerman, *Gott*, p. 155; J. Schaumberger, "Die neue Seleukiden-Liste BM 35603 und die makkabäische Chronologie," *Biblica* 36 (1955) 426-427; Goldstein, *1 Macc* , pp. 540-541. K. Bringmann [*Hellenistische Reform und Religionsverfolgung in Judäa. Eine Untersuchung zur jüdisch-hellenistischen Geschichte (175 - 163 v. Chr.)*, Abhandlungen der Akademie der Wissenschaften in Göttingen. Philologisch-historische Klasse, 3. Folge (Göttingen: Vandenhoeck & Ruprecht, 1983) pp. 15-28] claims that all dates in 1 Macc are based on the Seleucid Macedonian autumn era. His detailed argument is flawed, e.g. by his unprovable and probably false assumption that the Seleucid calendar year used in Jerusalem in the second century B.C. began neither in the month of Nisan nor even in the month of Tishri, but in Marheshvan. Concerning the problems of his chronological conclusions see the reviews by van der Woude in *JSJ* 15 (1984) 168 and Schunck in *TLZ* 111 (1986) 100-102.

[7]A. Geiger, *Urschrift und Übersetzungen der Bibel* (2d ed.; Frankfurt/Main: Madda, 1928) p. 206.

Sadducee.[8] Momigliano instead suggested that 1 Macc was written by one of the *Asidaioi*,[9] but he fails to account for the fact that no reconciliation between Hasmoneans and *Asidaioi* is reported after they parted company over the question of Alcimus' high priesthood (1 Macc 7:10-18). Even less convincing is Schunck's hypothesis that the author was a Pharisee, because of the emphasis on "zeal for the law" (1 Macc 2:26).[10] Bickerman rightly pointed out that 1 Macc represents not Pharisaic or Sadducean doctrine, but puts forward primarily the case of the Hasmonean family.[11] This thesis has further been strengthened by Goldstein who sees in 1 Macc above all a defense of Hasmonean dynastic claims.[12]

First Maccabees was composed between the latter years of John Hyrcanus (died 104 BCE), whose accomplishments are summarized in 1 Macc 16:23-24, and Pompey's conquest of Jerusalem in 63 B.C.E., after which a description of Roman conquests could hardly have been as favorable as that in 1 Macc 8.

A date before 120 BCE seems excluded because it is considered worth mentioning that the monument erected in Modein by Simon between 142 and 134 "remains to this day" (1 Macc 13:30). But there are no signs of the decline of the Hasmonean dynasty, and it is unlikely that at the time of composition there was, or had been, a Hasmonean king.[13] Therefore, a date late in the reign of Hyrcanus is most plausible, although a time when Aristobulus and Alexander Jannaeus were not considered kings is also possible.

First Maccabees has generally been viewed as trustworthy for the most part, although some of the documents, especially the correspondence between the Spartans and the Jews, may be unauthentic.[14] But everywhere we must try to detect the biases of the author and his sources which at times color the description and interpretation of events. Furthermore, rather than relying on 1 Macc

---

[8]So Geiger, *ibid.*, pp. 215-218; J. Le Moyne, *Les Sadducéens* (Paris: Gabalda, 1972) p. 75 (cites earlier proponents); T. Fischer, *Seleukiden und Makkabäer* (Bochum: Brockmeyer, 1980), p. 56.

[9]A. Momigliano, *Prime linee di storia della tradizione maccabaica* (Torino, 1931; reprinted Amsterdam: Hakkert, 1968), pp. 14-19.

[10]Schunck, *Quellen*, p. 80.

[11]*Gott*, pp. 29, 31, 145.

[12]*1 Macc.*, p. 77.

[13]Cf. 1 Macc 8:14 "not one of them (of the Romans) had put on a diadem or purple." The author represents this as a sign of virtue.

[14]Abel, *Macc.*, pp. 231-233; B. Cardauns, "Juden und Spartaner," *Hermes* 95 (1967) 317-324. The authenticity of the correspondence is defended by Goldstein, *1 Macc.*, pp. 447-452.

alone, we must consider the conflicting reports in 2 Macc and Josephus as well, because at times they use sources independent of 1 Macc.

Second Maccabees

Second Maccabees is a composite work consisting of a condensed version of Jason of Cyrene's five-volume history (see 2 Macc 2:23), with revisions and alterations, and prefaced by two letters (1:1-10a = Ep.1; 1:10b-2:18 = Ep. 2). It is our most important source for the pre-history of the Hasmonean revolt from the time of the high priest Onias III onward, and it describes events down to shortly before Judah Maccabee's death.

Jason's work was compressed into a one-volume *epitome* by an abridger (2:23) who claims to have followed the main lines of the original composition without doing any independent research of his own (2:28-31). To him we must attribute at least the introduction (2:19-32) and probably the conclusion (15:37-39).

Nothing can be learned about Jason of Cyrene from other sources. It is unlikely that he wrote after 63 BCE because the epitome of his work shows a favorable attitude toward Rome (2 Macc 4:11; 11:34) and asserts that from Judah's victory over Nicanor on, Jerusalem remained in Jewish hands.[15]

---

[15]15:37. This last statement is generally attributed to the abridger. It is hardly possible after Pompey's conquest of Jerusalem, but it seems to ignore also Bacchides' entry of Jerusalem (1 Macc 9:50-53) and the existence of a Seleucid garrison in the *Akra* (1 Macc 13:50-51) until 141 BCE, to say nothing of the entry of the city and destruction of its walls by Antiochus VII. Momigliano considered the statement untrue, tendentious, and meant only to justify the conclusion of the book at this particular point (*Prime linee*, pp. 99-100). Abel emphasized the religious concerns of the author: "La ville sainte considérée sous son aspect religieux pouvait être dite aux mains des Hébreux" (*Macc.*, p. 480).

These authors neglect the fact that the government of Judea (the *Akra* excluded?) was entrusted to Jews by Bacchides (1 Macc 9:25; see Goldstein, *1 Macc.* p. 376). Moreover, Jerusalem had been controlled by Jews before Nicanor's defeat, too, although Nicanor had easy access to it (1 Macc 7:27; 2 Macc 14:23), as did Bacchides later (1 Macc 9:50-53). The difference between the situations before and after Nicanor's death was not a legal but a practical one. Nicanor presented the last immediate threat to the Temple and its priesthood. The abridger here might seem to identify the fate of the Temple with that of Jerusalem itself, but more likely he was ignorant, or particularly anxious to strengthen the Jews' case for holding both city and Temple. Thus we come close to Abel's solution, though we must bear in mind that the Temple was a political as well as a religious center.

Many scholars consider Jason a contemporary or near contemporary of the events he described.[16] Their argument rests mainly on the way Eupolemus is introduced in 2 Macc 4:11. Undoubtedly the reader was expected to be acquainted with him. The closeness to the events would explain the often detailed information we receive even through the medium of the *epitome*.[17] Most of these scholars suppose that except for the documents in 2 Macc 11, Jason relied on his own knowledge or on oral traditions. However, a major stumbling block to this theory is the unexplained closeness between 1 Macc and 2 Macc. There is no evidence sufficient to show that 1 Macc relied on Jason's work,[18] or vice versa.[19] Yet the parallels between 1 Macc and 2 Macc cannot be explained by common subject matter and oral traditions. The two books share elements of common outline, have the same gap of silence between Lysias' capture of Antioch and Demetrius' takeover (1 Macc 6:63-7:1/ 2 Macc 13:26-14:1), speak of the *Asidaioi* on the same occasion (1 Macc 7:13/2 Macc 14:6), have the same reference to 2 Kgs 19:35 in Judah's prayer (1 Macc 7:41/2 Macc 15:22), and agree in many other details.

From these findings as well as from internal evidence of different layers in 2 Macc several writers have concluded that 1 and 2 Macc have some written source(s) in common.[20] Schunck and Bunge tried to prove the existence of a "Judasvita," possibly written by the above-mentioned Eupolemus, the historian, soon after the events.[21] Habicht admits the possibility that 2 Macc used a written source, perhaps the Jewish

---

[16]B. Niese, *Kritik der beiden Makkabäerbucher* (Berlin: Weidmann, 1900), p. 37; Schürer-Vermes-Millar 3, p. 532; Abel, *Macc.*, p. XLIII; Tcherikover, *Hellenistic Civ.*, pp. 385-386 (with detailed argument); Hengel, *Judaism and Hellenism* 1, p. 97; M. Zambelli, "La composizione del secondo libro dei Maccabei e la nuova cronologia di Antioco Epifane," *Miscellanea greca e romana* (Studi...Istituto Italiano per la storia antica, 16; Rome, 1965), p. 196; Habicht, 2 *Macc.*, p. 175.

[17]See 10:19-20; 13:24; 14:17 and Habicht, 2 *Macc.*, p. 178.

[18]A. Schlatter, "Jason von Kyrene," (1891), pp. 2, 43 (cited by Schunck, *Quellen*, p. 116). W. Kolbe, *Beiträge zur syrischen u. jüdischen Geschichte* (Stuttgart, 1926), p. 148; Niese, *Kritik*, p. 94. Most recent refutation of this view by Goldstein, *1 Macc.*, pp. 78-89.

[19]A. Geiger, *Urschrift*, p. 228; Goldstein, *1 Macc.*, pp. 80-89. Their assertion that 2 Macc is intended to refute 1 Macc finds no support in the evidence cited.

[20]J. Wellhausen, "Über den geschichtlichen Wert des zweiten Makkabäerbuches im Verhältnis zum ersten," *Nachrichten von der Gesellschaft der Wissenschaften zu Göttingen, Phil.-hist. Klasse* (1905), p. 158; Bickerman, *PW* 14.787; Momigliano, *Prime linee*, p. 113; Meyer, *Ursprung*, p. 458.

[21]Schunck, *Quellen*, pp. 74, 116-126; Bunge, *Untersuchungen* pp. 206-263.

History of Eupolemus.[22] Goldstein made two more elaborate, but less persuasive, attempts to distinguish in Jason's work several major sources and scattered borrowings from other authors.[23]

At present, it seems altogether too hypothetical to try to dissect sources in detail as Bunge and Goldstein have done.[24] Similarly hazardous are attempts to date Jason's work closely. If we consider the digest of earlier sources about the period between 175 and 161 BCE, and the favorable attitude toward Judah, we may date Jason's history between c. 155 and c. 106 BCE.

The date of the epitome has been linked by many writers to that of Ep. 1 (124 BCE),[25] since similar expressions are found in 2 Macc 1:7-9 and 10:3-6 to describe the celebration in the rededicated Temple. However, the author of 10:3-6 (Jason?) may have known the letter quoted in 2 Macc 1:7-8 (written in 143/2 BCE). He evidently knew of the connection between the (belated) celebration of Sukkot and the rededication of the Temple (2 Macc 1:9; 10:6; cf. 1:18). This, however, does not necessitate a direct connection between the epitome and Ep. 1. Furthermore, since Ep. 1 is based on a Hebrew or Aramaic original,[26] it is unlikely that it was composed in conjunction with a history written in Greek. Thus the relationship between Ep. 1 and the epitome remains doubtful.

The setting of the second letter (2 Macc 1:10b-2:18 = Ep. 2) just before the purification of the Temple must be considered fictional despite recent attempts to defend its authenticity.[27] Although its date is

---

[22]*2 Macc.*, pp. 177-178.

[23]Goldstein considers a work by Onias IV, written between April or May 131 and 129 BCE, to be the main source for the Tobiad romance (*Ant.* 12.154-236) and for 2 Macc 3-4. See "Tales of the Tobiads," *Christianity, Judaism and Other Greco-Roman Cults: Studies for Morton Smith at Sixty* (ed. J. Neusner; Leiden: Brill, 1975) 3.85-123; id., *2 Macc.*, pp. 35-37. While 2 Macc 3-4 may be derived from Oniad family traditions, a single reference to the Tobiad Hyrcanus (3:11) does not prove that the Tobiad romance comes to us through the same source. To the contrary, the Tobiad romance is discreditable to Onias II (*Ant.* 12. 158-167) and therefore not propaganda for the Oniads. Thus, Goldstein's hypothesis concerning authorship, date, and purpose of what he calls the work of Onias IV is not supported by the evidence. Also the fact that he speaks confidently about Jason's thought, while assigning to Jason only a few verses in all of 2 Macc, reminds us to be cautious in using his erudite and often useful commentaries.

[24]Bunge, *Untersuchungen* p. 310; Goldstein, *1 Macc.*, pp. 102-103; *2 Macc.* pp. 50-54. Against these see R. Doran, *Temple Propaganda*, pp. 12-23.

[25]Niese, *Kritik*, p. 25; Meyer, *Ursprung*, p. 455; Abel, *Macc.*, p. XLII; Bunge, *Untersuchungen* pp. 159-163, 204; Habicht, *2 Macc.*, p. 174.

[26]See Bickerman, Festbrief, p. 245 (= *Studies* 2, p. 148); Schunck, *Quellen*, p. 98; Bunge, *Untersuchungen* p. 62; Habicht, *2 Macc.*, p. 170.

[27]Bunge, *Untersuchungen* pp. 32-55; Similarly, B.Z. Wacholder, "The Letter from Judah Maccabee to Aristobulus. Is 2 Maccabees 1:10b-2:18 Authentic?"

uncertain,[28] its purpose is fairly clear. As Ep. 1, it is an exhortation to the Egyptian Jews to celebrate Hanukkah (2 Macc 1:18). The rededication of the Second Temple is compared to its original dedication (under Nehemiah!) and to the dedication of the First Temple under Solomon (2 Macc 2:8-12). The implicit criticism of the Oniad temple in Leontopolis has been recognized by many scholars.[29] It is not entirely clear, on what occasion this letter was attached to the epitome. Probably a redactor inserted it and at the same time transposed some parts of the epitome to fit the chronology of the epistle.[30]

Second Maccabees in its present form has often been called a Pharisaic work because of its belief in resurrection and strong emphasis on Jewish purity laws (5:27; 6:18-19; 7:1).[31] In fact, if 2 Macc represents the viewpoint of any known Jewish group, the Pharisees or the *Asidaioi* are the only possible candidates. We can prove this by negative selection:

(1)   The Tobiads: 2 Macc is not interested in them.

(2)   The Oniads: 2 Macc is silent about them after Onias III and implicitly criticizes their temple in Egypt.

(3)   The "Hellenizers": 2 Macc sees in them the origin of all evils.

(4)   The Dead Sea Sect/Essenes: 2 Macc affirms the purity of the Jerusalem Temple.

(5)   Other apocalyptic groups: 2 Macc shows little interest in apocalypticism.

(6)   The Sadducees: 2 Macc expresses belief in resurrection.

HUCA 49 (1978) 89-133; Fischer, *Seleukiden und Makkabäer*, pp. 92-94; Habicht (2 *Macc.*, p. 201) shows its chronological impossibility.

[28]See Habicht, 2 *Macc.*, pp. 176-177. E. Bickerman ("Ein jüdischer Festbrief vom Jahre 124 v. Chr. [II Macc. 1, 1-9]," *ZNW* 32 [1933] 234) dated it around 60 BCE on stylistic grounds, refuted by Bunge, *Untersuchungen* pp. 43-46. Goldstein's date "November or early December 103" (2 *Macc.*, p. 164) is too hypothetical to be trustworthy. Although any date between 124 BCE and 70 CE is possible, the first third of this time span has the greatest likelihood.

[29]Bickerman, Festbrief, p. 250; Grimm, 2 *Macc.*, p. 12; Cavaignac, *RHR* 80 (1945) 51-52; Bunge, *Untersuchungen* pp. 613, 528; Habicht, 2 *Macc.*, p. 186. The existence of such criticism has been denied by D. Arenhoevel, *Die Theokratie nach dem 1. und 2. Makkabäerbuch* (Walberberger Studien, Theologische Reihe, Bd. 3; Mainz: Grünewald, 1967), pp. 100-102.

[30]Habicht, 2 *Macc.*, p. 176.

[31]Wellhausen, Wert, p. 135; Abel, *Macc.*, pp. XXXIV, XLIV; Schunck, *Quellen*, p. 125 n.5; Bunge, *Untersuchungen* p. 615.

(7)   The Shechemites: 2 Macc is centered on Jerusalem and its Temple.

(8)   The Hasmoneans: 2 Macc is indifferent, if not hostile, toward all the Hasmoneans except Judah.

(9)   Diaspora Jewry: The content of the epitome, as opposed to its thoroughly Hellenistic form, shows no connection with the diaspora; rather it is focused entirely on Jerusalem and Judea. Although Jason (and the abridger) may have lived for some time in North Africa and been educated there, the epitome cannot confidently be called a work of the diaspora.

(10)   As for the *Asidaioi*, we have no positive evidence for their continued existence as an organized group after 162 BCE.

Thus, among all known groups the Pharisees are the most probable candidates. It has been thought that the Temple and the festivals connected with it are more at the center than would be expected in a Pharisaic work, and this would be correct if the Pharisees of 100 BCE were like their remote descendants, the rabbis of 100 CE (who were trying to adjust to the loss of the Temple). Since we know so little of the Pharisees of 100 BCE, it is hard to trust such criteria, but even harder to believe that a group at war with the Hasmoneans would have produced a work glorifying the first member of the dynasty. As we are dealing with a composite text of which we are not yet able to separate the strata precisely, it is safer not to make any firm attributions.[32]

The book's purpose has been defined in different ways. The explanations fall roughly into the following categories:

(1)   Cultic: (a) description of the origins of Hanukkah and of the Nicanor Day and exhortation to observe these festivals,[33] (b) affirmation of the holiness of the Jerusalem

---

[32]Tcherikover, *Hellenistic Civ.*, p. 383; Habicht, *2 Macc.*, p. 189, and Hengel, *Judaism and Hellenism* 1, p. 97, are similarly cautious. Doran (*Temple Propaganda*, p. 111) suggests that the author of 2 Macc "belongs to that educated group, influenced by Hellenism but loyal to Judaism in which Ben Sira and Eupolemus would have felt at home."

[33]Grimm, *2 Macc.*, p. XII; Abel, *Macc*, p. XLIV; Momigliano, *Prime linee*, pp. 96-97; Arenhoevel, *Theokratie*, pp. 113-114: purpose of Jason and of the latest redactor, but not of the abridger.

temple, addressed to Egyptian Jews, implying criticism of the Oniad temple in Leontopolis.[34]

(2)   Theological: proof of reward for goodness, punishment for evil deeds; desecration and restoration of the Temple being the paradigm.[35]

(3)   Historiographic: refutation of 1 Macc and affirmation of the veracity of Daniel 7-12.[36]

(4)   Propagandistic: temple propaganda (including, but not limited to, a cultic dimension).[37]

There is ample evidence for (1a) and (2). Concerning (1b), the exaltation of the Jerusalem Temple appears in every chapter except 7 and 12. In its present form, with its two introductory letters, 2 Macc does demonstrate the holiness and importance of the Jerusalem Temple. Yet, in 5:17-20, a passage that may be attributed to the abridger or to Jason, the Temple is subordinated to the fate of the people (5:19).[38] Ep. 2 was a particularly strong appeal to Egyptian Jewry because of its dramatic date and pseudepigraphic authorship. It is inconceivable that the author did not think of the Oniad temple, although open polemic was avoided.

For (3) the evidence is weakest. 2 Macc does express a viewpoint different from 1 Macc, especially in that its only Hasmonean hero is Judah while Mattathias is passed over in silence and a minor defeat of Simon is reported (2 Macc 14:17). This indicates that 1 Macc suppressed evidence unfavorable to the Hasmoneans while 2 Macc was not interested in the dynasty. However, if Jason wanted to contradict 1 Macc he was ineffective; few have recognized such polemic. There is no evidence for Jason's supporting the book of Daniel against 1 Macc. In his thorough study of 2 Macc, Doran shows some of the weaknesses of all earlier attempts to define its purpose.[39]

---

[34]See n. 29 above. Focus on the Jerusalem Temple is also emphasized by Bévenot, p. 36; Bickerman, *Gott*, p. 32; Mejia, *RevQ* 1 (1958/9) 64; Momigliano, *Prime linee*, p. 54.

[35]Arenhoevel, *Theokratie*, p. 122; Abel, *Macc.*, p. XLIV, Bickerman, *Gott*, pp. 32-33.

[36]Refutation of 1 Macc: Geiger, *Urschrift*, pp. 219ff; Goldstein, *2 Macc.*, p. 82. Confirmation of Daniel: Goldstein, *2 Macc.*, pp. 64-69. Goldstein's main argument for Jason's attempt to prove the veracity of Daniel is vagueness, which he considers to be deliberate.

[37]R. Doran, *Temple Propaganda*, p. 114.

[38]2 Macc 15:18 expresses a contrary opinion. According to Habicht (*2 Macc.*, p. 173) 5:19 belongs to the abridger, 15:18 to Jason.

[39]*Temple Propaganda*, pp. 105-112.

As to (4): Theological excursuses, apparitions, and legends have caused 2 Macc to be included in the category of "pathetic" or "tragic" history and have contributed to a low esteem for its historical value. But Doran has shown that both these characterizations are inappropriate. Though the title of his monograph is deliberately provocative and somewhat tendentious, he successfully demonstrates how cultic, theological, and historiographic elements in 2 Macc belong together. He stresses that 2 Macc is a city history in which the topos of epiphanic deliverance by the patron deity has a central function.[40]

Nevertheless, even when we take these factors into consideration, we find that much material in 2 Macc is of historical value. Outside evidence from Greek authors and from inscriptions more than once unexpectedly supports its statements.[41]

Josephus

The *Jewish War*
Between 75 and 79 CE Josephus completed Books 1-6 of his account "Concerning the Jewish War" (*Life* 359-361). He had previously written a similar work in Aramaic for τοῖς ἄνω βαρβάροις (*J.W.* 1.3), presumably meaning the Jews in the Middle East. For the Greek edition, intended for Greeks and Romans (1.6), he used assistants "for the sake of the Greek" (*Ag. Ap.* 1.50, Thackeray).

In style as well as in the approach to his subject, Josephus imitated the best Greek historians. He considered the Jewish War the most tragic of all times (*J.W.* 1.1/Thuc. 1.1), wanted to follow the highest standards of history writing (*J.W.* 1.30/Thuc. 1.22) and criticized the shortcomings of previous writers (*J.W.* 1.2/Thuc. 1.20-21/Polyb. 2.56.7). Josephus' concept of Tyche was probably adapted from Polybius, whose work he seems to have known.[42]

Josephus set the beginning of the *Jewish War* where "the historians...and our prophets conclude" (*J.W.* 1.18). Although the purpose of the *Jewish War* is to describe the war with the Romans (66-74 CE), *J.W.* 1.31-2.283 is an introduction covering the time from about 170 BCE to 66 CE. One consideration that led Josephus to begin with Judah may have been his alliance with Rome, the first treaty between

---

[40]R. Doran, *Temple Propaganda*, pp. 98-104.
[41]E.g. for Hegemonides (2 Macc 13:24) see C. Habicht, "Der Stratege Hegemonides," *Historia* 1958, pp. 376-378. For Heliodorus (2 Macc 3) see *Inscriptiones Graecae* XI.4.1112-1114.
[42]See H. Lindner, *Die Geschichtsauffassung des Flavius Josephus im Bellum Judaicum* (Leiden: Brill, 1972) p. 47.

Romans and Jews (1.38). This proved that relations between Rome and the "legitimate" representatives of the Jews were initially good. Secondly, Josephus was proud of the Hasmoneans and later claimed to be their descendant (*Ant.* 16.187; *Life* 2, 4).

In accordance with common practice, Josephus in the *Jewish War* did not identify his source(s). He may have been aware of 1 Macc, but did not use it. Nicholas of Damascus was his main source for the Herodian period.[43] When Josephus wrote the *Antiquities* he was acquainted with Nicholas' account about earlier history.[44] Hence many think Nicholas the major or sole source for the historical introduction of the *Jewish War* down to Herod.[45]

However, from the beginning of the Hasmonean revolt until just before Pompey's conquest of Jerusalem, the *Antiquities* mention Nicholas only in three places; in two of these the *Jewish War* differs[46] and in one it gives no parallel (*Ant.* 13.347). At least from 63 BCE onward both the *Jewish War* and the *Antiquities* seem largely based on Nicholas.[47]

The *Antiquities* (Books 12-14)

Josephus completed the first edition of his *Antiquities* by 94 CE (*Ant.* 20.267). In Books 12-14 he described events from the death of Alexander the Great to that of the last Hasmonean ruler, Antigonus. Some of his sources for this period are recognizable: he paraphrased the Letter of Aristeas (*Ant.* 12.11-118) and 1 Macc up to the beginning of Simon's rule (*Ant.* 12.241-13.214).[48] In some instances he added new

---

[43]*J.W.* 2.93 has many verbal agreements with a fragment of Nicholas' autobiography preserved in Constantinus Porphyrogenitus. Jacoby, *Fragmente* II A 90, F 136 end; also Stern, *Greek and Latin Authors* no. 97, lines 72-76. See Hölscher, *PW* 9.1946. *J.W.*'s exceptionally detailed information about, and bias in favor of, Herod is best attributed to Nicholas, Cf. *Ant.* 16.183-186; Schürer-Vermes-Millar, 1, p. 51.

[44]Cf. *Ant.* 1.94, 108, 159; 7.101; *Ag. Ap.* 2.84.

[45]Hölscher, *PW* 9.1944; Michel-Bauernfeind I p. XXV; H.St.J. Thackeray, *Josephus the Man and the Historian* (New York, 1929; reprint New York: Ktav, 1967) p. 40. Schürer-Vermes-Millar 1, p. 50.

[46]*J.W.* 1. 62; *Ant.* 13. 250; *J.W.* 1.123: (Antipater) "was of Idumean descent"; *Ant.* 14.9: "Nicholas of Damascus says that he (Antipater) was a descendant of the first Jews who arrived in Judea from Babylon."

[47]Cf. *Ant.* 14.104 and the close parallels *J.W.* 1.133-144/*Ant.* 14. 48-60; *J.W.* 1.150-178/*Ant.* 14.70-76, 79-103. *Ant.* used additional sources, especially Strabo to whom it has numerous explicit references: *Ant.* 13.284-287, 319, 347; 14.35-36, 66-68, 104, 111-112, 114-118, 138-139.

[48]See H. Bloch, *Die Quellen des Flavius Josephus in seiner Archäologie* (Leipzig, 1879; reprint Wiesbaden: Sandig, 1968) pp. 80-90. The argument for an

material[49] or corrected 1 Macc from another source.[50] Josephus did not use 1 Macc 14-16, perhaps because it was missing in his copy, or because he regarded another source (Nicholas?) as sufficient or superior, or because he wanted to diminish the role of Simon in favor of Jonathan, or because he feared to offend Agrippa II by recording that the Hasmoneans had been granted leadership of the people "forever – until a trustworthy prophet should arise" (1 Macc 14:41). He was not just a copyist, but reported Hasmonean history in accordance with his own (changing) outlook, and adapted it for his readers. S. Cohen lists some of these changes.[51] After paraphrasing 1 Macc, the *Antiquities* soon start running closely parallel to the *Jewish War* (*J.W.* 1.50/*Ant.* 13.225). Laqueur was first to analyze the relation between the *Jewish War* and the *Antiquities* thoroughly. He found that *Ant.* 14 relied mostly on *J.W.* 1 and that many of the differences could be accounted for by Josephus' change of opinion about his subject, especially about the Herodians.[52] A similar change of attitude, this time to a more favorable disposition toward the Pharisees, has been discovered by Smith.[53] These and similar changes probably reflect a different political and religious situation and Josephus' response to it, rather

---

intermediary source is chiefly based on inconsistencies between *Ant.* and 1 Macc, but these may be explained by Josephus' method of dealing with his *Vorlage*. He used a Greek text of 1 Macc; whether he had a Hebrew text in addition to it remains uncertain. See S.J.D. Cohen, *Josephus in Galilee and Rome: His Vita and Development as an Historian* (Leiden: Brill, 1979) pp. 34-35, 44-47.

[49]E.g., a request by the "Sidonians in Shechem" (*Ant.* 12.258-264), cf. 2 Macc 6:2; the death of Menelaus (*Ant.* 12.383-385), cf. 2 Macc 13:4-6. There is no evidence that he knew 2 Macc.

[50]See Cohen, *Josephus*, pp. 44-45.

[51]*Ibid.*, p. 46. Add to his list: *Ant.* 12.279-283 omits reference to Biblical heroes and instead fills Mattathias' deathbed speech (1 Macc 2:49-64) with philosophical considerations; *Ant.* 12.294 gives the king's liberality as reason for his shortage of funds, while according to 1 Macc 3:29 the ultimate reason was his abolishing the laws. Cf. also 1 Macc 3:55/*Ant.* 12.301: exemption from military duty; 1 Macc 3:58/*Ant.* 12.302-304: speech of Judah. On Josephus' tendencies in rewriting 1 Macc see I. Gafni, "On the Use of 1 Maccabees by Josephus Flavius," (Hebrew) *Zion* 45 (1980) 81-95. Less plausible is Goldstein's explanation (*1 Macc.*, pp. 55-61, 558-574). For a note of caution see Cohen, *Josephus*, p. 44 n. 77, and J.C. Dancy, *A Commentary on 1 Maccabees* (Oxford: Blackwell, 1954) p. 30.

[52]R. Laqueur, *Der jüdische Historiker Flavius Josephus* (Giessen, 1920, reprinted Darmstadt: Wissenschaftliche Buchgesellschaft, 1970) p. 132.

[53]M. Smith, "Palestinian Judaism in the First Century," *Israel: Its Role in Civilization* (ed. M. Davis; New York: Harper & Row, 1956) pp. 75-76. See further Cohen, *Josephus*, pp. 148-151.

than a different intended audience (cf. *J.W.* 1.6 and *Ant.* 1.5). The two factors are not mutually exclusive.

Laqueur's work has been carried further by S. Cohen in a detailed study of the literary relationship between the *Antiquities*, the *Jewish War*, and their sources, and the *Jewish War* and the *Life*. For the *Antiquities*, Josephus used Biblical texts, the letter of Aristeas, and 1 Macc in a similar fashion, generally avoiding verbal parallels, but following the outline of the source very closely.[54]

The relationship between *Ant.* 13-14 and *J.W.* 1 is more complex, as the *Antiquities* are more than twice as long as their *Jewish War* parallel. Undoubtedly in the *Antiquities* additional material was used, e.g. the documents in *Ant.* 14.185-267 and quotations from Polybius, Strabo, Timagenes, and Nicholas of Damascus. Close parallels can be explained by the use of a common source, by the use of the earlier work in the later one, or both. The common source theory does not account for the fact that *J.W.* 1 and *Ant.* 14 have extended verbal parallels, in spite of Josephus' tendency to change the wording of his source.[55] On the other hand, the *Antiquities* contain factual material not in the *Jewish War*[56] and attributable neither to dramatic expansion nor to a new source. Such material is most easily explained as derived from the source of the *Jewish War*. Thus, in writing the *Antiquities* Josephus had recourse to the *Jewish War*, to its sources, and to other material.[57]

Josephus' Reliability

As far as we can check, Josephus followed the outlines of his sources faithfully, but took liberties in details and interpretation of facts. Therefore we must be cautious about his evaluation of Herod and his family. Nicholas of Damascus was closely associated with and favorably disposed towards Herod. Josephus expressed this attitude in the *Jewish War*, but in the *Antiquities* made Herod a villain. These different attitudes toward Herod's family also affected the description of the struggle between Aristobulus II and Hyrcanus II (*J.W.* 1.120-174/*Ant.* 14.4-97). Since both reports are biased, we cannot *a priori* dismiss the *Antiquities* as secondary. Similar difficulties arise for many other reasons. First of all, his relations to the Romans, for even his account of early Jewish history is colored by his desire to influence his expected Roman readers to favor the Jews. Besides this, he was pro-Judean (vs. Samaritans, Idumeans, Galileans, and gentiles generally)

---

[54]Cohen, *Josephus*, p. 47.
[55]Cohen, *Josephus*, pp. 50-51; esp. n. 89.
[56]E.g., *Ant.* 14.275 has an explicit reference to Lydda and Thamna.
[57]Cohen, *Josephus*, p. 51.

and pro-Hasmonean (vs. Hellenizers and other aspirants to government).

While Laqueur was right in showing that the *Antiquities* depend largely on the *Jewish War*,[58] they have independent value because at times they seem to preserve Josephus' source(s) more fully than the *Jewish War* (see above).

Apart from such biases and occasional sloppiness, we have no reason to doubt Josephus' trustworthiness in relating his sources about early Hasmonean times. Thus, his historical reliability is primarily dependent on the accuracy of his sources, but liable to large secondary variations when his biases are involved – as they often are.

Other Literary Sources

There are numerous other sources which include information about the Hasmoneans and their times. Some of these works, such as Daniel and *1 Enoch* and some of the Dead Sea Scrolls were written in Palestine during the period under discussion.

Numerous Greek historians dealt with this period, but unfortunately, only fragments survive (e.g. of Polybius, Posidonius, Diodorus, Nicholas of Damascus, Strabo's *History*). At times we find valuable historical information in them that confirms, expands or rectifies accounts of the Books of Maccabees and Josephus. Memories of Hasmonean times are preserved in later rabbinic tradition especially in the Fasting Scroll (*Megillat Taanit*), but also in various other passages of the vast rabbinic literature.

It would be beyond the scope of this study to discuss these various sources in detail, but we shall make use of them and, whenever appropriate, discuss their reliability for individual aspects of Hasmonean history.

Generally, I have not cited sources that are late and unreliable, such as *Megillat Antiochus*, *Seder Olam Rabbah*, *Yosippon*, and the Samaritan Chronicles. They may corroborate, but hardly refute the data of our other sources, though admittedly they may contain remote reminiscences of actual events.

Non-literary Sources

The last few years have seen a tremendous increase in the quantity of archaeological data for the period under consideration. Excavations at various sites in Jerusalem, Jericho, Gezer, Mt. Gerizim, and elsewhere are yielding new material evidence from the Hasmonean period, much of it not yet published. Detailed surveys of Samaria are

---

[58]Laqueur, *Josephus*, p. 133 and passim.

revolutionizing our knowledge of rural settlements in the area. Wherever I have found the archaeological evidence helpful in reconstructing the political, social and religious history of the Hasmoneans I have tried to utilize it.

Last, not least, coins of the period offer valuable insights into Hasmonean policy and geographic expansion, while a few inscriptions and papyri give important background information.

Events Leading to the Hasmonean Revolt

The Situation Before the Persecution

The persecution of Antiochus Epiphanes has given rise to a vast literature. Here we are not concerned with the persecution and its causes as such. The start of the revolt, however, is of immediate interest to us. Traditionally, the killing of a royal official and of a Jewish collaborator by the priest Mattathias, as reported in 1 Macc, is considered the starting signal.

The situation was more complex, however. Bickerman and Tcherikover have pointed out that already in 168 BCE Jerusalem was in turmoil and that the capture of the city by the Mysarch Apollonius was in response to this.[59] Tcherikover tried to show that the revolt was the fruit of a civil war that raged in Jerusalem intermittently since 168 BCE or earlier.[60]

He considered the Hasidim the probable leaders in the fight of the Jerusalem *plebs* and Judean peasantry against the wealthy aristocracy, including the owners of large estates. The events of the Hasmonean revolt, however, belie any simple class struggle theory. Bickerman, instead, was correct in emphasizing the complex interplay of family feud, disagreements in points of principle, and foreign policy connections.[61] We can be certain that during the Syrian wars of the third century some people in Judea leaned toward the Seleucid side while others were loyal to the Ptolemies.[62] How continuous these political divisions were as decisive elements in Judean society, is hard to assess, because direct evidence for the first half of the second century

---

[59]*Gott*, p. 168; *Hellenistic Civ.*, p. 192; 2 Macc 5:5-7, 11, 24; cf. *J.W.* 1.31-32.
[60]*Hellenistic Civ.*, pp. 190-192.
[61]*Gott*, p. 69.
[62]Jerome in his commentary on Daniel, which is based on Porphyry's *Adversus Christianos*, alludes to such factions. See the text and Stern's commentary in *Greek and Latin Authors* 2.464L, 464N.

is lacking.[63] E. Meyer oversimplified matters when he asserted that the Hellenizers were pro-Seleucid, whereas the more traditional Jewish masses were pro-Ptolemaic.[64] In fact, when strife broke out in Judea some time early in the second century, it was not over religious issues, but had its origin in a family feud between the Tobiad Hyrcanus (who seems to have been more self-serving than pro-Ptolemaic) and his pro-Seleucid brothers (*Ant.* 12.228-229). The chronology and other details of these events are uncertain, but do not concern us here.

Second Maccabees, which is our most detailed though not always accurate source, ignores these feuds and at the outset depicts Jerusalem as being completely at peace under the benign rule of Onias III (3:1). The peace is broken by intrigues of a certain Simon, the captain of the Temple, for the sake of his own advancement (3:4; 4:1-3). While Onias is pleading his cause against Simon in Antioch, his brother Jason buys the high priesthood for himself from the new King Antiochus IV Epiphanes (175/4 BCE). Three years later Jason is ousted by a trusted subordinate, Simon's brother Menelaus. Menelaus outbids Jason by 300 talents, but to make good his promise and to pay various bribes, he has recourse to precious objects and funds deposited in the Temple treasury. Onias, the ousted high priest, denounces him publicly for this, but is treacherously murdered at the instigation of Menelaus. Up to this point (170 BCE),[65] the conflict appears to have been limited to a struggle between different individuals and factions of the local aristocracy (see also *J.W.* 1.31).

But the murder of the former high priest and especially the theft of Temple property caused a riot during which Lysimachus, a brother of Menelaus and Simon, was killed "by the crowd" near the Temple treasury (2 Macc 4:42). As a consequence of this riot three members of the Jerusalem Council of Elders (γερουσία) were executed, whereas Menelaus escaped any censure or punishment, reportedly through a bribe.

---

[63]See R. Doran, "Parties and Politics in pre-Hasmonean Jerusalem: A Closer Look at 2 Macc 3:11," *Society of Biblical Literature 1982 Seminar Papers*, ed. K.H. Richards (Chico, CA: Scholars Press, 1982) pp. 107-111. On the involvement of Ptolemy Philometor in Judean affairs, beginning no later than 152 BCE, see M. Stern, "The Relations Between the Hasmonean Kingdom and Ptolemaic Egypt in View of the International Situation During the 2nd and 1st Centuries BCE," *Zion* 50 (1984/5) 83, 87-93 (in Hebrew).

[64]*Ursprung und Anfänge des Christentums* (3 vols; Stuttgart/Berlin: Cotta, 1921-1923) vol. 2, p. 137. Against Meyer see Tcherikover, *Hellenistic Civ.*, pp. 76-79.

[65]For this date see Mørkholm, *Antiochus IV*, pp. 45, 141, n. 21.

According to 2 Macc 5:5, the first major armed conflict in Jerusalem arose when, upon false rumors of Antiochus' death, Jason attempted to reclaim his position as high priest. He was partially successful in that he forced Menelaus to retreat to the citadel (ἀκρόπολις). Josephus (*Ant.* 12.240) claims that Jason was supported by the majority of the people, but the fact is that he was soon forced to leave Jerusalem (2 Macc 5:7). Our sources are silent about who forced him to flee, but report that the king thereafter took action against the city as if it were in revolt. Since this seems difficult to understand if the king's appointee Menelaus had regained control, Tcherikover argued from the king's action that Jason was ousted by a popular revolt.[66] However, cities in which unsuccessful revolts were attempted could be punished for the attempt (see Acts 19:40). Consequently, a revolutionary party that ousted Jason need not be supposed (though it is not impossible). Furthermore, we do not know how long Jason was able to keep his hold on Jerusalem and how much time passed before Antiochus marched against Jerusalem. Jason's flight may have been linked to the approach of Antiochus' army. In any event, 2 Macc 5:7-16 is not a chronological account, since Antiochus must have been informed about the revolt in Judea (5:11) before Jason's odyssey (5:7-9) was over. Thus, Tcherikover's argument that Antiochus arrived some time *after* Jason had left Jerusalem, is not supported by 2 Macc.

Antiochus' troops took the city by storm, and killed or enslaved not only those who resisted, but also women and children; in addition, Antiochus is said to have entered the Temple with Menelaus as his guide, a pollution that would have been deeply resented by the pious. Even worse, the Temple was robbed of 1800 talents.[67]

A Phrygian commander, Philip, was left behind in Jerusalem and a certain Andronicus remained in Samaria (2 Macc 5:22-23). Both of them, in conjunction with Menelaus, reportedly maltreated the people (τὸ

---

[66]*Hellenistic Civ.*, pp. 187-189; so also Goldstein, *2 Macc.*, p. 250.

[67]2 Macc 5:11-21. The number of victims (80,000) seems grossly exaggerated. The same events are described in 1 Macc 1:20-22, but the dates differ: 1 Macc 1:20 gives 143 Sel. (fall 170/69 or spring 169/68 BCE), the time of the first Egyptian campaign, whereas 2 Macc 5:1 attributes the capture of Jerusalem to Antiochus' second Egyptian campaign which was ended by a Roman ultimatum in the summer of 168 BCE. Dan 11:28, 30 seems to suppose that Antiochus intervened in Jerusalem on both occasions, though it is not made explicit whether he was personally present. Josephus alone speaks of two visits of Antiochus in Jerusalem (*Ant.* 12.246-248), but his chronology is muddled. The details and the chronology of these events remain controversial. For recent assessments with some earlier bibliography see Schürer-Vermes-Millar, vol. 1, pp. 150-153, especially, n. 37; K. Bringmann, *Hellenistische Reform* pp. 32-40, 126.

γένος). This is an indication that both the king and 2 Macc considered Judea and Samaria closely related. 2 Macc deplores Philip's brutality. It is clear that all this was not borne with equanimity by the populace. Tensions must have grown not only between the garrison and the populace, but also between the followers of Menelaus who were supported by military force, and the rest of the population.

Some time later (between the fall of 168 and the summer of 167 BCE), the so-called Mysarch Apollonius[68] came to Jerusalem with an army. We are not told the reason for his coming. Both 1 Macc 1:30 and 2 Macc 5:25 state that he pretended to have peaceful intentions, but that he nonetheless killed many in the city. Tcherikover attributes this harsh treatment to the renewal of the supposed rebellion and thinks that Jerusalem had again "passed into the hands of the insurgents."[69] The fact, however, that Apollonius came in a peaceful guise and that people left the city to watch a parade of his troops (2 Macc 5:25-26) indicates that there was no *open* rebellion.

It is clear that by now in Jerusalem resentment against Seleucid rule was growing and lines between opposing Jewish factions were stiffening: Two high priests had been deposed, one of them murdered, the Temple had repeatedly been robbed,[70] political murders, riots, and executions had cost many lives. Property had been looted and destroyed. In spite of all this, no Jewish resistance movement is known to have been organized before the arrival of Apollonius.

He, however, took decisive action that transformed Jerusalem and changed the course of future events. He burned parts of the city, tore down the walls, and built a new fortified quarter, the *Akra* (1 Macc 1:33). There he settled Jewish as well as non-Jewish military and civilians who got control also of the Temple and stopped the traditional sacrifices.[71] First Maccabees informs us that many fled the city at this point; but it does not specify why they did so and whither they fled. Some homes had been burned, others may have been

---

[68]It is generally agreed that ἄρχοντα φορολογίας (1 Macc 1:29) instead of Μυσάρχην (2 Macc 5:24) is based on a mistranslation from the Hebrew. Note, however, A. Mittwoch, "Tribute and Land Tax in Seleucid Judaea," *Biblica* 36 (1955) 352-361.

[69]*Hellenistic Civ.*, p. 188.

[70]1 Macc 1:20-24; 2 Macc 4:39, 42; 5:15-16, 21; *J.W.* 1.32; *Ant.* 12.247, 249-250.

[71]Dan 11:31; 1 Macc 1:39; 1 Macc 1:34 speaks of "sinful people, lawless men" (ἔθνος ἁμαρτωλόν, ἄνδρας παρανόμους). At least the latter expression refers to Jews. Thus, Abel, *Macc.*, p. 17; cf. Goldstein, *1 Macc.*, p. 124. Josephus was more outspoken than 1 Macc about Jewish opponents of the Hasmoneans. *Ant.* 12.252 explicitly refers to apostate Jews in the *Akra*, possibly an inference from 1 Macc, or based on information independent of it. Cf. *Ant.* 12.362-364; 13.42.

dispossessed (cf. Dan 11:39) to make room for the new settlers. Other people may have fled in panic. First Maccabees exaggerates when it claims – in a poetic section – that Jerusalem was completely abandoned by its inhabitants (1:38), but the exodus must have been considerable.

Second Maccabees adds at this point a brief note about Judah Maccabee fleeing into the wilderness with about nine companions and living in the mountains, eating herbs like wild animals "so that they might not share the defilement" (5:27). This verse is puzzling because it has no connection with the context, mentions Judah for the first time in the narrative without introducing him, and above all, goes counter to the story of the Hasmonean rising as told in 1 Macc 2, *Ant.* 12.268-271, and *J.W.* 1.36. Furthermore, there was no reason before the decree of persecution to adopt a special diet in order to avoid defilement. 1 Macc 1:62-63 does speak of people who chose hardship and even death in order not to be defiled by unclean food, but this happened after the beginning of the persecution. It seems that Judah, before the revolt, was resident in Modein, and Modein seems to have been unmolested until the beginning of the persecution.[72] Since we know from two independent sources (1 Macc 2:28; *J.W.* 1.36) that Mattathias and his sons fled to the mountains after the beginning of the persecution, it seems best to suppose 2 Macc 5:27 another report of the same event.[73] There is nothing in 2 Macc to contradict this interpretation, because there, when we next hear of Judah, he is coming out of hiding to gather troops, after the persecution has begun (2 Macc 8:1).

Apollonius was partly successful in that he established in Jerusalem a citadel held solely by persons loyal to the Seleucid government. The rest of the city, unfortified, was immediately subject to disciplinary action from the *Akra* and also undefended against military forces that the government might bring against it. It was, however, also open to attacks by brigands and others. Moreover, the refugees from Jerusalem may have spread unrest to the Judean countryside, increasing the possibility of a revolt.

The Persecution of Antiochus IV and Reactions To It
    Not long after Apollonius' actions, further changes were made. Sometime in 167 BCE, observance of the Torah and possession of copies

---

[72]1 Macc 2:1 says Mattathias (presumably with his family) retreated from Jerusalem to his country estate in Modein in response to Apollonius' actions. *Ant.* 12.265 introduces him as resident in Modein.
[73]Similarly Bévenot, p. 197; Habicht, *2 Macc.*, p. 228; Goldstein, *2 Macc.*, p. 267; against Schunck, *Quellen*, p. 117, Bunge, *Untersuchungen* pp. 222-223, 648; Tcherikover, *Hellenistic Civ.*, p. 475, n. 27.

of it were outlawed under pain of death.[74] In addition, on 15 Kislev 145 a pagan structure (a new altar ?) was erected on the altar of the Jerusalem Temple.[75] The god of the Temple was identified as Zeus Olympius (2 Macc 6:2) and pagan forms of worship were introduced, drastically modifying the traditional Jewish Temple cult.

The questions as to the remote causes of these changes lie beyond the scope of this study. The question of immediate responsibility would be important for our purpose if it could be answered with assurance, but, as we have shown (n. 74 above), the primary sources and the scholarly interpretations of them are equally contradictory. What does seem certain is that the measures were widely represented in Jewish circles as due to the king, and were implemented in Jerusalem by his religious, civil, and military authorities alike. The religious authorities included many hellenizing priests of the Jerusalem Temple, as well as special royal commissioners for religious affairs. Finally, the hellenizing party among the priests had the support of many in the Jerusalem population.[76] These being indicated as the immediate agents of the "reforms" and the resulting persecution, we may now turn to the reactions to this situation.

---

[74]The sources disagree on who initiated these repressive measures: 1 Macc 1:41-57 (king); 2 Macc 6:1 (king through agent); Dan 11:31-33 (royal agents or the city government); *J.W.* 1.32-35 (king); *Ant.* 12.248-256 (king). Cf. *Jub.* 23:16-23 (strife between Jewish factions). 1 Macc attributes the change to the king and explains it as a result of his desire to unify the kingdom through unified customs. But there is no evidence for any forced change of customs or religious observances in any other part of the Seleucid empire. Dan 11:30 states that "he (Antiochus IV) will pay attention to (or, "come to an understanding with"?) those who forsake the holy covenant." This may be interpreted as a reference to the decisive role of Jewish "Hellenizers" in starting the persecution, but the context is not explicit as to what was due to their initiative, what to the king's (cf. 11:32). In *J.W.* 1.34 Josephus attributes the religious persecution to Antiochus' "lack of self-control" (ἀκρασία; Thackeray: "ungovernable passions") and to the memory of the sufferings he had undergone in the siege of Jerusalem. In his narrative in *Ant.* 12.251-256 Josephus gives no reason for the king's measures, but later on (12.384) he has Lysias claim that the high priest Menelaus had persuaded Antiochus IV to force the Jews to abandon their native religion. Similarly, Lysias put the blame "for all the trouble" on Menelaus according to 2 Macc 13:4. These accounts cannot easily be harmonized. The most important studies are Bickerman, *Gott,* 120-136, reviewed by I. Heinemann in *MGWJ* 82 (1938) 145-172; V. Tcherikover, *Hellenistic Civ.,* 175-203; more recently Hengel, *Judaism and Hellenism* 1.283-289; Bunge, *Untersuchungen* pp. 469-479; Goldstein, *1 Macc.,* pp. 125-160 and passim. K. Bringmann, *Hellenistische Reform* pp. 120-140; E. Will - C. Orrieux, *Ioudaïsmos-Hellènismos* (Nancy: Presses Universitaires, 1986) pp. 143-156, 169-175.

[75]1 Macc 1:54. Dec. 6, 167 BCE, if the Babylonian calendar was followed.

[76]1 Macc 1:11; Dan 11:30, 32; 2 Macc 4:9-16.

It has often been assumed that only two options were open to Jews: either to follow the line of the government and join the Hellenizers or to resist. It is easily evident that the situation was more complex. First it should be said that a wide variety of responses to persecution is possible. They may roughly be classified as follows: (1) active collaboration, (2) voluntary compliance, (3) compliance under compulsion, (4) paralysis, (5) evasion, (6) alleviation, (7) non-violent resistance, (8) armed resistance.[77] A careful reading of the sources suggests that all these possibilities were present at the time of Antiochus Epiphanes.

(1) *Active collaboration:* Menelaus continued to act as an agent of the Seleucid government. 1 Macc 1:52-53 specifically includes Jews among the perpetrators of the persecution. Jews were part of the garrison of the *Akra* (*Ant.* 12.252). Allusions to Jewish collaborators are also found in Dan 11:30 and *1 Enoch* 90:16.

(2) *Voluntary compliance* with the royal decrees must have been a fairly widespread phenomenon because we find it attested on several occasions.[78] Alcimus, the later high priest, may well fit into this category. Of him it is said that he had "voluntarily defiled himself" (2 Macc 14:3), but we are not sure whether this accusation applies to his actions before, during, or after the persecution.[79]

Often all those Jews who advocated or willingly accepted some aspects of the religious reforms during the time of Antiochus Epiphanes are called "Hellenizers." If taken literally, this term is misleading, because it suggests that familiarity with Greek language and culture meant a rejection of Jewish traditions and vice versa. But this was manifestly not so. In fact, those who changed their religious practices in accordance with Antiochus' decree included not only members of the Jerusalem aristocracy, but also villagers and soldiers of whom many,

---

[77]For part of my classification system I am indebted to R. Hilberg, *The Destruction of the European Jews* (rev. ed., New York: Holmes & Meier, 1985) Vol. 1, pp. 22-27. Although Hilberg analyzes only the pattern of reactions of diaspora Jews, we find a structural analogue in Palestine in the time of Antiochus IV. In adopting such a model I am aware of the qualitative differences between ancient, medieval, and modern persecutions. These differences however do not invalidate the model for possible *responses* to such persecutions. A similar but simpler classification system has been developed in the study of European colonialism and has been applied to reactions to hellenization by E. Will - C. Orrieux, *Ioudaïsmos - Hellènismos*, pp. 29-31.

[78]1 Macc 1:43; 6:23; Dan 11:32; *Ant.* 12.255.

[79]All three interpretations of ἐν τοῖς τῆς ἀμιξίας χρόνοις have been suggested. See Habicht, *2 Macc.*, p. 271. I doubt however that his order to execute 60 *Asidaioi* would have been described as voluntary defilement, as Habicht suggests.

presumably, knew little Greek. The Hasmoneans' raids were at first directed against country towns and villages.[80] On the other hand, other members of the Jerusalem aristocracy, apparently with Greek education, joined the revolt or offered non-violent resistance.[81]

(3) *Compliance under compulsion:* Certainly many people saw no other alternative than to comply with royal orders. Every month on the king's birthday, Jews were forced to participate in sacrificial meals, and during the festivals of Dionysus[82] they were compelled to participate in processions, wearing wreaths of ivy (2 Macc 6:7). All over the countryside shrines were erected and Jews participated in sacrifices under some measure of coercion.[83]

(4) *Paralysis:* When facing unexpected demands some people are so shocked that they are unable to comply or to resist. It is for this reaction – or non-reaction – that Hilberg uses the term "paralysis." He adds that it is a rare phenomenon which occurs during moments of crisis. We can not expect much evidence for this behavior, because usually people who do nothing find no place in the historical record. And yet, a mood of this kind seems to be captured in poetic form in 1 Macc 1:25-27: "Great sorrow came over Israel in all their dwelling places. Leading men and elders groaned, virgins and young men became weak, and the women's beauty faded. Every bridegroom raised his voice in lamentation, she who sat in the bridal chamber was in mourning!" Goldstein claims that the dirge, from which these lines are taken, "represents accurately the reaction of pious Jews to Antiochus' sack of Jerusalem."[84] Although I am not as confident on this point, it is plausible that an immediate reaction to different phases of Antiochus' intervention was dismay, lament, and mourning without knowing what to do or not to do.[85]

(5) *Evasion:* A means of escaping persecution was sought in evasion. The most natural form was flight to remote corners of the countryside.

---

[80]2 Macc 8:6; cf. 1 Macc 2:44-47.

[81]See 1 Macc 8:17; 2 Macc 4:11; 6:18; 14:37.

[82]Bickerman (*Gott*, p. 114) thinks that perhaps Dusares in meant.

[83]1 Macc 2:15, 23; *Ant.* 12.255, 268, 270; *As. Mos.* 8:1-5; cf. 1 Macc 1:44-51; *Ant.* 12.278.

[84]*1 Macc.*, p. 211.

[85]Cf. 1 Macc 2:7. Most MSS have καθισαι, which only means that Mattathias dwelt in Jerusalem at the time when city and Temple came under direct foreign control. Kappler-Hanhart and Abel (1949) emend the text on the basis of the Latin and Syriac versions to ἐκάθισαν, suggesting that Jerusalem's inhabitants "sat idle." The translation in Abel-Starcky (1961) follows the Greek MSS.

For many, apparently, this seemed the best way to remain true to their tradition and to escape harassment.

We are told that even before the persecution, all Jewish residents left Jerusalem and it became a settlement of foreigners (1 Macc 1:38), and later, that Israel was in hiding (1:53). Poetic license causes such exaggerations, but flight from the towns was fairly common, as the tragedy of those who strictly observed the Sabbath shows.[86] Many of them – reportedly one thousand – were killed in caves in the desert. Also Mattathias and his sons at first fled into the mountains.[87]

(6) *Alleviation:* Under the category of alleviation Hilberg subsumes different attempts to avert danger or to diminish the impact of persecution. One way was to dissociate oneself from the persecuted. An anticipatory measure in this direction was the removal of the sign of circumcision before the persecution began.[88]

Josephus relates another interesting instance of dissociation: The Samaritans who worshiped on Mt. Gerizim were afraid of being identified with the Jews of Judea. Therefore they filed a petition in which they disclaimed any connection with them.[89] Besides dissociation it contains an element of anticipatory compliance, namely the request that their temple on Mt. Gerizim be known as a temple of Zeus.[90] This was obviously an attempt to prove loyalty to the Seleucid government with the hope of avoiding harassment. The king's favorable response is quoted by Josephus.[91]

This correspondence, if genuine, shows that in Samaria there was a "Hellenizing" party, strong enough to influence the fate of the Gerizim temple. Apparently it was more successful than its Jerusalem counterpart in relations with the Seleucid government and with the local population. We do not hear of any imposed religious practices in

---

[86] 1 Macc 2:29-38; 2 Macc 6:11; *Ant.* 12.275, cf. 272.

[87] 1 Macc 2:28; cf. 2 Macc 5:27.

[88] 1 Macc 1:15; cf. *Ant.* 12.241; *As. Mos.* 8:3.

[89] *Ant.* 12.258-261; cf. 9, 291; 11.344. It may be worth noting that many Karaites escaped death during the Holocaust in a similar way. On January 9, 1939 the German Ministry of the Interior declared the Karaites non-Jews. Later several historians in the ghettos of Vilna and Warsaw reassured the German authorities that Karaites had indeed nothing to do with the Jews. This scholarly "adjustment" of history saved many lives.

[90] *Ant.* 12.261; cf. 2 Macc 6:2.

[91] *Ant.* 12.262-264. See E. Bickerman, "Un document relatif à la persécution d'Antiochos IV Epiphane," *RHR* 115 (1937) 188-223. Revised edition in E. Bickerman, *Studies in Jewish and Christian History*, Part 2 (Leiden:Brill, 1980), pp. 105-135.

Samaria. Modein, which had ties to Jerusalem, perhaps belonged to Judea (see chap. I n. 1 below).

A very different form of alleviation is found in the apocalyptic literature of the period, especially in Daniel. It interprets the persecution as a temporary trial that precedes the approaching new age.[92] By explaining the course of history as a preparation for a glorious future, the sufferings of the present are made more understandable and more bearable.[93] By the same token, the reader is encouraged to resist the temptation to abandon the "holy covenant" (Dan 11:30, 32). In this sense the Book of Daniel may be called "resistance literature."[94]

(7) *Non-violent resistance:* The heroes of the Book of Daniel are the "wise," who are willing to suffer and die for their convictions.[95] It is said that many will follow their teaching. These probably do not include the above-mentioned group of "a thousand" people who preferred to be burned in the caves where they had taken refuge rather than to fight on the Sabbath.[96] It seems likely that on any day other than the Sabbath they would have offered active resistance, since they are represented as persuading each other not to fight because of the Sabbath.

The sources agree also that the death sentence was carried out against men, women, and children who participated in circumcision and observed the dietary laws, but say nothing of armed resistance by these victims.[97] Second Maccabees lays great emphasis on martyrdom, of which it brings several detailed examples, though in largely legendary form.[98]

(8) *Armed resistance* is attested more than any other reaction. In fact, it led to the successful Hasmonean revolt, with which we will deal in subsequent chapters.

This is not a complete list of all possible or actual responses to the persecution of Antiochus, but it indicates the complexity of the Jewish side of the problem. This is not to say that each category of responses

[92]Dan 8:9-14, 25; 9:26-27; 12:1-13; *1 Enoch* 90:8-20.

[93]Dan 12:3; *1 Enoch* 90:30-38.

[94]So A.A. Di Lella, in L.F. Hartman and A.A. Di Lella, *The Book of Daniel* (AB 23; Garden City: Doubleday, 1978) 71, 294. I doubt that all apocalyptic literature can be called "resistance literature." To Daniel this term applies only in the limited sense outlined above.

[95]11:33, 35; 12:3. The frequent identification of these משכילים with the *Asidaioi* of 1 and 2 Macc rests on insufficient evidence. See Excursus on *Asidaioi*, below.

[96]1 Macc 2:29-38; 2 Macc 6:11; *Ant.* 12.275.

[97]1 Macc 1:60-63; 2 Macc 6:10; *Ant.* 12.256.

[98]2 Macc 6:18-7:42; 14:37-46.

reflects a different ideology, or that all reactions that can be subsumed under the same category reflect similar outlooks.

We have here a glimpse of the complex fabric of Judean society which until the time of Antiochus had been fairly stable. His interference in the high priestly succession gave practical importance to and promoted factionalism in the Jerusalem aristocracy which then had far-reaching repercussions for the whole population.

Several distinct factions emerge: Those who actively collaborated with the Seleucid government, and perhaps even instigated the persecution, under the leadership of Menelaus, plus their supporters (reactions #1 and 2); many who did not approve of the new policies but went along (#3); people who left their homes either because of expropriations or for religious reasons (#5); some of these may have advocated non-violent resistance (#7); others joined the incipient revolt based mostly in northern Judea and southern Samaria (#8). Relations with the rest of Samaria were strained even more than usual, at least temporarily (#6). We do not know what the supporters of Jason did, or those who later followed Onias IV to Egypt (*Ant.* 13.65, 73).

First Maccabees suggests that after the beginning of the revolt all good Jews joined ranks with the Hasmoneans in a united front against the evildoers, including both lawless Jews and Gentiles. That this was not so is evident, however, from the further course of events.

The persecution was probably fiercest in Jerusalem, where Menelaus' followers were strongest and the Seleucid garrison nearest. In fact, *J.W.* 1.34-36 and 2 Macc 6-7 give the impression that the persecution affected mostly people in Jerusalem and its immediate vicinity. The account in 1 Macc 1-2 instead stresses several times that people all over Judea were persecuted.[99] The picture in 1 Macc seems to be more complete.[100] The persecution, in fact, caused a second wave of refugees, this time not only from Jerusalem but also from the country towns. Only at this point our sources are for the first time explicit about organized opposition to the government at the grass-root level.

Both Dan 11:32-34 and *1 Enoch* 90:9 maintain that resistance started with devout Jews who met with little success, until they got help from others, presumably the Hasmoneans.[101] It has often been

---

[99]1 Macc 1:51-54, 58; 2:6, 15, 29-38.

[100]The focus of 2 Macc is generally more on Jerusalem and the Temple than on the countryside. But also the account in 1 Macc may be somewhat biased. In fact, 1 Macc generally emphasizes the importance of all Israel and of the revolt, which started in Modein, so that it may overstate the extent of the persecution in the country towns (1 Macc 1:51-58).

[101]So already Porphyry in Jerome's commentary on Dan 11:34 (Stern, *Greek and Latin Authors* 2.464R).

suggested that the "wise" in Daniel and the "lambs" in *1 Enoch* are the *Asidaioi* (=*Hasidim*) who joined the Hasmoneans early on in their fight (1 Macc 2:42).[102] The Book of Daniel and *1 Enoch* 85-90, however, represent substantially different views, especially with regard to the Temple. According to Daniel, one of Antiochus' greatest crimes was the desecration of the Temple (11:31; cf. 9:27; 12:11). *1 Enoch* instead considers the Second Temple defiled from the beginning (89:73) and expects a significant change only with the establishment of the "new" Jerusalem (90:29). These differences in outlook are all the more striking if both texts were written at approximately the same time.[103] Therefore, we cannot be sure that those whom the Book of Daniel called "the wise" would have seemed "lambs" to the author of *1 Enoch*, or *1 Enoch's* "lambs" been thought "wise" by Daniel. Again, there is no evidence to identify the group of strict Sabbath observers with the *Asidaioi*, as has often been done.[104]

1 Macc 2:42 reads as if the *Asidaioi* had been fighting before they joined the Hasmoneans. Probably neither was the only resistance group. 1 Macc 2:43 explicitly distinguishes from the *Asidaioi* the many others who fled from persecution, and whose resistance to it was probably not wholly passive. We should suppose that the religious and political situation produced a variety of groups which in moments of crisis collaborated, but rarely merged completely.[105] The Hasmoneans appear to have been one such group, which rose to become the major political force in the country for about a century and held the high priesthood from 152 to 37 and again briefly in 35 BCE.

---

[102]"The wise" = *Asidaioi*: L.F. Hartman and A.A. Di Lella, *The Book of Daniel* (AB 23; Garden City: Doubleday, 1978), pp. 43, 299; similarly Hengel, *Judaism and Hellenism* 2, p. 120, n. 490; O. Plöger, *Das Buch Daniel* (KAT 18; Gütersloh: Mohn, 1965), p. 165. "Lambs" = *Asidaioi*: Charles, *APOT* 2, p. 257; Hengel, *ibid.*, 1, p. 179.

[103]See Milik, *Aramaic Enoch*, p. 44; Hengel, *Judaism and Hellenism* 1.187; 2.116-117, n. 458. The military leader in *1 Enoch* 90:9-16, 31 who ushers in a new age can hardly be anyone but Judah Maccabee.

[104]See 1 Macc 2:29-38; 2 Macc 6:11; *Ant.* 12.272-275. A similar error is already found in 2 Macc 14:6, where Lysias speaks of Judah as the leader of the *Asidaioi*.

[105]So Grimm, *1 Macc.*, p. 44.

1

The Beginning of the Hasmonean Revolt

The Origin of the Hasmoneans

Very little is known about the origin of the Hasmonean family. Its traditional home was in Modein,[1] although both 1 Macc 2:1 and Josephus, *Ant.* 12.265, claim that Mattathias was originally from Jerusalem. It is, however, possible that he had lived in Jerusalem for some time before returning to Modein. If he was a priest of the clan of Joarib (1 Macc 2:1; 14:29), he would usually have to be in Jerusalem for Temple service several times a year.

---

[1] 1 Macc 2:70; 9:19; 13:25; *J.W.* 1.36. Modein is commonly identified with modern el-Medieh, about 7 miles east of Lod. See Abel, *Géographie* II p. 391; Möller, *Siedlungen*, p. 146. Judged by its geographic location, Modein is usually considered to have been part of the district of Lydda (Lod). See G. Beyer, "Die Stadtgebiete von Diospolis und Nikopolis im 4. Jahrh. n. Chr. und ihre Grenznachbarn," *ZDPV* 56 (1933) 234; M. Stern, *KS* 46 (1970) 97; Abel, *Macc.* p. 209. From this it follows that politically Modein belonged to Samaria until the time of Jonathan (1 Macc 11:34; 10:38; cf. 2 Macc 13:13-14). If correct, this conjecture would explain why the first military response to the Hasmonean rising came from Apollonius, the governor of Samaria (1 Macc 3:10; *Ant.* 12.287, 261). It may also explain why the attitude of Mattathias is contrasted with that of "the men of Judah" (1 Macc 2:18). On the other hand, Josephus calls Modein, perhaps anachronistically, a village of Judea (*Ant.* 12.265) and a resident of Modein is called *Ioudaios* (1 Macc 2:23). Also, apparently Modein was not affected by the favors granted by Antiochus IV in response to a Samaritan petition (*Ant.* 12.257-264). It may be that in southern Samaria a strong minority or even a majority of people were loyal to Jerusalem and considered themselves *Ioudaioi*. On the pre-Hasmonean use of *Ioudaioi* to refer to Shechemites, see Smith, *Palestinian Parties* pp. 189-190 and notes.

1 Macc 2:1 tells us that Mattathias was the son of John the son of Simon. Josephus calls Mattathias "a son of Asamonaios" (*J.W.* 1.36). This name never occurs in 1 or 2 Macc, but is frequently used by Josephus and in rabbinic literature in connection with the family of Mattathias. The Greek expression in *J.W.* 1.36 might be a translation from the Aramaic, meaning "a descendant of Asamonaios"; in *Ant.* 12.265, Josephus lists Asamonaios either as the name of Mattathias' great-grandfather or as the surname of his grandfather. In other passages he speaks of the descendants of Mattathias as *Asamonaioi* (*J.W.* 2.344; 5.139), or as "sons" or descendants of Asamonaios (*J.W.* 1.19; *Ant.* 11.111 and passim). Similarly, rabbinic literature speaks of בני or בית חשמונאי.[2] This should probably be translated "the clan of Hashmonay," though it can also be rendered "the clan of <the> Hasmonean."

Four explanations of this name have been proposed: (1) It was a personal name of an eponymous ancestor of Mattathias' family.[3] This would best accord with Josephus (*J.W.* 1.36) and with rabbinic texts, but the name never occurs outside this family. (2) It was the name of a family forming a subdivision of the priestly clan of Joarib.[4] This may account for Josephus' reference to Ἀσαμωναίων γένος,[5] but does not explain the name's origin. (3) It was an epithet added to the name of an ancestor of Mattathias. If an epithet, it might be based (a) on a place name such as Heshmon (Josh 15:27) or Hashmonah (Num 33:29, 30)[6] or (b) on a personal characteristic of the bearer. The derivation from a geographic name is possible, but no place with a similar name is connected with the family; similarly, no plausible explanation of what personal trait may be hidden in the name has been given. (4) It was an epithet of Mattathias similar to the epithets given to his sons. This possibility has been suggested by Goldstein on the basis of the *al hannissim* prayer, but against Goldstein, Josephus' usage does not imply this interpretation. In fact, Goldstein admits that Josephus may be correct in assigning that name (also) to Mattathias' grandfather or great-grandfather.[7] Thus a decision about the origin of the Hasmonean

---

[2]*m. Middot* 1:6 and elsewhere; see Goldstein, *1 Macc.* p. 18 n. 32.
[3]So H. Thackeray, LCL, *Life* 4, note.
[4]So J. Jeremias, *Jerusalem* pp. 188-189.
[5]*Ant.* 15.403. Niese conjectured Ἀσαμωναίου (singular) instead.
[6]Abel, *Macc.* p. IV; M. Stern, "Hasmoneans," *EncJud* 7.1455.
[7]1 *Macc.*, pp. 18-19. See also *Ant.* 20.238, which speaks of the "descendants of the sons of Asamonaios" in connection with Jonathan, the son of Mattathias. The text of *al hannissim* is not decisive; it contains errors only a late redactor could have made. See J. Heinemann, *Prayer in the Talmud* (Berlin/New York: De Gruyter, 1977) p. 241. J. Maier, *Geschichte der jüdischen Religion* (Berlin/New York: De Gruyter, 1972) 134.

family's name seems to be impossible on the basis of the available evidence.

Without doubt, however, the descendants of Mattathias claimed to belong to the priestly clan of Joarib, to which a Hasmonean redactor in 1 Chr 24:7 has given first place among the twenty-four priestly courses.[8]

Mattathias

The traditions about Mattathias, the first Hasmonean leader, are mostly included in 1 Macc 2. His name is not mentioned in 2 Macc. Because of this, Niese thought him to be literary fiction.[9] But this is unlikely since his rise is also described in the different and therefore probably independent account in *J.W.* 1.36-37.[10]

However, the account of Mattathias in 1 Macc 2 contains more direct speech and poetic material than any other chapter of 1 Macc. These are among the forms in which an author in the hellenistic period was least bound to historical accuracy.[11] Therefore we have to build mainly on the narrative sections, remaining wary of the pro-Hasmonean tendency of 1 Macc.

Our sources agree that Mattathias killed a royal official, then fled to the mountains[12] with his sons. There he was joined by others with whom he organized a resistance movement. He died not long afterwards, leaving his son Judah as military commander.[13]

---

[8]See 1 Macc 2:1; 14:29; *Ant.* 12.265. Concerning 1 Chr 24:7 see the decisive observations of Hölscher, "Levi," *PW* 12 (1925) 2191. Similarly J. Jeremias, *Jerusalem* p. 199. For a different view see Goldstein, *1 Macc.*, p. 17 n. 31.

[9]B. Niese, *Kritik der beiden Makkabäerbucher* (Berlin, 1900) 46.

[10]*J.W.* may follow popular legend. Mattathias is also mentioned in a document in honor of his son Simon (1 Macc 14:29). The Talmudic "Matityah, the High Priest" (*b. Meg.* 11a) is perhaps not our Mattathias, since he appears after and is distinguished from "Hasmonai and his sons". The passage suggests that later rabbis had more regard for the Hasmoneans than knowledge of them. Cf. J. Neusner *Rabbinic Traditions About the Pharisees Before 70* (3 vols. Leiden: Brill, 1971), Vol. 1 p. 39. His attribution of this passage to Samuel is erroneous; it is a Baraita introduced by במתניתא תנא.

[11]Josephus' rendering of 1 Macc 2 in *Ant.* 12.265-284 is a perfect example of this. He follows the narrative sections very closely, adding only a few names. But he shortens or alters speeches and poetic pieces at liberty. Cf. 1 Macc 2:7-13/*Ant.* 12.267; 1 Macc 2:49-68/*Ant.* 12.279-284. See I. Gafni, "On the Use of 1 Maccabees by Josephus Flavius," *Zion* 45 (1980) 81-95 (in Hebrew).

[12]εἰς τὰ ὄρη 1 Macc 2:28; *J.W.* 1.36; *Ant.* 12.271 has εἰς τὴν ἔρημον, practically equivalent.

[13]1 Macc 2:70; *Ant.* 12.285. Being an event of local history, it should be given according to Babylonian reckoning; 146 Sel. (Bab.) = 166/5 BCE.

First Maccabees adds important details to this outline. First it gives us a brief genealogy of Mattathias' family.[14] Unfortunately there are no clear explanations for the surnames of his five sons.[15] Secondly, 1 Macc describes at length the events that led Mattathias to kill a royal official. It specifies that this took place in Modein.[16] When the people came for the sacrifice, Mattathias and his sons came too.[17] Reportedly the king's officer asked Mattathias to be the first to sacrifice, because of his leadership in the community. In return for cooperation he offered honors and other rewards (2:17-18). The pro-Hasmonean author here had an opportunity to show the importance of his patron's family. Therefore his picture of Mattathias cannot be trusted, but may be true.

Mattathias refused to sacrifice, appealing to the "covenant of our fathers" and to "the Torah and the commandments" (2:20-22). When another Jew stepped forward in his stead, Mattathias reportedly killed both him and the royal official and tore down the altar. Josephus (*Ant.* 12.270) calls the royal official Apelles[18] and adds that Mattathias was assisted by his five sons, armed with choppers and that they also killed "a few soldiers." Obviously, Mattathias could not have single-handedly killed two men, torn down the altar under the eyes of a detachment of soldiers (unmentioned in 1 Macc, but presumably present), and got away with it. Josephus may have based his inventions on this assumption. Were the story in 1 Macc true, it would be surprising that there were no Hasmonean casualties, and that 1 Macc knew nothing of the free-for-all that must have ensued. 1 Macc certainly does not give us an accurate eyewitness account. But that is not its purpose. Rather, it is structured to parallel the story of Phinehas in Numbers 25: invitation to pagan sacrifice, sin of one conspicuous

---

[14]1 Macc 2:1-5; cf. *Ant.* 12.265-66. On the historical value of the genealogy see Schunck, *Quellen* p. 63 n. 3.

[15]Especially Judah's surname "Makkabaios" has been the subject of much study. The majority of scholars connects it with מקב ("hammer"), but there are several other proposals, e.g. a derivation from the root נקב interpreted as "fixed" (sc. made certain, permanent by the Lord). So Abel, *Macc.* p. III.

[16]1 Macc 2:15-25. *J.W.* 1.36 seems to imply that Mattathias had remained in Jerusalem. In *Ant.* 12.268, however, Josephus follows 1 Macc in locating these events more correctly in Modein.

[17]Goldstein translates 1 Macc 2:16b "Mattathias and his sons were brought into the gathering" and thinks that the passive is used deliberately (*1 Macc.*, p. 232). In 1 Macc, however, συνήχθησαν is commonly used as middle, "came together"; see 2:42; 3:46; 7:22, and passim, and Abel's warning against over-interpretation (*Macc.*, p. 35).

[18]For the tendency to identify unnamed persons see R. Bultmann, *The History of the Synoptic Tradition* (Rev. ed.; New York: Harper & Row, 1976) pp. 241, 260, 310.

Israelite, slaying of Israelite and gentile seducer while they are caught in the sinful act. These parallels are deliberate, as the several references to Phinehas show (1 Macc 2:26, 54), and serve a definite purpose. Phinehas and his descendants received the (high) priesthood because of his zealous act (Num 25:13; 1 Macc 2:54), not because of his descent from Aaron. Therefore, the descendants of Mattathias are heirs of Phinehas and have the right to be (high) priests.[19]

In *J.W.* 1.36, Josephus gives a largely different account, which is clearly popular legend: Mattathias in Jerusalem, with a band of kinsmen (μετὰ χειρὸς οἰκείας) including his five sons, killed the king's general, Bacchides, and forthwith took to the hills. Nothing is said of the occasion of the slaying. For the tendency of popular legend to substitute famous for obscure figures and telescope events, one may compare the remarks of Thucydides (6.54) on the legend prevalent in his time about the murder of Hipparchus, less than a century before.

1 Macc 2:28-30 sets the escape of the Hasmoneans in sharp contrast to the flight of a group of "Seekers of Justice and Judgment." The former left their belongings in the town and fled to the mountains, the latter chose to go down to the desert, taking not only their wives and children, but also their herds along.[20] Mattathias was accompanied not only by members of his family, but he also gathered a group of "friends" around himself, consisting perhaps in part of fellow villagers who had fled Modein with him, in part of like-minded individuals from elsewhere.[21] If 2 Macc 5:27 has any historical value, it may indicate that the original group was very small indeed: around ten men. It also, like *J.W.*, writes as if the departure were from Jerusalem - probably because it too reflects legend.

Many of the "Seekers of Justice and Judgment" (1 Macc 2:38 speaks of 1000) were killed in the desert caves where they had taken refuge,

---

[19]See V. Aptowitzer, *Parteipolitik der Hasmonäerzeit im rabbinischen und pseudoepigraphischen Schrifttum* (Vienna/New York: Kohut Foundation, 1927) pp. 4-12; Arenhoevel, *Theokratie*, p. 45.

[20]See Goldstein, *1 Macc.*, p. 235, but his assumption that the "Seekers of Justice and Vindication" were opposed to armed resistance is unwarranted because the only stated reason for their inactivity was the Sabbath. See 1 Macc 2:34; 2 Macc 6:11. On "Justice and Judgment" (= "Torah observance") see the passages collected by Abel and his commentary (*Macc.*, p. 39).

[21]Schunck (*Quellen*, p. 59) would substitute "Judah and his friends" for "Mattathias and his friends" in 1 Macc 2:39, 45 and thereby attributes 2:29-48 to Judah. This emendation is unwarranted because it supposes the author is using an account of Judah as the basis of his story about Mattathias. There is no evidence of such a source. The story about Mattathias seems free creation on the basis of popular tradition or legend. But, in any event, there is no reason to doubt that Mattathias started immediately to gather a following (cf. 2:27).

because they refused to violate the Sabbath rest in any way.[22] Thus they did not even attempt any self-defense. First Maccabees reports that in order to avoid similar disasters in the future, "Mattathias and his friends" took counsel together and jointly decided to defend themselves even on a Sabbath (1 Macc 2:39-41). Josephus says that many of the Sabbatarians escaped and joined Mattathias (1 Macc knows nothing of this) and that Mattathias *instructed them* to fight in self-defense on the Sabbath, a rule which remained in effect until Josephus' own days (*Ant.* 12.276-277). The transference of the joint decision to Mattathias would be expected in oral transmission, but the report that members of the Sabbatarian group escaped and joined Mattathias is surprising. *Prima facie* it is plausible that in such a situation Mattathias and his followers would have decided that preserving life was more important than observing the Sabbath rest. Problems arise, however, when we compare their decision with the evidence for its implementation. Second Maccabees does not refer to such a decision.[23] Furthermore, it reports that in 161/0 BCE Nicanor still thought that on the Sabbath he could attack Judah and his men with complete impunity (2 Macc 15:1). The first time we hear about a battle on a Sabbath is when Bacchides attempted to trap Jonathan and his men at the Jordan (c. 160 BCE).[24] It is possible that a decision made by Jonathan on the spot (1 Macc 9:44) was later justified by attributing a pertinent ruling to "Mattathias and his friends." Elsewhere Mattathias is cited as an authority figure for the later Hasmonean claim to the high priesthood (cf. 1 Macc 2:54) and for the policy of forced circumcision (cf. 1 Macc 2:46). If a decision to fight on the Sabbath was not taken until after Judah's death, we could more easily explain the fact that *Jubilees* 50.12 prohibits, on pain of death, any Sabbath violation, specifically including warfare, yet seems to judge Judah's wars favorably. This observation is valid only, if this text of *Jubilees* is to be dated after 161 BCE.[25]

---

[22]Cf. 2 Macc 6:11; *Ant.* 12.275.

[23]That it says Judah and his men refrained from pursuing their enemies on the Sabbath (8:26; cf. 12:38) is not relevant, since what was permitted was only *defensive fighting*. Presumably aggression remained forbidden.

[24]1 Macc 9:43-49. The reference to the newness of the situation in v 44b may be meant as a justification for the order to fight (for the first time?) on the Sabbath. According to *Ant.* 13.12, Bacchides did not expect any resistance because of the Sabbath. See Abel, *Macc.*, p. 170.

[25]Such a date is suggested by J. VanderKam, *Textual and Historical Studies in the Book of Jubilees* (Harvard Semitic Monographs 14) Missoula, MT: Scholars Press, 1977, pp. 217-238, 283-284; similarly Schürer-Vermes-Millar 3.313; a date around 168 is preferred instead by G.W.E. Nickelsburg in *Jewish Writings of*

B. Bar-Kochva has recently challenged the accepted view that Mattathias and his men were the ones to decide that self-defense on the Sabbath should be permitted. He starts out from the plausible argument that the question must have arisen earlier, because of the Syrian wars that touched Judea and because of the many Jews who served as mercenaries in various armies. He is probably correct in attributing the capture of Jerusalem by Ptolemy I on a Sabbath to a ruse rather than to a reluctance of the Jews to defend themselves on that day.[26] He is also correct in pointing out that Sabbath observance *per se* and not only self-defense was at issue in the attack on the strict Sabbath-observers in the caves (1 Macc 2:34). Yet he cannot explain away the fact that, according to 1 Macc 2:41, the decision of Mattathias and his men was specifically concerned with self-defense on the Sabbath.[27]

One fact that Bar-Kochva overlooks is the gradual progression and sectarian diversity in the interpretation of what would be permissible on the Sabbath. For example, 2 Chr 23, though it modifies the story of 2 Kgs 11 considerably, does not criticize the pious priest Jehoiada for choosing to start the bloody coup against Athaliah on a Sabbath. The Sabbath observance of Jewish soldiers in foreign armies is not discussed in our sources before the time of John Hyrcanus I (cf. *Ant.* 13.250-252), and the first exemptions from military service were granted to Jews by the Romans in the mid-first century BCE[28] From the available evidence it appears that warfare on the Sabbath was not yet considered problematic in the fourth century BCE (see 2 Chronicles). The issue is addressed for the first time in *Jubilees.* The decision of the Hasmoneans to allow defensive warfare by no means settled the issue, because it was raised again and again, even in Josephus' time, usually without any reference to the Hasmoneans.[29]

---

the Second Temple Period, ed M. Stone (Compendia Rerum Iudaicarum ad Novum Testamentum, Section 2 Vol. 2) Philadelphia: Fortress, 1984, pp. 102-103.

[26]Cf. *Ant.* 12.4 with Stern, *Greek and Latin Authors* 1, No. 30a-b.

[27]B. Bar-Kochva, *The Battles of the Hasmoneans. The Times of Judas Maccabaeus*, Jerusalem: Yad Izhak Ben-Zvi Publications, 1980, pp. 331-342, esp. 336 (Hebrew).

[28]See E.M. Smallwood, *The Jews Under Roman Rule from Pompey to Diocletian*, Leiden: Brill, 1981, pp. 127-128.

[29]*Life* 161; *Ant.* 18.323. On the whole issue see M.D. Herr, "The Problem of War on the Sabbath in the Second Temple and the Talmudic Periods," (in Hebrew) *Tarbiz* 30 (1960/61) 244-245. R. Goldenberg, "The Jewish Sabbath in the Roman World," *ANRW* II.19.1 (1979) pp. 430-433.

After relating the decision to fight on the Sabbath, 1 Macc continues by introducing a new group of allies of Mattathias: the *Asidaioi* (see Excursus below). We do not know the numerical strength of either the *Asidaioi* or the other allies of Mattathias. Later on the *Asidaioi* are represented by Alcimus (according to 2 Macc 14:6) as the most conspicuous contingent of Judah's forces. Since it is 1 Macc – a work of Hasmonean origin – which says that they joined Mattathias, we might even consider it possible that in fact Mattathias and his men took the initiative and joined them. The author of 1 Macc may have introduced the *Asidaioi* deliberately in connection with the decision to fight on the Sabbath. This would give added proof to the legitimacy of the new interpretation of the Torah, especially if the *Asidaioi* were connected with any group challenging Hasmonean legitimacy.[30]

Others, besides the *Asidaioi*, who joined the Hasmoneans in the mountains included "all those who fled the troubles" (1 Macc 2:43). It is worth noting that 1 Macc explicitly distinguishes these from the *Asidaioi*. Its author envisioned – or, at least, wished his readers to envision the Hasmoneans as the representatives and leaders of a variety of groups, potentially, of all good Israelites. Many other passages show the same purpose.[31]

First Maccabees attributes to Mattathias and his followers raids designed to restore observance of the Torah in Judea. The enemies are not named but defined by their negative attitude toward Torah (ἄνομοι, i.e. "lawless ones")[32] and by their sinfulness (ἁμαρτωλοί). Abel and especially Renaud have pointed out that Jews and only Jews are defined with reference to the Torah (ἄνομοι), whereas Gentiles are more generically called "sinners."[33] Arenhoevel, however, has shown that there is at least some inconsistency in this usage.[34] In fact, in the Septuagint both ἄνομος and ἁμαρτολός most frequently translate Hebrew רשע and the Hebrew text of 1 Macc may simply have used two nearly synonymous terms.[35]

---

[30]This is no proof that they were connected with the later Pharisees, but *may* point in that direction.

[31]E.g., 1 Macc 2:70; 3:10-11; 4:25; 5:62-64; 9:20-21.

[32]1 Macc 2:44. This may reflect the view of the Greek translator only, since Hebrew has no exact equivalent of ἄνομος.

[33]Abel, *Macc.*, p. 44; B. Renaud, "La loi et les lois dans les livres des Maccabees," *RB* 68 (1961) 45-49. See above, *Introduction* n. 71.

[34]See Arenhoevel, *Theokratie* p. 4 n. 6.

[35]1 Macc 2:43b and 44 look like close translation of two verses with *parallelismus membrorum*. It is not difficult to render καὶ ἄνδρας ἀνόμους ἐν θυμῷ αὐτῶν ("and <they smote> lawless men in their anger") as ואנשי בליעל באפם, and the fact that two of the three stresses are needed for אנשי בליעל would explain

Those of the enemies who were able to escape Mattathias' troops allegedly fled "to the Gentiles" (1 Macc 2:44). Later on, such refugees were to play an important political role. Observance of the Torah as a residence requirement in Judea is frequently found in sources of the Hasmonean period.[36]

The statement that "they [Mattathias and his followers] circumcised by force all the uncircumcised boys they found within Israel's borders" (1 Macc 2:46) is not simply exaggeration. Ascribing to the founder of the dynasty the origins of a policy that clearly caused some opposition, could go a long way toward explaining and perhaps justifying it.[37] Mattathias may well have forcibly circumcised some children, but the statement as it stands may be thought to reflect the policy followed by John Hyrcanus and his successors, because Mattathias' area of operation was in no way coterminous with "Israel's borders," whereas Hyrcanus could claim that he was reestablishing Jewish Law within these borders. However Mattathias may have thought Judea the *de facto* territory of "Israel," as Judah seems to have thought in bringing refugees from Gilead to Judea.

In spite of 1 Macc's claim that Mattathias subdued his enemies and rescued the Torah from the Gentiles, the truth is that his military success was very limited.[38] Thus, 1 Macc 2:47-48 again displays the tendency to attribute to Mattathias events that occurred later, but were considered of paramount importance for the history of the dynasty.[39]

First Maccabees concludes the account of Mattathias' life with his farewell speech addressed to his sons. After a brief exhortation to show zeal for the Torah (v 50), its first part (vv 51-61) is a recapitulation of the merits of the Fathers, similar to Sir 44-50.[40] This section again is written in balanced cola, though the balance is less carefully

---

the lack of a second verb to balance ἐπάταξαν ("they smote"). If this conjecture be correct, we glimpse as one element of 1 Macc a heroic poem in Hebrew, celebrating the revolt. Cf. 1 Macc 3:3-9; 14:4-15. Whether these poetic sections represent a separate source is debatable. G.O. Neuhaus assumes without question that all poetic sections were composed by the author of 1 Macc (*Studien zu den poetischen Stücken im 1. Makkabäerbuch* [Würzburg: Echter, 1974] p. 180).

[36]See 1 Macc 13:48 and the discussion of circumcision p. 143 below.

[37]Pella was destroyed by Alexander Jannaeus "because the inhabitants refused to change to the native customs of the Jews" (*Ant.* 13.397).

[38]1 Macc 2:47-48. The contrast with the more somber mood in the following verses (49-50) is so abrupt that one may think of a different source for the farewell speech, or of omission of material that formerly intervened.

[39]Cf. Abel, *Macc.*, p. 45. Again, the style is marked by balanced cola that may reflect Hebrew verse.

[40]Cf. also Heb 11; *m. Abot* 1-2.

observed.[41] It gives not only models of faith, of obedience to the Law, and of zeal for it but it also establishes a link between the forefathers and the Hasmonean heroes, especially through Phinehas "our father who by being greatly zealous received the covenant of an eternal priesthood" – and so provided a basis for the later Hasmonean claims. It is significant that of the eight other examples mentioned, in three cases the reward was rulership, in two deliverance from dangers, in one possession of the land. The emphasis on deliverance from danger, rulership, and (high) priesthood, may suggest that this material originated in the time of Simon or the early days of Hyrcanus. This would explain the preeminence of Simon.

The second part of Mattathias' speech contains general admonitions (vv 61-64) and practical advice for the sons (vv 65-68). Simon is given a role of prominence, he is to be regarded as father,[42] although he never takes center stage in the account of 1 Macc until 142 BCE His position may result from the fact that his descendants continued the Hasmonean dynasty. Judah therefore takes second place. The last advice to the sons is to rally around themselves all those who observe the Torah (v 67) and to be observers of the commandments themselves (v 68). The emphasis on Torah thus provides a framework for the entire speech. The ensuing death and burial of Mattathias are described in terms similar to the conclusion of the lives of biblical heroes.[43]

The account of Mattathias' life is thus far from a mere description of events. Though undoubtedly based on some factual and legendary material, it is a skillful presentation of the origin and legitimacy of the dynasty and a defense for some of its central tenets: It claims the right to the high priesthood, asserts complete and zealous dedication to Torah, represents the dynasty's rise to power as resultant from its founder's defense of Torah and leadership of those anxious to defend it, and affirms that changes in observance, at least of the Sabbath, are legitimate when necessitated by the circumstances. Considering this, our knowledge about Mattathias himself is rather slim.

---

[41]The cola are paired, but in most pairs the first is markedly longer. This is characteristic of the Hebrew *Qinah* meter, dominant in Lamentations, but also in Ps 65, a hymn of thanksgiving. See N.K. Gottwald, "Poetry, Hebrew," *IDB* 3.834.

[42]Abel describes this as Hebraism (*Macc.*, p. 50).

[43]Gen 50:10 (Jacob); Deut 34:5-8 (Moses); Judg 8:32 (Gideon); 1 Sam 25:1; 28:3 (Samuel); 2 Chr 35:24 (Josiah).

Extent of Support for the Hasmoneans at Mattathias' Death

Mattathias had gained support from different quarters. The core of his movement consisted of his sons and other family members (1 Macc 2:17). Around them there was an initial group of friends (v 39). It probably consisted of fellow townsmen from Modein and surrounding villages. This circle was expanded by the joining of a company of *Asidaioi* (v 42). Additional support came from scattered refugees (v 43), many of them probably former inhabitants of Jerusalem (1 Macc 1:38, 53), where the persecution was most directly felt. Nothing is known about their identity, but it is a fair guess that among others they included displaced Temple personnel (priests, levites, others). Some of them may have been personal acquaintances of Mattathias.

Apparently all these different elements were referred to as Mattathias' "friends" (1 Macc 2:45). They constituted a coalition of groups and individuals which later on split and regrouped several times. Interestingly, there is no indication of the geographic area in which Mattathias operated, other than "Israel's borders" (v 46). His guerilla activity apparently did not reach Jerusalem and was probably limited to the mountainous area to the north and northwest of the city.[44]

While religious beliefs and economic interests are not invariably congruent, we may plausibly suppose that many of Mattathias' sympathizers and supporters were (1) members of the Jerusalem Temple staff who found themselves on the losing side in the many changes there, especially those who favored the old ways against hellenistic innovations; (2) rural landowners either pinched or dispossessed by extension of monetary economy, royal taxation, Greek moneylending, and perhaps expropriations to create estates for royal "friends," (3) rural peasantry, traditionally hostile to city ways and rulers, and glad to follow local leaders in revolt.[45]

---

[44]See M. Avi-Yonah, *Carta's Atlas of the Period of the Second Temple*, p. 25, map 30.

[45]For the economic factors of the Hasmonean revolt see H.G. Kippenberg, *Religion und Klassenbildung im antiken Judäa* (Göttingen: Vandenhoeck & Ruprecht, 1978) pp. 87-93; H. Kreissig ("Der Makkabäeraufstand, zur Frage seiner sozialökonomischen Zusammenhänge und Wirkungen," *Studii Clasice* 4 [1962] 143-175) accuses others of focusing exclusively on religious aspects of the revolt, but his own socio-economic interpretation, strongly influenced by Marxist theory, goes too far in the opposite direction.

Excursus: Who Were the Asidaioi?

Scholarly consensus derives the word ἀσιδαῖοι (1 Macc 2:42; 7:13; 2 Macc 14:6) from the Hebrew חסידים ("pious"), probably through the Aramaic emphatic plural form חסידיא. Especially since the discovery of the Dead Sea Scrolls, the *Asidaioi* have often been related to the Essenes, and more specifically to the Qumran community; many scholars also consider them the forerunners of the Pharisees.[46] The main arguments for connecting the *Asidaioi* with the Essenes are their piety and the similarity of their names. It is assumed that the Syriac word *hase* existed in Palestinian Aramaic and was used as a substitute for Hebrew/Aramaic חסיד and that the Greek forms ἐσσηνοί (*J.W.* 2.119 and passim) and ἐσσαῖοι (Philo, *Quod omnis probus liber sit* 13 and passim) may have been influenced by the Syriac plurals *hasen* and *hasayya* respectively.[47] But the word is not attested in Palestinian Aramaic with the meaning of "pious."[48] Therefore, the relation between *Asidaioi* and Essenes is at best uncertain. Furthermore, the *Asidaioi* are not directly related to the "pietists of old" (חסידים הראשונים) of rabbinic literature,[49] nor does available evidence permit us to link them with writings such as Daniel, *1 Enoch,* and *Jubilees.*[50] In fact, we have no evidence that the *Asidaioi* were interested in apocalyptic speculation and their acceptance of Alcimus as high priest rather suggests the opposite. Similarly, the connection between the *Asidaioi* and the Scribes or Pharisees is unprovable because 1 Macc 7:12-13 which speaks first of Scribes and then of *Asidaioi* should probably be read as distinguishing between the Scribes assembled by Alcimus and Bacchides to restore the Law (?), and the *Asidaioi* who, *because* of this demonstration of concern for the Law, *thereupon* sought peace with Alcimus.

In many attempts to link the *Asidaioi* with other later groups there seems to be a tacit assumption that Josephus' statements about the existence of three and only three Jewish sects is true not only for the

---

[46]For recent discussion and for literature see Hengel, *Judaism and Hellenism* 1, pp. 175-180; 2, pp. 116-120 nn. 453-490.

[47]So Schürer, *Geschichte* 2 (1907) p. 655, followed by many scholars.

[48]Schürer-Vermes-Millar 2, p. 559; for other derivations of the term "Essene" see *ibid.*

[49]See S. Safrai, "The Teaching of the Pietists in Mishnaic Literature," *JJS* 16 (1965) 15-33, especially pp. 15, 20.

[50]It is often assumed that these works stem from the same circles, but Dan 11:31 affirms the holiness of the Second Temple, while *1 Enoch* 89.73 denies the validity of the sacrifices offered in it. *Jub.* 50.12 forbids any fighting on the Sabbath, while the *Asidaioi* are said to have approved of it.

early first century CE, but also, without change, for the mid-second century BCE, and that therefore by the time of Jonathan (d. 143/2 BCE) all religious Jews in Palestine had become either Pharisees or Essenes or Sadducees.

Davies and Meyer consider ἀσιδαῖοι/חסידים a term designating a wide variety of individuals or religious groups for whom piety was a central concern.[51] This may be true for the several occurrences of the term in canonical and non-canonical psalms,[52] but the fact that the term is not translated in either 1 or 2 Macc suggests that it was not used in its generic meaning, but designated a specific group. There is no indication that the strict Sabbath observers (1 Macc 2:29-38; 2 Macc 6:11) belonged to it.[53]

Our negative assessment of the connections between *Asidaioi* and other known Jewish groups may be disappointing, but seems to be required by the state of the evidence. It is shared by a growing number of scholars.[54]

Having had to discard all other texts adduced as evidence, we can rely only on the explicit references to a group called *Asidaioi* which existed in Judea in the 160s BCE: 1 Macc 2:42; 7:13-18, and 2 Macc 14:6-10. From these passages we learn that a company of *Asidaioi* joined the Hasmoneans early in their struggle. Second Maccabees has Alcimus later tell King Demetrius that "those of the Jews who are called *Asidaioi*, whose leader is Judah Maccabee, are maintaining war and stirring up rebellion," and goes on to say that they are causing great

---

[51]P. Davies, "Hasidim in the Maccabean Period," *JJS* 28 (1977) 127-140; R. Meyer, *TDNT* 7.39 n. 27.

[52]E.g., Ps 79:2; 148:14; 149:1, 9; Ps 154.12 (11QPs^a xviii.10) may refer to a specific group, but חסידים is only one of its many titles. See J.A. Sanders, *The Psalms Scroll of Qumran Cave 11 (11QPs^a)* (DJD 4; Oxford: Clarendon, 1965) pp. 68, 70. Sanders considers the psalm "perhaps proto-Essenian or Hasidic."

[53]Josephus does say that those who survived the Sabbath massacre joined Mattathias and appointed him their leader (*Ant.* 12.275). In his account these refugees take approximately the place that the *Asidaioi*, whom he never mentions, take in 1 Macc. The *Asidaioi*, however, joined Mattathias as an organized group (συναγωγή) and not as scattered refugees (1 Macc 2:42). Therefore one cannot confidently base any conclusions about them on Josephus.

[54]See M. Smith, in *Der Hellenismus und der Aufstieg Roms. Die Mittelmeerwelt im Altertum II*, ed P. Grimal (Fischer Weltgeschichte 6; Frankfurt/Main: Fischer, 1965) p. 383 n. 365; M. Stone, *Scriptures, Sects and Visions* (Philadelphia: Fortress, 1980) p. 73; G.W.E. Nickelsburg, "Social Aspects of Palestinian Jewish Apocalypticism," in *Apocalypticism in the Mediterranean World and the Near East*, ed. by D. Hellholm (Tübingen: Mohr, 1983), pp. 647-654.

suffering to the people and so long as Judah survives there can be no
peace (2 Macc 14:6-10). According to 1 Macc 7:8-10, Demetrius I then
sent Bacchides (according to 2 Macc 14:12-13, Nicanor) with Alcimus to
put down the revolt and restore peace. Only 1 Macc 7:13-14 tells us that,
when Alcimus and Bacchides arrived, the *Asidaioi* entered into
negotiations with Alcimus – presumably they gave up their alliance
with Judah when they did so. In spite of an oath, Alcimus had sixty of
them executed. After this tragedy, both 1 and 2 Macc are silent about
the *Asidaioi*. Concerning their attitudes the cited passages tell us only

(a)   that they temporarily cooperated with the Hasmoneans,

(b)   that they were "volunteering for (Goldstein: in defense of)
         the Torah,"[55]

(c)   that they were represented as stirring up the war and

(d)   that they (or, at least some of them) made peace when
         Demetrius sent Alcimus whom they thought – reputedly
         because of his Aaronic ancestry – a legitimate high priest
         with authority to restore the Torah.

The author of 1 Macc called the *Asidaioi* "men of strength" (2:42
ἰσχυροὶ δυνάμει). This suggests that they were considered an
important addition to the military power of the Hasmoneans, probably
that they had prior military experience.

---

[55]πᾶς ὁ ἐκουσιαζόμενος τῷ νόμῳ (perhaps from Hebrew כל המתנדב לתורה) means
that "each one who volunteered" was a member of this group. The Greek text
may be a mistranslation or a tendentious overstatement, because there were
people other than the *Asidaioi* who were zealous for the law (e.g., the
Hasmoneans; cf. 1 Macc 2:50 and passim). Therefore NEB translates "everyone
of them a volunteer in the cause of the law" (my italics). A similar expression
occurs in Neh 11:28; 2 Chr 17:16 and in 1QS 5.1-2.

2

Judah Maccabee

We are in the fortunate position of having a number of independent sources for the time of Judah Maccabee. Of these, 1 and 2 Macc are the main ones, but the Book of Daniel, *1 Enoch*, and the works of Josephus offer important independent information. Unfortunately these sources differ on the relative chronology of events, especially whether the rededication of the Temple, the first campaign of Lysias, and Judah's early expeditions outside Judea occurred before or after the death of Antiochus IV.

These chronological problems have given rise to a vast literature, but unfortunately the evidence is so ambiguous that the areas of consensus are few. Since however a precise chronology is generally not central to my thesis, I shall limit myself to presenting what seems to me a plausible outline of events, listing a selection of different views in footnotes.[1]

---

[1]Major treatments of the period are found in: F.-M. Abel, *Macc.*; B. Bar-Kochva, *The Battles of the Hasmonaeans. The Times of Judas Maccabaeus* (Jerusalem: Yad Izhak Ben-Zvi, 1980).E. Bickerman, *Gott*; K. Bringmann, *Hellenistische Reform und Religionsverfolgung in Judäa* (Göttingen: Vandenhoeck & Ruprecht, 1983); Bunge, *Untersuchungen*; T. Fischer, *Seleukiden und Makkabäer* (Bochum: Brockmeyer, 1980); J.A. Goldstein, *1 Macc.*; *id .*, *2 Macc*; C. Habicht, *2 Macc.*; M. Hengel, *Judaism and Hellenism*; O. Mørkholm, *Antiochus IV of Syria* (Classica et Mediaevalia, Dissertationes 8; Copenhagen; Gyldendal, 1966); P. Schäfer, "The Hellenistic and Maccabean Periods," in J.H. Hayes and J.M. Miller, *Israelite and Judaean History* (Philadelphia: Westminster, 1977); Schürer-Vermes-Millar; V. Tcherikover, *Hellenistic Civ.*; S. Zeitlin, *The Rise and Fall of the Judaean State* (3 vols: Philadelphia: JPS, 1968-78) vol. 1; More detailed bibliographies may be found in these works.

Early Achievements

The transition of leadership from Mattathias to Judah seems to have been smooth. Simon, who was given a privileged position in Mattathias' last discourse (1 Macc 2:65), is portrayed as following Judah's directions (1 Macc 5:17). 1 Macc 3:2 stresses that all his brothers and all those who had joined his father helped him.

Second Maccabees, which never mentions Mattathias, tells us that Judah and his men secretly entered villages by night to call their relatives and those who had remained faithful to Judaism. Reportedly they gathered 6,000 men (2 Macc 8:1).

The outline of the progress of the revolt in 1 Macc is rather schematic, though more detailed than in 2 Macc: Apollonius set out to fight against Israel. Judah defeated his army and killed him (1 Macc 3:10-12; *Ant.* 12.287). Then Seron, styled "commander of the Syrian troops" (1 Macc 3:13), came with a stronger army to fight against "Judah and those with him who disregarded the King's command." He brought with him "a strong company of ungodly men to help him punish the children of Israel."[2] Seron was defeated in an ambush at Bethhoron and fled with his remaining troops back to the coastal area (1 Macc 3:23-24; *Ant.* 12.292).

Probably in the following spring, 165 BCE, Antiochus IV set out on his ill-fated eastern campaign, leaving Lysias in charge of affairs in the west. Soon afterward, Ptolemy the son of Dorymenes, the governor of Coele-Syria and Phoenicia, dispatched a sizable army under Gorgias and Nicanor to Judea.[3] Judah rallied his troops at Mizpah, then took the Seleucid camp near Emmaus in a surprise attack. The survivors fled,[4] including a large detachment under Gorgias that had been searching in vain for Judah and his men.

---

[2]1 Macc 3:14-15. Since this "company" (παρεμβολή) is clearly distinguished from Seron's forces, and since 1 Macc commonly used "ungodly men" (ἀσεβεῖς) for Jewish opponents (e.g. 3:8; 6:21; 7:5, 9; 9:73), it would seem that refugees from the Hasmoneans, with their friends and supporters, formed a considerable group in Syria already by the time of this campaign (*Ant.* 12.289). However, the "company" may have included many people displaced during the fighting between the priestly competitors, who hoped now to gain restoration by supporting the government.

[3]According to 2 Macc 8:8 the initiative came from Philip, the *Epistates of Jerusalem* (see 2 Macc 5:22 and Habicht ad loc.), who requested assistance from the governor. According to 1 Macc 3:38-39 it was Lysias who ordered Ptolemy (and Nicanor and Gorgias) to intervene. The two accounts are not mutually exclusive.

[4]1 Macc 4:15: to Gezer, Idumea, Azotus, Jamnia.

The account of 1 Macc passes from the battle of Emmaus immediately to the first campaign of Lysias against Judea, which it places "in the following year."[5] It is evident that several months, probably the winter of 165/4 BCE, passed between these events.

Second Maccabees on the other hand places Lysias' first (and second) campaign under Antiochus V, therefore not earlier than 163 BCE This however can easily be explained as a misreading of the documents in 2 Macc 11. As they stand, they are lumped together with events under Antiochus V, whereas only one letter (11:22-26) belongs to that period. The other letters document the exchanges which took place in 148 Sel. Mac. (165/4 BCE) under Antiochus IV.[6]

The earliest document is a letter of King Antiochus to "the *Gerousia* of the Jews" (i.e. of Jerusalem) "and to the other Jews" (2 Macc 11:27-33). It grants limited amnesty to those who return home and permits Jews to observe again their δαπανήμασι (dietary regulations?)[7] and other laws. According to the letter, Menelaus had informed the king that the Jews (including the *Gerousia*?) were anxious to return to their properties; he was sent by the king to Jerusalem, presumably to announce the terms of the amnesty.[8] Whatever the date of the amnesty,

---

[5]Kolbe, *Beiträge zur syrischen und jüdischen Geschichte* (Berlin, 1926) pp. 79-81 and Mørkholm, *Antiochus IV of Syria*, pp. 152-154, have argued that Lysias invaded Palestine only once, after the death of Antiochus IV, and that the accounts in 1 Macc 4:28-35 and 2 Macc 11:1-12 are doublets of 1 Macc 6:20-49, designed to neutralize the defeat suffered by the Hasmoneans at Beth-zechariah in 163 BCE. This explanation does not hold for 2 Macc and has not been accepted by others. See Schürer-Vermes-Millar 1, p. 160 n. 59; Bunge, *Untersuchungen* p. 416.

[6]The most plausible explanation of these letters and their chronology is given by Habicht (*Harvard Studies in Classical Philology 80* [1976] 1-18, esp. 14-17), whom I follow here. He argues convincingly that the letter of Antiochus IV *to the Gerousia* is not a sequel to Lysias' letter *to the revolutionaries* (πλῆθος). Goldstein (2 *Macc.*, pp. 426-428) provides a less likely reconstruction, since it requires, e.g., that Antiochus V, less than ten years old, produced a document in opposition to Lysias, his guardian. Fischer (*Seleukiden und Makkabäer*, p. 71) dates all documents in 2 Macc 11 (except vv 27-33) between the death of Antiochus IV and the rededication of the Temple in Jerusalem. In order to accomplish this, he has to reject the accepted date of the death of Antiochus IV (late fall 164 B.C.), which is based on the only plausible reading of the Babylonian king list (Sachs-Wiseman, *Iraq* 16 [1954] 208-209) and confirmed by 1 Macc 6:16.

[7]So Abel, *Macc.* p. 430. Habicht (2 *Macc.* p. 259 n. 31a) and Goldstein (2 *Macc.*, pp. 421-422) follow Wilhelm's conjecture διαιτήμασι ("way of life").

[8]The date of this letter is problematic, especially since the end of the amnesty period (30 Xanthicus) is too close to the date of the letter (15 Xanthicus, 148 Sel. Mac.). Furthermore, a letter of Roman ambassadors which reflects a different situation is dated on the very same day (2 Macc 11:38). Thus, at least one of the

it had no effect on Hasmonean activity, and it is doubtful whether others took advantage of it.[9]

"In the following year" (1 Macc 4:28) Lysias mustered a large force to combat the insurgents. Reportedly, Judah's army had in the meantime increased to ten thousand combatants (1 Macc 4:29). Lysias took a roundabout way and approached Jerusalem from the south. This strongly suggests that the northern and western approaches to Jerusalem were by now under Hasmonean control or at least considered unsafe for a Seleucid army.[10]

The troops engaged each other at Beth-zur, a village on the southern border of Judea (1 Macc 4:29-35; 2 Macc 11:5-12; *Ant.* 12, 313-315). The accounts in 1 and 2 Macc agree on the site and the outcome of the battle – victory for Judah – but differ on the number of Seleucid troops and casualties involved and other important details. 2 Macc 11:5-6 states that Beth-zur was a fortress and that Lysias besieged it. According to this report, Judah was in the vicinity of Jerusalem when he heard of the siege and came to the rescue of the defenders, routing Lysias' troops (11:8-12). First Maccabees instead states that Lysias encamped at Beth-zur[11] and was engaged and defeated by Judah and that Judah fortified Beth-zur only later, after the rededication of the Temple.[12] The archaeological evidence is inconclusive but the excavators favor the account of 1 Macc over that in 2 Macc which may

---

dates is incorrect. If the date of Antiochus' letter is wrong, one may look for a different occasion for it altogether. The only time when a Jerusalem *Gerousia* both needed an amnesty and had a chance of getting one was after the murder of Lysimachus and the execution of the *Gerousia*'s envoys sent to excuse it (2 Macc 4:47) and before Jason's seizure of the city (5:5-7) in 169/8 BCE. The weightiest argument against such a date is the permission granted in the letter to observe the Jewish laws (2 Macc 11:31), which would not have been meaningful before their abrogation in 167 BCE. Thus, there is some likelihood that the year if not the month of the letter (148 Sel. Mac. = 165/4 BCE) is correct.

[9]It is possible that the period of amnesty included Passover (so Abel ad loc.); Josephus in fact identifies the month Xanthicus with Nisan (*Ant.* 3.248), but this may reflect a development of the first century CE (See Bickerman, *Chronology* p. 25; cf. p. 20). Habicht (*2 Macc.* p. 258 n. 27a) thinks that the amnesty was intended primarily for former followers of Jason; but it is unlikely that in 165/4 BCE they still carried any political weight and would have wanted to return "to their own laws as in former times" (2 Macc 11:31).

[10]Abel prefers protection of Idumea as primary cause of the detour ("Topographie" *RB* 32 [1923] 510-511). But 2 Macc 10:15 suggests that the conflict with Idumea started after Judah had captured Jerusalem.

[11]1 Macc 4:29. *Ant.* 12.313 specifies that it was a village.

[12]1 Macc 4:61. The Greek text printed by Kappler here is patently corrupt. See the plausible conjecture by Abel (*Macc.*, p. 88) and the less plausible one by Goldstein (*1 Macc.*, p. 288). Cf. *Ant.* 12.326.

have been influenced by the situation during Lysias' second attack on Beth-zur (2 Macc 13:19).[13]

Shortly after his defeat, but before the end of 148 Sel. Mac. (fall 164 BCE), Lysias received two emissaries with Hebrew names, John and Absalom, sent by what he called the πλῆθος ("multitude" or "association") of the Jews, meaning a part of the Jewish people or perhaps "the majority," by contrast to the royalists in the *Akra*. They brought an authoritative document – probably a statement of terms. Some terms he granted and he sent back with the emissaries both emissaries of his own to carry on the discussion and a conciliatory letter (2 Macc 11:17-21) promising further favors if the Jews "continued friendly." It has been recognized that this letter was addressed to the insurgents because of its unofficial addressee and because the negotiators bear Hebrew, not Greek names.[14] That these insurgents who showed friendliness to the Seleucid government and negotiated with it were the Hasmoneans is not certain.[15]

Shortly thereafter, two Roman envoys sent a letter to the Jews (2 Macc 11:34-38), approving the terms already granted by Lysias, and asking the Jewish stand on the points to be referred to the king, so as to decide what position they would take on these.[16] No immediate effect of this letter is known. If authentic, it documents the earliest contact between Rome and the Hasmoneans. Moreover, since the Seleucid government would not have brought the Romans into its dealings with the Jews, the approach to them was almost certainly made by the Jews. Again, we cannot be sure that these Jews were the Hasmoneans, but this is the common and likely assumption.

Before Antiochus IV could answer any of Lysias' requests he died in the East, in November or early December of 164 BCE. In the meantime, however, Judah and his men attacked Jerusalem and got control of the Temple area and other parts of the city though not of the *Akra*. According to 1 Macc 4:38, the Temple was in a state of abandonment; priests (selected by Judah) cleansed it and removed the stones of the

---

[13]R. Funk, "The History of Beth-Zur with reference to its Defenses," *AASOR* 38 (1968) 9-10. The date assigned to the fortification (165 BCE) is too early by at least a few months.

[14]Habicht, *Harvard Studies* p. 10; differently Tcherikover, *Hellenistic Civ.* p. 438 n. 24.

[15]See Goldstein, *2 Macc.*, pp.409-410.

[16]For discussion of the letter's authenticity and for earlier bibliography see Habicht, *2 Macc.* p. 260; Goldstein, *2 Macc.*, 422-426. The date of this letter, 15 Xanthicus, 148 Sel., is identical with that of the previous letter by Antiochus (2 Macc 11:33) and is likely to be secondary, because a Roman document would not be dated according to the Seleucid era.

defiled altar, and built a new one.[17] They also rebuilt the *cella* of the temple and restored of its equipment the lampstand, incense altar, table of shewbread, and curtains (1 Macc 4:48-51; 2 Macc 10:3).

On 25 Kislev, 148 Sel. Bab. (about December 14, 164 BCE) sacrifices were offered for the first time on the new altar.[18] This occasion was to be commemorated every year for eight days (1 Macc 4:59; 2 Macc 10:8) and later became known as the Festival of Hanukkah ("Dedication").

The origin and meaning of this best-known postbiblical Jewish festival has long occupied scholars, but attempts to find connections with winter-solstice celebrations, with a New Age festival of Zeus-Kronos, or with Dionysiac celebrations have been unconvincing, chiefly for lack of evidence. It is also doubtful whether Bickerman was correct in suggesting that Judah imitated the Greek practice of commemorating important events and that "this was the first step along the path which was to constitute the historic mission of the Hasmoneans – the introduction of Hellenic usages into Judaism without making a sacrifice of Judaism."[19] Hellenistic custom commemorated the birthdays of gods and kings monthly, but there is no evidence for an annual commemoration of the dedication of a temple.

The closest extrabiblical parallel seems to be the ancient Roman observance of the *dies natalis* of temples, the annual celebration of

---

[17]1 Macc 4:43-47; cf. 2 Macc 10:2-3; *m. Middot* 1:6. See Goldstein, *1 Macc.* p. 284 ad 4:38; contrast Bickerman, *Gott*, pp. 109-110. The removal of the *soreg* (lattice-work) may have been part of these cleansing operations (*Megillat Taanit*, 23 Marheshvan). See Lichtenstein, Fastenrolle, p. 279.

[18]The Julian date is correct only if Jerusalem followed the Babylonian calendar exactly, including its intercalations. This is somewhat doubtful for this period. For a different hypothesis see Goldstein, *1 Macc.* p. 23, 276-280. Bunge, *Untersuchungen* pp. 402-457 distinguishes between the purification of the Temple in Marheshvan or Kislev (late fall) 165 BCE, and a joyous celebration on 25 Kislev, 164 BCE, to commemorate the recent death of Antiochus IV as well as the earlier rededication of the Temple. This elaborate hypothesis is based on several unprovable and probably false presuppositions so that we better leave it aside. Bringmann too dates the rededication of the Temple in 165 BCE, reading the year 148 as a Seleucid Macedonian date (*Hellenistische Reform* p. 26). Such an interpretation has the great advantage of enabling one to maintain the sequence of events in 1 Macc 4-6: dedication of the Temple (165 BCE), expeditions outside Judea (spring/summer 164 BCE) and death of Antiochus IV (late fall 164 BCE). It requires however to disregard the most natural reading of several dates given in 1 Macc and is therefore not convincing. Against Bunge see Schäfer pp. 566-568; Habicht, *2 Macc.* pp. 199-202; cf. Goldstein, *1 Macc.* pp. 82-83; against Bringmann see above, *Introduction* n. 6.

[19]From Ezra to the Last of the Maccabees (New York: Schocken, 1962) p. 121.

their dedication or rededication.[20] It would be rash, however, to assume direct Roman influence on the institution of Hanukkah. An anniversary celebration of the dedication of a shrine is known from Palmyra, but since the temple of Bel involved was probably founded in 32 CE it teaches us nothing about the origins of Hanukkah two centuries earlier.[21]

It is therefore better to look primarily for Biblical precedents for Hanukkah, and the parallels to the dedication of the first Temple as described in 2 Chr 7:1-10 are indeed striking. The eight-day duration, the connection with Sukkot (emphasized in 2 Macc 1:9,18; 10:6) and elements of the liturgy, including the musical accompaniment, have been noted.[22]

For our present study, some questions relating to the rededication of the Temple are particularly relevant. According to both 1 and 2 Macc, Judah Maccabee initiated the cleansing and rededication of the Temple. In 1 Macc, however, where we would expect his role to be emphasized, he is only said to have selected suitable priests to cleanse the Temple (4:42) and, after its dedication, to have decided together with "his brothers and the whole assembly of Israel" to commemorate the event every year for eight days (4:59). In the best manuscripts, there is no reference to Judah in 1 Macc 4:43-58, i.e., during the cleansing and rededication of the Temple. This fact is particularly significant if we compare it with the active role assigned to Simon in the conquest and cleansing of the *Akra*.[23]

In light of the relative independence maintained by the Jerusalem priesthood until the time of Simon, it is indicative that in 1 Macc 4:43-53 the priests who cleanse the Temple are the grammatical subject. The decision concerning the disposal of the stones of the defiled altar is attributed to them (or to "the elders," in two late mss.), not to Judah.

Without overinterpreting the text of 1 Macc, we may conclude that Judah is presented in the extant sources as the military leader of the revolt, but even though priestly descent is claimed for his family, he never assumes a priestly role, perhaps because of its incompatibility with his military function. Jerusalem priests cooperate with him, but maintain relative independence. This is evident again a few years

---

[20]See K. Latte, *Römische Religionsgeschichte* (Munich: Beck, 1960) pp. 419, 432-443 ("Natales Templorum"); evidence is discussed in *Dizionario epigrafico di antichità romane* ed. E. De Ruggiero, vol. 1 (Rome, 1894) pp.147-149.
[21]R. Du Mesnil du Buisson, *Les Tessères et les Monnaies de Palmyre* (Paris: Boccard, 1962) pp. 571-572.
[22]See J. VanderKam, "Hanukkah: Its Timing and Significance According to 1 and 2 Maccabees," *JSP* 1 (1987) 33.
[23]1 Macc 13:50-52. See pp. 114-115 below.

later when priests show Nicanor the sacrifices they are offering for the Seleucid king, but do not cooperate in his search for Judah.[24]

The rededication of the Temple was an important event which might have concluded the Hasmonean revolt, if restoration of the Torah and of the Temple had been or remained its only goals. Yet at least by now the revolt had become larger in scope. Not only was Mount Zion fortified in order to protect the Temple area. Beth-zur too was fortified as an outpost against invasions from or through Idumea (1 Macc 4:60-61). Here then for the first time a switch from guerilla-type warfare to territorial defense is evident in Hasmonean strategy.

Around the same time the young Antiochus V became sole king with Lysias managing his affairs. A letter concerning privileges (φιλάνθρωπα), customary at the beginning of a new reign, was formally addressed by the boy-king to Lysias confirming that the Jews were permitted to follow their own customs. The Temple was restored to them, in recognition of the *status quo* created by Judah and his men.[25] The authenticity of this letter is generally accepted but it is dubious because the terms it concedes are very similar to those Lysias is made to propose to the king as a novel suggestion only a year later, when anxious to make peace with Judah in order to meet the attack of Philip (1 Macc 6:55-61; 2 Macc 13:23). These terms included freedom to live according to the Torah and approval of the restored Temple cult, the primary (but evidently no longer the only) goals of the revolt. It is surprising that Lysias, as regent, should have made unnecessarily, at the very beginning of the king's reign, an offer to which he later would turn only in order to meet a crisis. At all events, if the offer was made, it was rejected by Judah. After the initial successes[26] the goal of the revolt had been expanded to include autonomy not only in the strictly religious sphere but in political (and fiscal) matters as well.

---

[24]1 Macc 7:33-38; 2 Macc 14:31-36.

[25]This letter (2 Macc 11:22-26) is generally dated *after* Lysias' second campaign, parallel to 1 Macc 6:59, but Habicht has rightly pointed out that there is no reference to a previous armed conflict and the death of Antiochus IV is mentioned as a recent event (*Harvard Studies* pp. 16-17; so already Schürer-Vermes-Millar 1, p. 164; for dissenting opinions see Habicht, *ibid.*). The letter is undated, as was customary for copies. It may have been received 28 Adar, 163 BCE (*Megillat Taanit*). Differently Goldstein, 2 *Macc.*, p. 418.

[26]Tcherikover (*Hellenistic Civ.* pp. 206-207) thinks that from the beginning the revolt had strong political overtones. H. Kreissig one-sidedly stresses socio-economic reasons for the outbreak of the revolt ("Der Makkabäeraufstand, zur Frage seiner sozialökonomischen Zusammenhänge und Wirkungen," *Studii Clasice* 4 [1962] 143-175).

Expeditions Outside Judea

After Jerusalem and Beth-zur were fortified, Judah had for a while control over most of Judea. From this territorial base he was able to launch expeditions to other areas. These campaigns are lumped together in 1 Macc 5, whereas in 2 Macc they are reported on different occasions but evidently not in the correct order.[27]

Synopsis[28]

1 Macc			2 Macc	
			8:30-32	Treatment of enemies and of spoils (Examples: Timotheus, Bacchides)
5:1-2	Rededication of Temple causes Gentiles to plot against Jews.	≠	10:14	Gorgias, local *strategos*, gathers mercenaries against Jews.
3	Judah's victories: Idumea (Akrabatene)		15-17	Idumeans along with refugees from Jerusalem are defeated.
			18-21	Simon's men bribed
4-5	"Sons of Baian" destroyed in their forts in retaliation		22-23	People in forts destroyed
6-7	Timotheus in Ammon	≠	24-31	Timotheus in Judea (?)
8	Iazer taken		32-38	Timotheus & brother killed in "Gazara"
Cf.	1 Macc 4:28-35		11:1-12:1	Judah defeats Lysias at Beth-zur, Lysias makes peace (various documents).
			12:2	Timotheus and local *strategoi* harass Jews.
			3-7	Jews of Joppa are killed, retaliation by Judah.
			8-9	Preemptive strike against Jamnia.

---

[27]8:30-33; 10:16-38; 12:5-45. See Habicht, 2 *Macc.* pp. 250-251 ad 10:11; Abel, *Macc.*, pp. 393-394, 415; Schunck, *Quellen* p. 115.

[28]≠ indicates contradiction; = indicates close parallel.

5:9-13	Israelites in Gilead attacked by Gentiles led by Timotheus, flee to Dathema ("the Fort").		
	All Jews in Toubias' region killed.	≠ Cf.	2 Macc 12:17
	Request for Judah's aid.		
14-15	Jews *in* Galilee are attacked by people from Ptolemais, Tyre and Sidon, Galilee.		
16-20	Decision to send Simon to Galilee, Judah & Jonathan to Gilead, Joseph & Azariah to stay in Judea.		
21-23	Simon fights in Galilee, brings Jews from Galilee & Arbatta to Judea.		
24	Judah to Gilead,	≠ 12:10-12	Thence against Timotheus,
25-27	meets friendly Nabateans	≠	Judah defeats Arabs, makes alliance.
	1 Macc 5:36	= 13-16	Judah takes Kaspin
28	captures Bosora		
29-33	relieves "the Fort,"	17-18	relieves Toubian Jews in "the fortified camp."
34	routs Timotheus' army.	19	Dositheus and Sosipatros rout Timotheus' troops.
35	Judah takes Alema (?)		
36	Judah takes Chaspho, Maked, Bozor, and the remaining towns of Gilead.	=	2 Macc 12:13-16
37-43	Timotheus defeated near Raphon, his troops flee to Karnain.	20-21	Timotheus pursued, sends women and children to Karnion.
		22-25	Timotheus defeated, captured by Dositheus & Sosipatros, freed.

5:44	Judah conquers Karnain and its sacred precinct	12:26	Judah conquers Karnion and the temple of Atargatis.
45	Judah brings "all Israel" from Gilead to Judea.		
46-51	Judah takes Ephron,	27-28	Judah's troops take Ephron,
52	passes Beth-shan (= Scythopolis) safely,	29-31a	spare Scythopolis because friendly to Jews,
53-54	returns to Jerusalem with refugees.	31b	return to Jerusalem before Pentecost.
55-60	Meanwhile, Joseph & Azariah had attacked Jamnia, were routed by Gorgias. ≠	32-34	Jews now attack Gorgias, *strategos* of Idumea. Some are killed.
		35	Gorgias escapes to Marisa.
61-64	Judah & family the only proper leaders, win many supporters.		
65-67	Judah & brothers fight Edomites, ravage Hebron and Marisa.	36-37	Judah assists hard pressed Esdrias, defeats Gorgias' men.
		38	Judah retreats to Odollam for Sabbath.
		39-45	Death of those who fell is punishment for wearing Jamnian amulets. Resurrection affirmed.
68	Judah destroys altars, images of gods in Azotus, returns to Judea.		

This synopsis shows the differences between 1 and 2 Macc, but with equal clarity it indicates that both accounts use similar clusters of stories and arrange them in similar order. This is true not only for Judah's campaign in Gilead where both reports are especially close to each other (1 Macc 5:24-54;2 Macc 12:10-31), but also for his earlier dealings with the Idumeans and with a Timotheus (1 Macc 5:3-8; 2 Macc 10:14-38). The differences in the sequence of events concern (a) a misplaced summary note involving Timotheus,[29] (b) Lysias' first campaign which is clearly out of place in 2 Macc,[30] and (c) expeditions to Idumea which 1 Macc 5:55-68 dates in part during Judah's war in Gilead, while 2 Macc 12:32-38 puts them after his return. The intention of the author of 1 Macc to dissociate Judah and his family from an ignominious defeat is reason enough for such a transposition (see 1 Macc 5:61-64). 2 Macc 12:38-40 solves the problem differently by glossing over the defeat and giving idolatry as the reason of the casualties.

This agreement between the two outlines – in spite of substantial differences in the treatment of the material – presents an interesting problem for source criticism. The parallel accounts of the expedition to Gilead are similar enough to make their derivation from a common source plausible.[31] The major divergences in the other sections, however, seem to indicate that 1 and 2 Macc, independently of each other, agreed that the Hasmoneans, after beating off the Seleucids, first fought against neighbors in Idumea and the coastal plain, then turned to the East and North, and then returned to Idumea and the coast. Without trying to go beyond these stories to the facts, we may here conclude:

(1) Our reconstruction of Judah's wars with neighboring peoples cannot rely on 1 Macc alone, but must equally consider 2 Macc which represents a different viewpoint.

(2) In various places outside Judea Jews who were sympathetic to the Hasmonean cause were harassed, threatened, sometimes killed. Areas for which this is specifically mentioned include the coastal plain, (Western) Galilee, Idumea, and Gilead.[32]

---

[29]2 Macc 8:30-33 does not stand in chronological order because it interrupts the narrative about Nicanor's defeat 8:29, 34. It is linked to the context by topic and language: the disposal of booty and punishment of wicked enemies. Schunck (*Quellen* pp. 110-111) and Bunge (*Untersuchungen* pp. 285-287) insist that 8:30-33 stands in the correct place and refers to events before the death of Antiochus IV, on the basis of the reference to a Timotheus in 2 Macc 9:3. Habicht (*2 Macc.*, p.244) and Goldstein (*2 Macc.*, p. 351) maintain that Timotheus' name has been interpolated there. On literary questions see Doran, *Temple Propaganda*, pp. 58-59.

[30]2 Macc 11. Differently Bunge, *Untersuchungen* pp. 287-290.

[31]So Schunck, *Quellen* p. 113 (with bibliography); Bunge, *Untersuchungen* p. 247. See however Doran, *Temple Propaganda*, pp. 14-15.

[32]*Jamnia:* 2 Macc 12:8-9; *Joppa:* 2 Macc 12:3-7; *Arbatta* (1 Macc 5:23) is generally identified with Narbata, a few miles inland, just south of Mt. Carmel. See Goldstein, *1 Macc.* p. 300; M. Avi-Yonah, *Gazetteer* p. 82 with bibliography.

Galilee: 1 Macc 5:14-15. The enemies come *from* Ptolemais, Tyre, Sidon, and "the Galilee of foreigners," but the Jews attacked are in Galilee only. If there is any truth to the story, it would indicate that the Jewish settlements in Western Galilee were strong enough to be a concern for the rulers of the coastal towns.

It is striking that Jews in such diverse regions should have been attacked at approximately the same time. Second Maccabees lays the main blame on local (Seleucid?) commanders[33] who simply did not let the Jews live in peace. First Maccabees, instead, speaks of the enmity of the Gentiles round about, who were angered by the restoration of the Temple.[34]

Neither of these explanations seems to be adequate. An examination of 2 Macc shows that Gorgias and "Timotheus" are the only commanders mentioned in connection with specific military operations. Furthermore, Gorgias is accused of fomenting war (2 Macc 10:14), but the clash occurs between Judah's men on one side and Idumeans and refugees from Jerusalem on the other. Gorgias' troops have no role in the fighting until much later in the narrative when they are attacked by followers of Judah.[35]

The problem of the identity of "Timotheus" in 1 and 2 Macc, which has caused considerable debate,[36] does not concern us here directly, but the question of the role played by the individual or individuals bearing this name is of interest for an understanding of Judah's operations. According to our sources, a Timotheus fights Judah in Gilead (1 Macc 5:11,34-44; 2 Macc 12:20-25), in Ammonite territory in connection with the town of "Iazer" (1 Macc 5:6-8), and in "Gazara" (2 Macc 10:32), which normally means the well-known Gezer. The question of whether

---

There does not seem to have been any trouble with the (more hellenized?) Jews who lived in the coastal cities.

Idumea: 1 Macc 5:3; 2 Macc 10:15. The location of Akrabattene is debated. It may be connected with the Ascent of Akrabbim, southwest of the Dead Sea (this is the majority position according to Abel, *Macc.,* p. 89 ad 5:3), but Goldstein (*1 Macc.,* p. 294) and others prefer to identify it with the district of Akrabatta in Southern Samaria.

The identity of the "sons of Baian" (1 Macc 5:4) is unknown. Normally such a formulation refers to a tribe or territory, but occasionally it may mean inhabitants of a town (cf. 2 Esdras 2:21-34) as the pronoun αὐτῆς (1 Macc 5:5) would indicate. Galling thinks of a semi-nomadic tribe near Jericho (*PJ* 36 [1940] 52-53); cf. Abel, *Macc.,* p. 90.

Gilead: 1 Macc 5:9-12. 2 Macc has no petition for help from Gilead, but stresses Judah's fight against Timotheus and his men.

[33]τῶν δὲ κατὰ τόπον στρατηγῶν 12:2; cf. 10:14. See Bickerman, *Institutions* p. 65. Goldstein, 2 *Macc.,* p. 432.

[34]1 Macc 5:1-2, 9, 15. Galling considers these verses characteristic for one of two sources for 1 Macc 5 (*PJ* 36 [1940] 45).

[35]2 Macc 12:32-35; cf. 1 Macc 5:58-60.

[36]Goldstein (*1 Macc.* pp. 296-297; 2 *Macc.* pp. 338-340, 395-397), Schunck (*Quellen* pp. 111-115), and others posit two Timothei, whereas Zambelli (Composizione, p. 277; bibliography pp. 272-273), Habicht (2 *Macc.* p. 251), Bar-Kochva (*Battles* pp. 353-357) and others relate all references to one and the same Timotheus.

there were one or more persons bearing the name "Timotheus" arises because of the apparently different areas of operation and different functions of "Timotheus," and especially because his death in "Gazara" is reported in 2 Macc 10:37, whereas a "Timotheus" is again active in 2 Macc 12:2,20-25. A literal interpretation of the sources would require the existence of two or three "Timothei," because the commander of a large army who dies in "Gazara" would have to be distinguished from the commander(s) in Ammon and Gilead.

Strategically it would have made sense for Judah to take Gezer, a principal stronghold on the western approach to Jerusalem. A superficial reading of 2 Macc clearly locates "Timotheus" there. But if Judah did conquer Gezer, one would expect to find some reflection of it in 1 Macc and in the further course of events. Instead, Simon is credited with (and accused of) the conquest of Gezer, the removal of its anti-Hasmonean population, and the relocation of Torah-observing settlers there (1 Macc 13:48; 14:7,34; 15:28).

Most scholars consider the defeat (and death) of Timotheus in "Gazara" a doublet of Judah's taking of "Iazer." Generally it is thought that the less well-known Iazer near Heshbon is meant and, consequently, that "Timotheus" operated only in Transjordan. Even Goldstein, who distinguishes two "Timothei," locates both of them there, one in Ammon, the other in Gilead.[37] Whether there were one or two Timothei, it appears that Judah encountered not only local but regionally organized opposition during his one or two expeditions across the Jordan.

From the Timotheus stories as well as from other evidence one can gather that Seleucid control in Transjordan was generally weak.[38] It is therefore unlikely that the central government was involved directly in Judah's wars with the neighboring Gentiles. This confirms the impression conveyed by Antiochus V's letter to Lysias of the spring of 163 BCE (2 Macc 11:22-26) which makes no reference to an armed conflict. Instead, we have strong indications in both 1 and 2 Macc that conflicts arose in different cities and areas between Gentiles and Jews. But the restoration of the Temple was hardly the reason for this, despite such a claim in 1 Macc 5:1. If events are in correct order in 1 Macc 5, Timotheus may have been provoked by Judah's attack on Ammonite territory and may have tried to retaliate against a Jewish (pro-Hasmonean) minority in Gilead.

---

[37] *2 Macc.* pp. 393-395, 433.
[38] See the positions of Hyrcanus the Tobiad (*Ant.* 12.222, 229-236) and Aretas (2 Macc 5:8).

The question of why these conflicts arose is a complex one and may best be considered case by case. 1 Macc 5:3-5 claims that Judah's expedition against Idumea and "the sons of Baian" was meant to counteract previous harassment. 2 Macc 10:15 adds that refugees from Jerusalem fought on the Idumean side. These refugees were probably Jews, perhaps members of Menelaus' party who had been driven out of the city when Judah conquered it.[39] Thus the conflict was not between Jews and Gentiles as such, but between the supporters of the Hasmoneans and their Gentile and Jewish opponents.

Reportedly, Judah and his men made several raids into Idumea, with varying success. These raids did not result in conquests, and some may not have occurred. Since 1 Macc knows nothing of the destruction of the Jews in Joppa, we may question the report (in 2 Macc 12:3-9 only) that the harbors of Joppa and Jamnia were burned. The raids into Idumean territory may be overextended in 1 Macc's claim that the territory of Hebron, Azotus, and even Marisa was ravaged. Considerable booty was doubtless carried off (1 Macc 5:68). Booty may well have been a principal motive of whatever raiding occurred, and there were probably raids on both sides. The breakdown of Seleucid control left the area open for looting and for the expression of long-standing local hostilities.

Both 1 and 2 Macc are careful to shield Judah from the blame for the casualties among his men. First Maccabees claims that not one of them fell during the expedition to Gilead (5:54). It even provides an alibi for Judah by placing the defeat in Idumea during his absence in Gilead (5:55-62) and emphatically dissociates the defeated generals from the Hasmonean family. Only the more successful part of the Idumean campaign is dated after his return (5:65-68). Second Maccabees instead makes Judah arrive on the scene in time to avert defeat (12:36-37). However, the fact that he retreated to Odollam (2 Macc 12:38) and only later returned to bury the dead indicates anything but victory.

The report of the persecution of Jews in Galilee and Simon's subsequent rescue mission there and to [N]arbatta has roused suspicion because of 2 Macc's ignorance of this important event, the uncharacteristic lack of detail and the similarity to Judah's campaign in Gilead.[40] Abel noted the use of formulae from Deuteronomy and Joshua.[41] In addition, the number of slain enemies equals the number of men assigned to Simon. Since praise of Simon is a recurrent feature of 1 Macc, there has to be some doubt about the authenticity of this report

---

[39]Complaints over expulsions are reported in 1 Macc 6:24; 7:6.
[40]1 Macc 5:14-15, 17, 20-23; Wellhausen, *Wert*, pp. 148-149.
[41]*Macc.* p. 95.

which in its present form is designed to put him almost on a par with Judah.[42]

As already remarked, the reports of Judah's wars in Gilead in 1 and 2 Macc suggest a common source. According to both accounts, Judah relieves a fort in which Jews have gathered, takes Chaspho/Kaspin, defeats Timotheus near Karnain/Karnion, conquers Ephron, and returns to Jerusalem by way of the plain of Beth-shan/Scythopolis. All these events are reported in almost identical sequence. First Maccabees names several more places that Judah attacked, all except Bosora located in a fairly small area of Gilead, east of the Sea of Galilee. Beyond that, however, 1 Macc 5:36 asserts that Judah captured "all the remaining towns of Gilead," a gross overstatement which should make us cautious concerning conquests not reported in 2 Macc.

Second Maccabees has serious flaws too. Strength of troops is routinely exaggerated and sometimes the narrative is incoherent because vital elements have been left out or misplaced by the editor (epitomizer?). Thus, there seems to be a lacuna between 2 Macc 12:9 and 10, because events shift abruptly from Jamnia to Gilead. Other differences are difficult to evaluate: 2 Macc 12:10-12 speaks of a fight with a band of Arabs before they establish friendly relations with Judah, while in 1 Macc 5:25 Nabateans are immediately friendly. When 2 Macc favorably mentions several commanders in Judah's army who are apparently not members of the Hasmonean family this has no evident motive and is therefore probably reliable.[43] This, together with the mention of the maligned Azariah as "leader of the people" indicates that there was a growing circle of senior officers aside from the Hasmonean family.[44]

The most striking difference between the two accounts of the expedition to Gilead is in the central issue: according to 2 Macc it is essentially a war against Timotheus, whereas 1 Macc states as the purpose the rescue of oppressed Jews. That goal is stated at beginning and end (5:16-17, 45), and most of the places he captured were places in which, he had been told, the Jews had been shut up.

Second Maccabees never explicitly mentions any Jews from Gilead. But the report that Timotheus held parents and brothers or sisters of some of Judah's men hostage indicates that they were local people (2

[42]Conversely, however, Simon is treated unfavorably in 2 Macc (10:20; 14:17). Therefore a successful mission of his may have been suppressed.
[43]2 Macc 12:19, 24: Sosipater and Dositheus are leaders (ἡγεμόνες). The latter is probably to be distinguished from the brave Toubian cavalryman Dositheus (12:35).
[44]1 Macc 5:18, 55-62; cf. also Joseph (1 Macc 5:18 and passim) and Zacchaeus (Zechariah?) (2 Macc 10:19).

Macc 12:24-25). Thus Judah seems to have picked up supporters as he went along. We need not doubt the fact that he ventured to Gilead in order to assist Jews in distress. Besides refugees, Judah brought a fair amount of plunder back, but that was hardly the primary purpose since, as Wellhausen observed, he could have had that closer to home.[45]

Why the Jews were suddenly attacked (in Gilead and *possibly* in Joppa and Galilee) is a question to which our sources give no adequate answer. We can only guess that there were either local quarrels or a surge of antagonism against those who supported the Hasmonean revolt. The many instances of anti-Jewish outbreaks, of which 1 and 2 Macc speak vaguely, are not said to have been caused by government policy, and were not directed against all Jews as such, since some Jews participated in a request for Seleucid intervention against the Hasmoneans (1 Macc 6:21-27).

Notable is also the fact that no clashes between the Hasmoneans and the Samaritans are reported. Apparently some kind of mutual understanding existed between the two groups, at least permitting peaceful passage of Judah's forces through Samaria on his way from Beth-shan to Jerusalem (1 Macc 5:52-54; 2 Macc 12:30-31).

After the conquest of Jerusalem and the rededication of the Temple, the Hasmoneans were free to settle some old accounts with their neighbors, especially in the south. Their rescue of Jews who were in trouble in Gilead and perhaps in Galilee added to their fame as leaders, secured them the allegiance of many of the rescued Jews, and encouraged others to turn to them for help. Refugees may have been settled in Judea on land formerly belonging to people close to Menelaus. These refugees gave the Hasmoneans additional military strength and political clout. Other people were impressed by their achievements and added their support too: "The man Judah and his brothers were greatly honored among all Israel and among all the Gentiles, wherever their name was heard; and people joined them praising them" (1 Macc 5:63-64). At the same time, however, Hasmonean military activity widened the rift between them and their Jewish opponents who joined with Gentiles to regain their property (2 Macc 10:15; 1 Macc 6:24; 7:6). Territories outside of Judea were not occupied by the Hasmoneans at this time.

Renewed Fighting for Control of Judea

While Judah was campaigning outside Judea, the *Akra* in Jerusalem continued to be occupied by his enemies. The relations between the

---

[45]Wert, p. 148.

people of the *Akra* and the Hasmoneans are enigmatic to us, due to the spotty coverage in our sources. After the conquest of the Temple area of Jerusalem, Judah left a garrison of unknown strength in Judea (1 Macc 5:18).[46] Whatever the strength of the remaining Hasmonean troops, the conflict with the people of the *Akra* did not get much attention until after the completion of the campaigns outside Judea. Whether in the interim there existed a formal or tacit agreement between the Hasmoneans and the *Akra* we do not know. If it existed, it was of short duration. First Maccabees of course, in line with its basic outlook, represents the conflict between the two parts of the city as constant and implacable.[47] This it may have been, since the garrison of the Temple was probably composed of Hasmonean stalwarts picked for guard duty in a strategic post adjacent to an enemy stronghold. But a distinction must be supposed between the Hasmonean fighters and the rest of the Judeans.

In the spring or summer of 163 BCE Judah attempted to take control of the *Akra*.[48] He gathered troops to besiege it, but was unable to conquer it. The besieged, Gentiles according to 1 Macc, but Jews according to Josephus, were able to send messengers to the royal court to ask for help; they were joined by Jewish opponents of the Hasmoneans, perhaps still living in the countryside, perhaps already refugees

---

[46]B. Bar-Kochva (*The Seleucid Army: Organization and Tactics in the Great Campaigns* [Cambridge/New York: Cambridge Univ. Pr., 1976], pp. 185-186) estimates it at 10,000, based on the casualty figure of 2,000 in the battle against Gorgias (1 Macc 5:60). It is unlikely, however, that this figure is reliable. Bar-Kochva's statement (*ibid.*) that it serves no ulterior purpose, is false. It serves to show how great was the disaster that occurred when leaders other than the Hasmoneans tried to take control (5:61-62, explicitly). The parallel (?) in 2 Macc 12:34 says that only "a few" Jews fell, but it, too, has an apologetic purpose, to show that *only* those were killed who had been wearing amulets of pagan gods (2 Macc 12:40). Moreover, it dates the battle after Judah's return (and this suggests that 1 Macc's account may be an attempt to exculpate the Hasmoneans from responsibility for a defeat). If so, the number of Jewish combatants involved would tell us nothing of the number left in Judea during Judah's absence.

[47]1 Macc 6:18; cf. *Ant.* 12.362 which dramatizes the *Akra*'s misdeeds.

[48]In 150 Sel. according to 1 Macc 6:20. In 2 Macc 13:1 instead, the ensuing campaign of Lysias is dated to 149 Sel. These dates may be reconciled if one assumes that 1 Macc was using the Macedonian fall era and 2 Macc the Babylonian spring era. It is more plausible, however, that the siege of Jerusalem started in 149 Sel. by the Macedonian reckoning because the Seleucid response probably came by early autumn of 163 BCE. So Bickerman, *Gott*, p. 157.

abroad.[49] In spite of several years of Hasmonean activity and in spite of the flight of many of their opponents, there were probably still some Jews loyal to the Seleucids among the rural population.[50] *A priori* it would be surprising if *no* crypto-Hellenizers had survived in the countryside and amazing if the increase of the Hasmoneans' power had not made them at least some enemies who hoped for help from the Seleucids. Further, it is incredible that the *Akra* could have held out for so long without regular provisioning from the countryside.

The mission to the royal court had the desired effect. Lysias decided to overpower the revolt through intervention with a strong army. As often, numbers indicating enemy strength are unreliable. The totals for Lysias' infantry and cavalry vary between 55,000 and 120,000.[51] In any case, the presence of Lysias, who had become regent for the young King Antiochus V, and the deployment of battle elephants, indicate a major operation. The Hasmonean troops had little chance of withstanding this onslaught. 2 Macc 13:13-17 reports a Hasmonean victory in a night attack on the Seleucid camp near Modein. If any such attack happened,[52] it had no noticeable effect, because the royal troops continued their march southward to Beth-zur where they besieged the Hasmonean garrison. After a siege, Beth-zur was taken by Lysias. According to 1 Macc 6:49-50, lack of provisions because of the Sabbath year led to the surrender. 2 Macc 13:19-22 instead affirms that Judah had sent in enough provisions and that the fortress fell only through one man's treason.

The decisive battle occurred near the village of Beth-zechariah, on the southern approach to Jerusalem. Judah's troops were heavily outnumbered and easily defeated, in spite of their bravery. The story of the death of Judah's brother Eleazar became very popular. Reportedly, he was crushed by an elephant he had stabbed because he thought the king was riding on it. There are at least two independent versions of the story. On one hand, 1 Macc 6:44 glorifies Eleazar's deed and attributes to him classical Greek as well as Israelite motives: "He gave himself

---

[49]1 Macc 6:21, of which *Ant.* 12.364 may be an unreliable interpretation and expansion. That Josephus was using a separate source is possible, but not likely.

[50]Cf. 1 Macc 2:44: flight of enemies of Hasmoneans; 6:24: pro-Seleucid Jews killed and their property taken; 7:6: all pro-Seleucid Judeans killed or scattered; 2 Macc 10:15: flight to Idumeans.

[51]*J.W.* 1.41 (55,000); 2 Macc 13:2 (115,300?); 1 Macc 6:30 (120,000); *Ant.* 12.366 copies 1 Macc 6:30.

[52]The reference to the slaying of the leading elephant (2 Macc 13:15) appears to belong to the battle of Beth-zechariah and indicates confusion in the account of 2 Macc. Cf. 1 Macc 6:43-46 and *J.W.* 1.42-44, which is independent of 1 Macc.

in order to save his people and to gain eternal fame."[53] On the other hand, *J.W.* 1.42-45 considers Eleazar's daring an act of folly and attributes the final defeat of Judah not only to the enemies' superior numbers but also to their good fortune.[54]

After the battle Judah and his men fled. In *Ant.* 12.375 Josephus asserts that Judah retreated to Jerusalem, but since 1 Macc is strangely silent about him, Josephus' earlier report (*J.W.* 1.45) is more trustworthy, namely, that Judah and his men fled to the district of Gophna on the border of Samaria, not far from Modein.

Lysias' troops moved on to besiege the Temple area of Jerusalem where only a small remnant of defenders held out. Others had returned to their homes in the country. Both besiegers and besieged suffered from a severe food shortage because of the sabbatical year.[55] A decision was brought about by a new development elsewhere. Philip who, it was claimed, had been made regent by Antiochus IV on his deathbed (1 Macc 6:14-15), was trying to seize control of Syria. The news of this threat induced Lysias to negotiate quickly a peace with the defenders of the Temple. Judah was not present and was not consulted in the course of the negotiations, although 2 Macc 13:24 reports that he was graciously received by the king.[56]

It would be important to know who negotiated this peace treaty, but all our sources are silent on this. This silence is strong evidence that the Jewish negotiators did not include Judah. Mölleken has acutely observed the problems raised by the account in 1 Macc and, by inferences from these has tried to reconstruct the original sequence of events in 1 Macc 6:60-9:4. He thinks these events included negotiations between the king and the *Asidaioi*, who accepted the appointment of Alcimus as high priest. To maintain this opinion he has to assume that the editor of 1 Macc cut the text in front of him apart and put it back together very differently in order to discredit Alcimus, and that this editorial process can now be traced, the original pieces distinguished,

---

[53]*Ant.* 12. 373-374 otherwise follows 1 Macc closely, but omits this sentence. In the Hebrew Bible apparently no hero acted for the sake of gaining fame, but David is said to have made a name for himself through his military exploits (1 Sam 18:30; 2 Sam 8:13). Mordecai disclaims desire for fame according to the Greek text of Esth 4:17d (Rahlfs) = 13:12 (RSV).

[54]Josephus may here reflect the viewpoint of his source. But he may also have had reasons of his own for this interpretation: To attribute a victory to fortune exculpates the defeated, and the hostility to suicide may be connected with his excuse for his behavior at Jotapata (*J.W.* 3.361-391).

[55]1 Macc 6:53, 57; cf. *J.W.* 1.46; 2 Macc is silent on this score.

[56]Arguments for the unhistorical character of this meeting may be found in W. Mölleken, "Geschichtsklitterung im I. Makkabäerbuch (Wann wurde Alkimus Hoherpriester?)" *ZAW* 65 (1953) 218; Bunge, *Untersuchungen* pp. 267-268.

and their original order restored. These assumptions are not adequately supported and seem unlikely.

It is presumable that the Temple area was defended by people sympathetic to the Hasmoneans, but it is unlikely that, while besieged, they were able to communicate with Judah before their surrender. There is no evidence that the defenders were *Asidaioi*. Under the circumstances, anyone might have surrendered when offered reasonable conditions, for the defenders probably did not know that because of Philip's invasion of Syria Lysias needed a peace agreement as much as they did.

Both 2 Macc and Josephus state that the high priest Menelaus was deposed and executed in Beroea in connection with Lysias' campaign. 2 Macc 13:3-8 relates his execution at some length, at the beginning of the campaign, whereas Josephus puts it after its conclusion and connects it with the appointment of Alcimus and the flight of Onias IV to Egypt.[57]

Lysias and Antiochus V departed from Jerusalem early in 162 BCE,[58] whereas Demetrius I did not seize power until the end of that year or early in 161.[59] Both 1 and 2 Macc are strangely silent about this interval and resume their narrative precisely at the same point, when Demetrius comes to power and Alcimus goes to complain to him against Judah and his men. Again, this is strong indication that both books drew on a common source, especially since they contain reminiscences of events in the intervening period (1 Macc 7:6; 2 Macc 14:3, 9).

---

[57]*Ant.* 12.383-388. This is one of the few sections in *Ant.* 12.241-13.214 that are not taken from 1 Macc. Cf. *Ant.* 20.235. Since 1 Macc is silent on the appointment of Alcimus by Lysias, some scholars mistakenly take 1 Macc 7:9 ἔστησεν αὐτῷ τὴν ἱερωσύνην to mean that Demetrius appointed him high priest. The usage of 1 Macc however contradicts this, since the above phrase always refers to confirmation in office (11:27, 57; 14:38), whereas a new appointment is usually indicated by the verb καθίστημι with two accusatives, one of the person appointed, the other of the office to which he was appointed (1 Macc 10:20; cf. 1 Macc 11:59; 15:38; 4 Macc 4:16). 2 Macc 14:13 shows that this latter construction can also be used for reinstallation of an already appointed office holder, but does not show that the former construction was ever used for a new appointment.

[58]Probably on 28 Shebat (March 5 if the Babylonian calendar was followed exactly). So Zeitlin, *Megillat Taanit*, pp. 80-81; Goldstein, *1 Macc.*, p. 325. Lichtenstein, Fastenrolle pp. 287-288 connects this day with the withdrawal of Antiochus VII, but that took place shortly after Sukkot (*Ant.* 13.241-248). The 18th of Adar instead refers to the earlier end of the persecution. Contrast Lichtenstein, Fastenrolle p. 279.

[59]The last document referring to Antiochus V as king is dated January 11, 161 BCE. See A.R. Bellinger, *American Numismatic Society Museum Notes* 1 (1945) 43. Antiochus V may have been deposed a short time before then.

Judah's Last Years

Judah's position seems to have suffered greatly as a consequence of Lysias' campaign. Beth-zur received a Seleucid garrison and the fortifications of Jerusalem were destroyed (1 Macc 6:50, 62). Judah and those who had remained with him fled to the mountainous area whence the revolt had started, the district of Gophna north of Jerusalem near the border with Samaria (*J.W.* 1.45). All of his last battles took place in that area.[60]

There is a general consensus that Judah controlled Jerusalem during most of the last period of his life. Close analysis of the sources, however, raises strong doubts in this regard. The razing of the fortifications recently built by Judah returned military control of the city to the garrison of the *Akra*. In fact, if 1 Macc 7:8-19 is correct, Bacchides entered Jerusalem without encountering any opposition. Furthermore, 1 Macc 7:22-24 states that Alcimus gathered a large following and was able to extend his control of Judea to some extent, but Judah then went about the hills, took revenge on those who had deserted him, and prevented his enemies from going further into the country. Thus, when Alcimus requested help from the king and Nicanor was sent, it was not because Alcimus had been driven out of Jerusalem, but because the countryside was unsafe for his loyal subjects. In fact, Nicanor fled *to* the "city of David" after a minor defeat near Capharsalama (1 Macc 7:32). He had easy access to the Temple where priests were offering a sacrifice for the king (1 Macc 7:33). These priests, though portrayed sympathetically in both 1 and 2 Macc, were certainly not under the direction of Judah, who was at war with the royal army.

Judah's shortlived friendship with Nicanor who urged him to get married and settle down, allegedly gave him easy access to Jerusalem.[61] But it is made clear that Judah went there as a guest of Nicanor, not in a position of authority. When he realized that Nicanor's attitude had changed he retreated with his companions to the region of Samaria (2 Macc 15:1). After the death of Nicanor, 1 Macc 7:47 reports that his head and right hand were exhibited *outside* (παρά) Jerusalem. Similarly, 2 Macc 15:35 states that Judah displayed

---

[60]For Capharsalama (1 Macc 7:31), Dessau (2 Macc 14:16), Adasa (1 Macc 7:40) see Abel ad loc. Concerning Beth-zaith/Beerzeth/ Berzetho (1 Macc 7:19; 9:4; *Ant.* 12.397, 422) and Elasa (1 Macc 9:5) see C. Möller and G. Schmitt, *Siedlungen Palästinas nach Flavius Josephus* (Wiesbaden: Reichert, 1976) pp. 46-48.

[61]2 Macc 14:23-25. See n. 75 below.

Nicanor's head *outside* the *Akra*. This act does not necessitate possession of the city. Judah's control of the Temple area however is assumed in 2 Macc 15:30-34. According to this passage, Judah convoked an assembly in or near the Temple, with priests prominently present in front of the altar, and cut out Nicanor's tongue. This passage may be a dramatization of the known fact that Nicanor's head was displayed publicly. Since any reference to Judah's possession of Jerusalem is lacking in 1 Macc,[62] and since Judah's action as described in 2 Macc would have meant a blatant defilement of the Temple and its priests,[63] we cannot rely on this account. In fact, 2 Macc 15:34 also claims that the Temple was not defiled. Thus it is likely that Judah was reduced to guerilla warfare, restricted primarily to the area around his home town.

As the territory under his control shrank, so did the number of his active supporters. In 1 Macc 7:40 and 9:5 he has no more than three thousand men under arms compared with six to ten thousand or more in earlier times.[64] This marked decline was partly due to casualties and individual desertions, but a major cause seems to have been the loss of support from those who accepted Alcimus as high priest.[65] They did so in spite of the fact that he was appointed by a foreign ruler and not in the senior line of succession of the Oniad family that had held the high priesthood for several generations. Indeed, he may not have been an Oniad at all.[66] They obviously also recognized him as highest civil

---

[62]1 Macc 8:22 designates Jerusalem as the ultimate destination of a copy of the treaty with the Romans, but does not necessarily imply Judah's possession of the city at the time.

[63]Cf. Num 19:11-16; 2 Kgs 11:15-16; *Ant.* 11.298-301; *m. Oholot* 1:7; 2:1; 11QTemple 45.17.

[64]2 Macc 8:1 (6,000); 1 Macc 4:29 (10,000); cf. 1 Macc 5:18-20 (well over 11,000, but Simon's contingent of 3,000 may be spurious).

[65]1 Macc 6:54. The interpretation of αὐτομολῆσασι (7:24) is not certain – it may refer to deserters or to renegades from Jewish law – i.e., Hellenizers. Abel (*Macc.*, p.136) takes it to refer to those who left Judah and accepted Alcimus as high priest.

[66]The legitimate successor of the Oniads eventually went to Egypt (*Ant.* 12.387; 13.62-73). The main reasons for thinking Alcimus an Oniad are (1) that neither 1 nor 2 Macc complains that he was not (but see *Ant.* 12.387); (2) that he was appointed to the office traditionally held by the family; (3) that the *Asidaioi* accepted him. That 1 Macc 7:14 does not mention his family, but simply makes him "a priest from the seed of Aaron" is understandable. The text is a defense of the Hasmoneans who had meanwhile seized the priesthood. They could not pretend to be Oniads, but did claim to be Aaronide priests. Consequently, the author makes Alcimus' claim to the office no better than theirs and argues by implication that those who accepted Alcimus *qua* Aaronide should accept the

authority and representative of the central government in the now again "autonomous" province of Judea. Sabbath-observing Jews served in Nicanor's army. Even though they are said to have been compelled into service (2 Macc 15:2) they were considered loyal enough to fight against Judah. Their refusal to join battle applied to the Sabbath only (15:2-4).

According to 1 Macc 7:12, Alcimus' legitimacy was implicitly accepted by an "assembly of scribes" (συναγωγὴ γραμματέων) who gathered to "seek what is right."[67] If this assembly was convoked or permitted by royal authority, the legitimacy of Alcimus could not have been one of the questions it discussed, because a royal appointment would not have been subject to discussion. The text is silent about the agenda of the assembly,[68] but ἐκζητῆσαι δίκαια ("to seek what is right") indicates legal concerns. Among the most pressing problems may have been practical ones, such as property rights of refugees, compensation for damages, amnesty, calendar adjustments, etc., as well as the more general question of Torah observance. Several new customs had been introduced by the Hellenizers before the Torah was outlawed as a whole (2 Macc 4:11). Also, a decision about the lawfulness of Hasmonean innovations concerning Sabbath, Temple, and holidays may have been considered urgent (cf. 1 Macc 2:41; 4:42-59; 2 Macc 10:2-8). It is possible but not certain that the "assembly of scribes" influenced the decision of the *Asidaioi* to recognize Alcimus as high priest.

Hasmoneans for the same reason. The question was a lively one at about the time the work was written (cf. *Ant.* 13.288-292; *b. Qidd.* 66a).

[67]See Bickerman, *Gott* p. 85. It is clear that the assembly of scribes has to be distinguished from the Jerusalem *Gerousia*, but we cannot be sure whether it was in any way connected with the "Men of the Great Assembly" (*m. Abot* 1:1) or with the later Sanhedrin. The "Great Assembly" that confirmed the powers of the Hasmonean Simon had a different origin and composition. Scribes are not even mentioned among its members (1 Macc 14:28). The history of the Sanhedrin(s) is an unsettled question since Tannaitic times, as can be gathered from the often vague and contradictory character of the sources, from Mantel's survey of literature prior to his work, and from that work itself: H. Mantel, *Studies in the History of the Sanhedrin* (Cambridge: Harvard Univ. Pr., 1965). See also I. J. Schiffer, "The Men of the Great Assembly," in *Persons and Institutions in Early Rabbinic Judaism*, ed. W. S. Green (Brown Judaic Studies 3; Missoula: Scholars Pr., 1977) 237-283.

[68]Enactments attributed to the "Great Assembly" by rabbinic literature deal with matters of liturgy (*b. Meg.* 2a; *b. Ber.* 33a), recording and classification (?) of texts (*b. B. Bat.* 15a) and with duties of scribes (*b. Pes.* 50b). The scribes who met with Alcimus may have dealt with these matters, too, but they must have had other and more pressing concerns which the rabbinic traditions about the "Great Assembly" do not mention at all.

According to 1 Macc 7:13, "the *Asidaioi* were the first (or, foremost) among the Israelites and they sought peace" (from Alcimus and from the royal envoy Bacchides). This is commonly taken to mean they "were the first Israelites to try to make peace with them."[69] As the text stands, this occurred after Alcimus had been confirmed in office by Demetrius,[70] and after the assembly of scribes had met under his presidency. That, after these events, the leading groups among Judah's supporters (in 1 Macc's terms, "among the children of Israel"), should make peace with Alcimus was a serious loss to Judah. He had previously refused to negotiate because of the large army that accompanied Alcimus, and because of his suspicion that the offer was a ruse. Consequently, 1 Macc is quick to point out that Judah's distrust was justified: Soon after Alcimus had assured the *Asidaioi* under oath that he would not harm them or their friends, he apprehended sixty of them and executed them on the same day.[71]

What became of the remaining *Asidaioi* we do not know. The statement attributed to Alcimus that "the *Asidaioi*, whose leader is Judah Maccabee, are maintaining war" (2 Macc 14:6), has sometimes been used as evidence for a reconciliation between Judah and the *Asidaioi*.[72] Such a supposed reconciliation however is in contrast with the sharp decline of Judah's active supporters. Rather, Alcimus' statement may reflect, as Tcherikover has noted, the situation before

---

[69]This interpretation does not even consider the hellenizers, who were surely on Alcimus' side. See Abel, *Macc.*, p. 133, reviewing other opinions. A statement that the *Asidaioi* were "foremost among the Israelites" would be somewhat unexpected in 1 Macc (cf. 5:62), but is possible. A belated acknowledgment of the greatness of one's former ally is not uncommon.

[70]Mölleken (Geschichtsklitterung p. 214) has argued that we have here an intentionally misplaced reference to the earlier peace negotiations with Lysias. There is no substantial evidence for this argument.

[71]1 Macc 7:15-16. Josephus puts the responsibility for the execution of sixty people on Bacchides (*Ant.* 12.396). I am not sure whether Josephus intends to exculpate Alcimus, whom he treats slightly more favorably than 1 Macc does (*Ant.* 12.398), or whether he simply operated on the assumption that Alcimus served as a puppet of the Seleucid authorities. Josephus' deviation from 1 Macc is certainly not based on independent information. Josephus does not identify those sixty victims as *Asidaioi*, but a little later he remarks that Alcimus "had put to death many of the good and pious (ὅσιοι) men of the nation" (*Ant.* 12.400). Yose ben Yoezer is often considered one of these victims, but the midrashic story of his martyrdom (*Gen. Rab.* 65:22) is at variance with the main elements of the report in 1 Macc. For an elaborate attempt to reconcile the evidence see Goldstein, *1 Macc.*, pp. 334-336, 393.

[72]See Habicht, *2 Macc*, p. 272 n. 7a. J. Efron's argument that there never was a division between Hasmoneans and *Asidaioi*, is contradicted by the further course of events (*Studies on the Hasmonean Period* [SJLA 39, Leiden: Brill, 1987] pp. 24-26).

the split, when the *Asidaioi* represented the largest element in Judah's army.[73]

To be sure, Judah did retain a substantial following and the Seleucid government thought him so dangerous that it continued to send Alcimus military support. Judea was temporarily put under the command of a *strategos*. Nicanor, an experienced army officer, was the first to hold that post.[74] At first he avoided military confrontation with Judah. The description of the friendship that developed between these two men (2 Macc 14:23-25) is unusual, though hardly fictional, because Nicanor was ultimately regarded as an archvillain after he turned against Judah.[75]

Although Nicanor defeated a detachment of Hasmonean forces under Simon (2 Macc 14:17), the guerilla troops under Judah eluded him. They remained victorious in two engagements. After the second battle, in which Nicanor lost his life, Judah picked up the temporary support of the villagers who joined in the pursuit of the fleeing Seleucid army and shared in the loot (1 Macc 7:46-47).

The cruel treatment of Nicanor's body is somewhat unusual though not unique.[76] It was not only a sign of revenge against a former friend, but also an eloquent, if ineffectual, warning to the people in the *Akra*. The last victory over Nicanor, on 13 Adar, was considered important enough to be commemorated annually, an honor given to no other military exploit of Judah.[77]

---

[73]*Hellenistic Civ.* pp. 229-230; Tcherikover thinks that a reconciliation must have occurred, but adduces no evidence for this opinion.

[74]2 Macc 14:12. See Habicht, *2 Macc*, p. 239 n. 9a; p. 272 n. 12c.

[75]2 Macc 15:3. I see no reason why 2 Macc should have invented this friendship. Instead, it is plausible that 1 Macc omitted this episode, because it does not fit its image of the totally hostile gentile world.

[76]Similar treatment of the chief enemy is found in the nearly contemporary story of Holofernes (Judith 14:11) and in the earlier accounts about Goliath (1 Sam 17:54) and Saul (1 Sam 31:8-10).

[77]1 Macc 7:49; 2 Macc 15:36; *Megillat Taanit* 13 Adar. Scholars are almost evenly divided about the year of Nicanor's death. 161 BCE: Bickerman, *Gott*, p. 15; Schürer-Vermes-Millar 1, p. 170 n. 30; Goldstein, *1 Macc.*, pp. 341-342. 160 BCE: Abel, *Macc.*, p. 144; Abel-Starcky, p. 144; Bunge, *Untersuchungen* p. 630. The year of the battle is nowhere given, but the events described in 1 Macc 7 and 2 Macc 14-15 cannot all have occurred during the winter of 162/161 BCE (Demetrius may have left Rome in the fall, but did not come to power until winter. See note 59 above) On the other hand, the author of 1 Macc supposed a very short time span, "a few days" (7:50), between the death of Nicanor and the events leading to Judah's death, which occurred in the spring of 160 BCE. This time reckoning, however, may not be taken literally. The only argument Goldstein adduces against the later date is the unfounded assumption that Judah could not have sent ambassadors to Rome before he defeated Nicanor.

Second Maccabees ends on this auspicious note, whereas 1 Macc recognizes that this victory provided only temporary respite (1 Macc 7:50). Bacchides' retaliatory campaign came only a few weeks later, in the first month of 152 Sel. Bab.[78] The Seleucid army at first encountered some resistance in the area of Arbela, probably not in Galilee, but in the border area between Judea and Samaria.[79] From there it marched to the vicinity of Jerusalem, but Judah was not there. So Bacchides tracked him down, according to 1 Macc 9:5 near Elasa.[80] Judah reportedly had three thousand men with him of whom all but eight hundred fled when they saw the approaching Seleucid army. Even if this number is understated, Judah's men were clearly outnumbered.[81] After some initial successes they were encircled and routed. Judah fell. His brothers Jonathan and Simon buried him in the family tomb in Modein (1 Macc 9:19) probably after having agreed to a truce with Bacchides (see *Ant.* 12.432).

First Maccabees claims that "all Israel greatly lamented Judah" (1 Macc 9:20-21), but this cannot conceal the fact that most of his supporters had either been killed or had left him and that it would be several years before Jonathan could again muster a substantial following.

The chronological problem is best solved if one recognizes that Demetrius' escape from Rome in 151 Sel. (1 Macc 7:1) is reckoned according to the Macedonian era (= 162/1 BCE). The author of 1 Macc interpreted it as a Babylonian date (= 161/0 BCE) and routinely attributed the Day of Nicanor to that year (13 Adar, 151 Sel. Bab. = March 160 BCE).

[78]1 Macc 9:3. April/May 160 BCE. See Goldstein, *1 Macc.*, p. 372; Abel, *Macc.*, p. 159; Schaumberger, Seleukiden-Liste, p. 435. Differently Schürer-Vermes-Millar 1, p. 173.

[79]1 Macc 9:2; against *Ant.* 12.421 see Möller-Schmitt, *Siedlungen*, p. 22.

[80]For a discussion of the proposed locations of Elasa see Möller-Schmitt, *Siedlungen*, pp. 47-48; for an analysis of the battle see B. Bar-Kochva, *Battles*, pp. 288-307.

[81]B. Bar-Kochva (*Battles*, pp.60-73) argues that the number of Seleucid soldiers is frequently exaggerated and the number of their Jewish opponents consistently understated throughout 1 Macc. These allegations correctly identify the unreliability of numbers in our sources. However, in trying to be more specific, Bar-Kochva bases his case on the unproven assumption that the hellenizers were a statistically insignificant group and that basically all the rest of the population was ready to actively support Judah. His further assertion that there was no drop in support toward the end of Judah's life is disproven by the further course of events.

Excursus: Judah's Embassy to Rome

Judah's relations with Rome have been the subject of voluminous research.[82] It is now generally accepted that Judah did send ambassadors to Rome in 161/0 BCE to ask for assistance against Demetrius. This fact emerges not only from 1 Macc 8:17-32, but is independently confirmed by other sources.[83] A favorable outcome of the embassy is indicated by a statement in Justin that "after they (the Jews) had defected from Demetrius, they requested the friendship (*amicitia*) of the Romans and became the first of all the eastern peoples to receive liberty, since the Romans at that time easily granted what was not theirs."[84] While there is little doubt about the existence of relations between Judah and Rome, the character of these relations has received much critical attention. During the past generation most scholars have followed Täubler's assessment that the text in 1 Macc 8:23-30, though differing somewhat in form from other treaties, is basically an authentic rendering of a Roman document of 161/0 BCE.[85] Formal difficulties are usually explained by pointing out that the text went through three translations: from Latin to Greek to Hebrew/Aramaic and back to Greek.

This view has been challenged by Gauger (n. 82 above). Though he admits that the text is based on an authentic document, he does not believe that the Romans would have committed themselves as early as 161/0 BCE to enter a formal alliance with the Jews as the text states. Gauger argues that because Rome was noncommittal in its support for Timarchus (161 BCE) and Alexander Balas (c. 153 BCE), it would not

---

[82]J.-D. Gauger, *Beiträge zur jüdischen Apologetik*, pp. 153-328; *idem*, "Zur Rekonstruktion der römisch-jüdischen Beziehungen im 2. Jh. v. Chr.," in *Studien zur Alten Geschichte* ed. H. Kalcyk *et al.* vol. 1 (Rome: Giorgio Bretschneider, 1986) 261-291. M. Smith, "Rome and Maccabean Conversions: Notes on 1 Macc 8," in C. K. Barrett et al., *Donum Gentilicium* (Oxford: Oxford U.P., 1978) 2-3. Goldstein, *1 Macc.* pp. 346-369.

[83]See 2 Macc 4:11; *Ant.* 14.233 with Gauger pp. 168-177.

[84]Justin 36.3.9; cf. (36.1.10). See Stern, *Greek and Latin Authors* 1, p. 342. Cf. Diodorus 40.2.2 and *J.W.* 1.38. These texts, too, seem to be independent of 1 Macc.

[85]E. Täubler, *Imperium Romanum. Studien zur Entwicklungsgeschichte des römischen Reichs*, vol. 1 (Leipzig: Teubner, 1913) 239-254. The authenticity of vv 31-32, which in 1 Macc form the end of the document, is doubtful because this clause is lacking in Josephus' text (*Ant.* 12.417-418) and does not conform to Roman practice in style or content. See Abel, *Macc.*, p. 157; Goldstein, *1 Macc.*, pp. 368-369 defends the authenticity of the passage.

have entered into a formal commitment with the less illustrious emissaries of Judah.[86]

Gauger overlooks that Rome was more likely to promise assistance to a smaller power than to a potentially powerful (and dangerous) king.[87] Moreover, the possibilities he suggests are less convincing than the diverse and independent reports that a treaty was made in Judah's time. Therefore we have no adequate reason to deny the basic authenticity of the document in 1 Macc 8:23-30. As is well known, however, the treaty had no immediate consequences. Demetrius' policy of aiming at full control of Judea did not change appreciably, except that perhaps he intensified his efforts.[88]

For the concern of this study, however, the treaty shows that, contrary to biblical precept as traditionally interpreted, Judah and his men were willing to enter into a formal relationship with a Gentile power outside of Palestine.[89] Furthermore, both envoys bore Greek names, though their fathers had Hebrew ones (1 Macc 8:17). About Jason we know nothing else. Eupolemus *may* be identical with the historian by the same name, although certainty on this issue is impossible. His family belonged to the priestly aristocracy, as can be gathered from the fact that he belonged to the priestly clan of Hakkoz (Ezra 2:61; Neh 7:63) and that his father had negotiated royal privileges for the Jews (2 Macc 4:11). Thus the revolt attracted not only peasants, country priesthood, and other lower-class people, but also aristocrats with considerable knowledge of Greek speech and manners. It must be remembered that such knowledge did not entail any willingness, not to say desire, to neglect the traditional Mosaic law. On the other hand, it may be that the power struggle among different factions of the higher priesthood had led some moderate Hellenizers into Judah's camp.

First Maccabees puts the embassy to Rome shortly before Judah's death in the spring of 160 BCE. But, as has been pointed out frequently, 1

---

[86]*Apologetik*, pp. 243-250, 327-328. He further argues with Willrich that according to a letter of Julius Caesar the friendship between the Jews and Rome started after the conquest of Joppa (*Ant.* 14.205). But, as he himself admits, this argument is weak because chronological accuracy was not of great concern (*ibid.*, pp. 253-257); also, the reference to "when they made (the treaty of?) friendship with the Romans" may refer to a subsequent treaty or other accord.

[87]See E. Badian, *Foreign Clientelae* (264-70 B.C.) (Oxford: Oxford U. Pr., 1958) p. 112: "The cities, unlike the kingdoms, would normally be sure of (Rome's) protection: for their protection was the humiliation of the kings."

[88]See E. Bickerman, *From Ezra to the Last of the Maccabees* (New York: Schocken, 1962) pp. 133-134.

[89]See M. Smith, "Rome and Maccabean Conversions", p. 3.

Macc 8 is an intrusion in the context. It is generally believed that a letter of the Consul Gaius Fannius to the magistrates of Cos refers to Judah's envoys (*Ant.* 14.233). If this is so, their stay in Rome can be dated between March 15, 161 and March 15, 160 BCE.[90] Therefore it is impossible that the envoys left Judea only after the victory over Nicanor. Perhaps the vigorous intervention of Bacchides and/or Nicanor caused Judah to send an embassy to ask for Rome's friendship, i.e., support. It is in that sense that the author of 1 Macc 8:18 understood the envoys' mission. Whether or not they returned before Judah's death we do not know.

Conclusions

Judah's Supporters

As we have seen above, Mattathias had drawn support from a variety of groups. Judah, to whom leadership of the movement passed apparently without controversy, was able to enlarge the circle of supporters considerably. He recruited a substantial army from the Judean countryside. Priests who opposed the changes in the temple and the abolition of the Torah joined, though at least some of them maintained a degree of independence (1 Macc 5:67). At least after Judah's initial successes, members of the Jerusalem aristocracy became active supporters of the Hasmonean movement. Eupolemus, a descendant of an important family, became one of the movement's spokesmen. Other members of the aristocracy were sufficiently associated with anti-Seleucid circles (probably the Hasmoneans) to cause Bacchides to take their sons hostages.[91]

The most conspicuous additional support for Judah came from refugees brought to Judea from Transjordan and perhaps from Galilee. Some of them were trained soldiers. Judah assisted them with food and probably settled them on lands previously owned by "Hellenizers." Judah's supporters from Transjordan included a group of "Toubians" perhaps connected with the anti-Seleucid branch of the Tobiad family.[92]

---

[90]See Broughton, *Magistrates* 1.443. The expression στρατηγὸς ὕπατος at that time could mean either *consul* or *proconsul*. See R.K. Sherk, *Roman Documents from the Greek East* (Baltimore: Johns Hopkins, 1969) nos. 14.60, 62, 70; 31.1; p. 250 n. 1. Since the letter seems to originate in Rome, Fannius appears to have been consul at the time.
[91]1 Macc 9:53; 10:6, 9. This occurred after Judah's death but before Jonathan came to power.
[92]See 2 Macc 12:17, 24-25, 35(?); 1 Macc 5:13 claims, wrongly, that all of them were slain before Judah could bring assistance.

Judah maintained friendly relations with Jews in other areas as well, as the example of the Jewish community of Beth-shan (Scythopolis) shows (2 Macc 12:29-31). He did not despise friendship with foreigners either. He actively sought Rome's support and fostered good relations with the Nabateans. Even with Nicanor he developed a shortlived friendship (2 Macc 14:24-25).

Judah's Achievements and Failures

After the midpoint of his career, rededication of the Temple and successful expedition to Gilead, Judah's following decreased considerably through casualties, desertions, and through the split with the *Asidaioi.*[93] Before his last battle, Judah was abandoned by all but a few hundred stalwarts. How desperate the situation of the Hasmoneans was, can be gauged from the course of further events. Judah's enemies were in control in Jerusalem and in most of the rest of the country. The revolt was at its nadir. And yet, Judah had accomplished three important goals:

(1) Through their military actions, he and his followers had put the Seleucid government on notice that opposition to the decrees of Antiochus IV was strong and resilient. The revolt induced the government to restore the legal validity of the Pentateuch. The new high priest was an Aaronide and perhaps of a branch of the high priestly family. The dietary laws and other Pentateuchal provisions (for circumcision, Sabbath observance, etc.) perhaps were not enforced, but at least could now be observed by those who wanted to observe them.

(2) Judah rededicated the Jerusalem Temple, making it fit again for the traditional cult of Yahweh, and he restored that cult. Other forms of worship were discontinued in the Jerusalem Temple.

(3) Judah gained a following from diverse quarters. Though in the end he lost the active support of many, a small but dedicated core remained. Moreover, he had become a symbol of national and religious resistance and as such had established ties with a large number of influential Judeans. The heroic picture of him in 2 Macc shows how much he was admired even by people who did not think highly of the rest of his family.

Under the leadership of Judah's brother Jonathan the core continued to operate, at first as outlaws, then officially recognized and tolerated. When more favorable conditions arose they formed the backbone of a reemerging Hasmonean movement, to which, in time,

---

[93]*J.W.* 1.47 claims that before his last battle Judah got many new recruits, but the other evidence does not support this contention.

others rallied who had formerly cooperated or sympathized with the Hasmoneans.

3

Jonathan

Eclipse and Reorganization

After Judah's death his remaining companions were for a while in complete disarray. If, as Josephus suggests, they had negotiated a truce with Bacchides for the burial of their slain leader (*Ant.* 12.432), it was of short duration. Apparently, Bacchides attempted to root out all opposition and used Jewish collaborators to hunt down "Judah's friends." Those who were found were treated mercilessly (1 Macc 9:26; *Ant.* 13.4). What was worse, a great number of Jews rallied to the government's side (1 Macc 9:23). A famine, undoubtedly increased if not caused by war activity, forced many country dwellers (who, as we have seen, had hitherto been the Hasmoneans' mainstay) to make what terms they could with the city people and the government who controlled most of the imported and – probably more important – of the stored food. Therefore, it is understandable that 1 Macc 9:24 reports that "the country went over to their side." The Hasmoneans, apparently the only ones who continued their resistance, seem to have shrunk to a tiny group. Many of their pious neighbors – and friends – probably considered the results of the revolt sufficient and any further bloodshed futile (cf. 2 Macc 15:37). Therefore, Abel's characterization of the situation as a "triomphe du parti grec" is somewhat misleading.[1] The collapse of the revolt was so complete, that the author of 1 Macc could state that this situation was the greatest crisis since the time when prophets had ceased to appear.[2]

---

[1]Abel, *Macc.*, p. 164.

[2]1 Macc 9:27. Josephus interprets this phrase freely and calls it the greatest calamity since the return from Babylon (*Ant.* 13.5). We do not know whether 1 Macc espoused the later rabbinic view that prophecy ceased after Malachi (*b.*

Of the events of the following years we know very little. Evidently not much occurred that was considered worth memorializing by the Hasmonean family. Jonathan was chosen by "all the friends of Judah" to succeed his brother in the leadership of the Hasmonean cause.[3] But not even the hills of northern Judea were safe for Jonathan, because Bacchides was in virtually complete control of the country and tried to seize him (1 Macc 9:32; *Ant.* 13.7). Therefore Jonathan and his men went into hiding in the desert of Tekoa, at a water hole called Asphar, southeast of Jerusalem (1 Macc 9:33; *Ant.* 13.8). This was not far from Beth-zur where Judah had earlier established a stronghold (1 Macc 4:61), later taken by Lysias (6:49-50). Even there, however, they did not feel completely safe, for Jonathan charged his brother John to convey their baggage and probably their wives and children to the Nabateans. The caravan was intercepted, however, by the (perhaps Nabatean) tribe of Jambri from Medaba in Transjordan. John was slain, the goods were taken, and according to *Ant.* all his companions were killed too.[4] In *J.W.* 1.47 Josephus tells us that "John died through a plot of the partisans of Antiochus." The reference to Antiochus is wrong. It is possible, however, that this was not merely an act of highway robbery. Rather, the attackers may have been in collusion with Bacchides, who preferred to rely on local collaborators instead of regular armies whenever possible.[5]

Jonathan and his men took revenge on the tribe of Jambri by attacking a large bridal party, killing many of them, taking the spoils, and vanishing into the Jordan valley.[6] Bacchides, however, was informed about their position and attacked them at the river's edge, on a Sabbath. But after some fighting they escaped across the Jordan.[7]

Yoma 9b), nor when and why its disappearance was thought to have caused a crisis.

[3]1 Macc 9:28-31 (The similarity with Judg 10:18; 11:6-11 may be deliberate); *J.W.* 1.48; *Ant.* 13.5-6. We do not know why Jonathan was preferred over Simon, his older brother. But now Simon is mentioned more often, mostly in conjunction with Jonathan. He is completely absent from the story of Judah in 1 Macc, with the exception of his alleged campaign in Galilee (1 Macc 5:17-55) – a fact which adds to the suspicion with which that report should be regarded.

[4]1 Macc 9:35-36, 38; *Ant.* 13.10-11 (somewhat dramatized). On Jambri see Abel, *Macc.*, p. 168.

[5]Cf. 1 Macc 9:25-26, 60; *Ant.* 13.4, 24-25. See n. 18 below.

[6]1 Macc 9:37-42; *Ant.* 13.18-21 (the number of the slain [400] is added by Josephus).

[7]1 Macc 9:43-49 (with a brief heroic speech); *Ant.* 13.12-14. This is the first reported instance of actual fighting on a Sabbath. Cf. 1 Macc 2:40-41; see pp. 32-33 above.

After his return to Jerusalem, Bacchides devised a network of new fortresses and strengthened existing ones in order to insure full control over the country (1 Macc 9:50-52). The heaviest concentration was in northern Judea and southern Samaria, i.e., the area where the Hasmoneans had scored their initial successes. Avi-Yonah thought that the fortresses were placed so as to control the major access roads to Jerusalem. Abel, however, located all except Beth-zur (and the *Akra*) north of Jerusalem.[8] If Abel's locations are correct, effective control of the local population and prevention of rebel infiltration appear to have been the primary goal and this seems somewhat more likely, since Jerusalem was not in danger of outside attack.

Bacchides shrewdly realized that the guerilla fighters could not be effectively defeated by a mobile army, however large, but that the staging areas for their raids had to be controlled. Furthermore, he realized that the voluntary or forced cooperation of the local population was of paramount importance. By taking the children of prominent citizens hostages, he assured himself of their acquiescence.[9]

While Bacchides apparently held the governance of the province of Judea firmly in his hands, Alcimus was reduced to a secondary position, but kept the supervision of the Temple, until the spring of 159 BCE when he died of a stroke. His death was interpreted as punishment for alterations of the Temple architecture that he had ordered.[10] Apparently he wanted to ease access to the inner court of the Temple. This was considered a grave offense. The proper layout of the Temple, as well as strict observance of purity regulations were considered of great importance in many circles, though there was wide disagreement as to details.[11]

First Maccabees does not state who succeeded Alcimus in the high priesthood. Josephus instead has two contradictory versions. According

---

[8]Carta's Atlas of the Period of the Second Temple (Jerusalem: Carta, 1966) p. 30 map 42. Avi-Yonah identified Tephon (1 Macc 9:50) with Tekoa on the basis of *Ant.* 13.16 and also located Timnah in the south. Abel instead (*Géographie* 2. 475-476, 481-482) identified the two localities with Tappuah and Timnat-Serah, north of Jerusalem.

[9]1 Macc 9:53; *Ant.* 13.17.

[10]1 Macc 9:54-56; *Ant.* 12.413. Cf. J. Maier, *Die Tempelrolle vom Toten Meer* (UTB 829; Reinhardt: Munich/Basle, 1978) p. 94. Bunge dates Alcimus' death in 160 BCE on the basis of *Ant.* 20.237 ("Zur Geschichte und Chronologie des Untergangs der Oniaden und des Aufstiegs der Hasmonäer," *JSJ* 6 [1975] 14-27). I follow Abel (*Macc.*, p. 174) and Goldstein (*1 Macc.*, p. 391) and the majority of scholars on the basis of 1 Macc 9:54.

[11]Compare Ezek 40-46 with 11QTemple 30-47. See Goldstein, *1 Macc.*, pp. 387-393.

to one, Alcimus died before Judah, and Judah succeeded him.[12] In this view, after Judah's death the high priesthood was vacant for four years (*Ant.* 13.46). Later Josephus corrected himself and added to the vacancy the three years previously assigned to Judah, for a total of seven years without a high priest (*Ant.* 20.237).

This later view of Josephus was generally accepted as accurate until challenged by Stegemann's thesis that the Teacher of Righteousness was high priest in the interim.[13] Stegemann would explain the silence of 1 Macc about Alcimus' successor by the unsupported and unlikely conjecture that 1 Macc would not have been interested in the high priesthood of the Teacher. *Damnatio memoriae* is also unlikely because Alcimus, a great enemy of the Hasmoneans, is mentioned by name. Stegemann further asserts that all later literature depended on 1 Macc. This is almost certainly false; Josephus' list of high priests seems to have been derived from archival sources.[14] Certainly false is the assertion that as a title in postexilic literature "the priest" (הכהן) *always* designates a high priest.[15]

It is impossible that both Ezra "the priest" (Ezra 7:11) and Meremoth "the priest" (Ezra 8:33; cf. Neh 3:20-21) were high priests at the same time. The appointment of Shelemiah "the priest" as one of three treasurers of the storehouses (Neh 13:13) does not befit a high priest. Thus, there is no evidence that the Teacher of Righteousness was ever considered high priest in Jerusalem (though he may have functioned as chief priest for the Qumran community). If a high priest had been appointed after Alcimus' death, he would certainly have had to be acceptable to the people of the *Akra* because at that time they had effective control over Jerusalem. The Teacher of Righteousness would almost surely have been unacceptable to them.

In any event, it is more likely that, as Josephus states and 1 Macc implies, from 159 to 152 there was no high priest.[16] Bacchides was not

---

[12]*Ant.* 12.414, 419, 434.

[13]*Die Entstehung der Qumrangemeinde*, Bonn (diss.) 1971, pp. 210-225.

[14]Stegemann, *Entstehung* p.219. See Hölscher, *Hohenpriesterliste* pp. 7-8. Admittedly, the Temple archives were long controlled by the Hasmoneans, but the list has no indication of polemical omissions.

[15]Stegemann, *Entstehung* pp. 102, 210.

[16]The lack of a high priest is unusual but not unique. It is unlikely that Menelaus was allowed to officiate while Judah was in control of the Temple (cf. 1 Macc 4:42). Thus at least on Yom Kippur of 163 BCE a problem had arisen. Similarly it is unlikely that a rival was officiating on Yom Kippur before Jonathan entered office on Sukkot 152 BCE (1 Macc 10:21). In later years, a substitute could perform the functions of the high priest, if the latter was unable to do so (*m. Yoma* 1:1). For a more detailed refutation of Stegemann's

authorized to appoint a successor for Alcimus, the appointment and confirmation of high priests being a royal privilege.[17] If Bacchides left for consultations in Antioch, and no suitable candidate, loyal to the government and capable of uniting Jerusalem, could be found, the decision to make no appointment from either the "Hellenizers" or the "Traditionalists" may have helped to keep both parties on good behavior while hoping for the reward.

Even if this scenario is basically correct, we are still left with a series of problems: Who controlled the Temple? Was there a compromise between the people of the *Akra* and more traditional Jews to permit common worship? Some people regarded the Second Temple as defiled (see *1 Enoch* 89:73), but we suppose that for most Jews it was the center of Jewish worship. Since peace with the government's forces and acceptance by the local populace was necessary for smooth operation, we also suppose that the Temple priesthood tried to please as many factions as possible (see 1 Macc 7:33).

Jonathan's Rise to Power

A major challenge – and an unprecedented opportunity – arose for Jonathan when Bacchides again intervened in Judean affairs. The nature of his intervention, especially its beginning, is obscure.[18]

---

thesis see H. Burgmann, "Das umstrittene Intersacerdotium in Jerusalem 159-152 v. Chr.," *JSJ* 11 (1980) 135-176.

[17]See 2 Macc 4:7-8, 23-24; 1 Macc 10:20; 11:27, 57.

[18]According to 1 Macc 9:58, Bacchides was called into the country by local foes of Jonathan who contended that he could apprehend Jonathan and his men in a one-night operation. ἀπῆρε τοῦ ἐλθεῖν μετὰ δυνάμεως πολλῆς (1 Macc 9:60) means that Bacchides "set out to come with a large army." (Vulgate: *et surrexit ut veniret*). Whether he *did* come is not stated. Commentators have generally taken for granted that he did, but this creates a problem that is easily overlooked; if he himself came with an army to apprehend Jonathan and his men (v 60a), why did he send letters ordering his Judean allies to do so (v 60b)? Perhaps he hoped to have Jonathan on hand, in chains, for his arrival, and so be spared the nuisance of a campaign when a show of power would be sufficient.

1 Macc continues by saying that "they" (presumably the allies) were not able to capture Jonathan and his men "because *their* scheme became known. And *they* seized up to fifty men of the originators of the trouble, from the men of the countryside, and killed them. And Jonathan left the district" (1 Macc 9:60-62). It is generally thought that the last "they" refers to Jonathan and his men, the preceding ones to Bacchides' allies (so Abel, Zeitlin, Goldstein, RSV, NAB). However, there is no textual basis for this change of subject, and against it is the fact that, when Jonathan is introduced immediately afterwards, he is named. The common interpretation results from the description of the men killed as "originators of the trouble" (τῶν ἀρχηγῶν τῆς κακίας 9:61); since "the

Whatever the precise sequence of events was, there is no reason to doubt that Jonathan and his men barricaded themselves in the fortress of Bethbasi, on the edge of the Judean desert between Bethlehem and Tekoa.[19] Together with the information about their earlier hiding place near Tekoa this indicates that the center of their operations had been shifted from northwestern to southeastern Judea. Judah's earlier occupation of Beth-zur would suggest that supporters of the Hasmonean cause were to be found in this area as well. It is not certain, however, how much freedom of movement Jonathan and his companions had because the north was more heavily guarded by Bacchides' fortresses.

Jonathan and his men repaired and strengthened the fortifications of Bethbasi. As soon as Bacchides found out about this, he is said to have gathered his army and summoned his Judean allies and come to besiege Bethbasi.[20] Despite the use of war engines and a protracted siege he was unable to take the fortress. While Simon remained inside, Jonathan was even able to slip out with a number of men. It may plausibly be supposed that he wanted to get provisions and reinforcements, but by making trouble in the countryside he also put added pressure on Bacchides who may not have had enough manpower to effectively carry on the siege and guard the countryside. Such evidence of Seleucid weakness may have induced many people to switch their support to Jonathan. Such was probably the case of the tribes of Odomera and "the children of Phasiron."[21] As the text stands, Jonathan "smote" these tribes "and they began to beat and they went up

---

trouble" in this context is usually understood to be the proposal to call in Bacchides, the originators are thought to have been Bacchides' allies. But if "the trouble" was the fact that their plans became known to Jonathan and their attempts to seize him failed, then its originators would have been Jonathan's friends, and the text would make perfect sense if *they* were taken in all instances to refer to Bacchides' allies (as the Greek would normally be understood). Another possibility is that the obscurity of the text results from a change of the sources used. The author may be conflating several accounts and 1 Macc 9:61 may be a doublet of 9:69. Josephus made Bacchides responsible for the executions in both instances (*Ant.* 13.25, 31). There is no easy solution to the problems and any reconstruction has to remain conjectural.

[19]1 Macc 9:62; *Ant.* 13.26 has instead Bethalaga which is usually identified with Beth-Hogla near the northwest corner of the Dead Sea (So Abel, *Géographie*, 2.265; Möller-Schmitt, *Siedlungen*, pp. 42-43). Josephus' relocation of the site does not seem to be based on independent evidence and is probably wrong.

[20]1 Macc 9:63. The parallel with 9:60 again suggests a doublet.

[21]We know nothing about these tribes and even their names are unexplained. See Abel-Starcky, p. 159, n. b.

in the forces."[22] This we should understand to mean that these tribes joined Jonathan in the fight against Bacchides. Meanwhile Bacchides was unambiguously attacked by Simon's men who sallied from Bethbasi, burnt his siege engines, and reportedly got the better of him, so that he decided to raise the siege and to return to Syria (1 Macc 9:67-69). His decision may be taken as evidence supporting our conjecture (above) that he did not have sufficient troops to continue the siege and keep the country under control at the same time. Before leaving, he executed "many" of those men who had called him into the country.[23]

When Jonathan became aware of Bacchides' intention to leave, he sent emissaries to him to negotiate an agreement. The exact terms are not known, but Bacchides agreed to return prisoners he had taken in Judea. The hostages who were being held in the Akra however were evidently not included in the transfer.[24] Furthermore, Bacchides promised not to make any more trouble for Jonathan. What Jonathan

---

[22] 1 Macc 9:66: ἐπάταξεν...καὶ ἤρξαντο τύπτειν καὶ ἀνέβαινον ἐν ταῖς δυνάμεσι. The manuscript tradition shows that already ancient copyists had problems with this verse: Some MSS instead of ἐπάταξεν have ἐπέταξεν, which may be rendered "he added" (scil. these tribes to his own troops); hardly "he commanded," pace Goldstein (1 Macc., p. 395), for there is no indication that he was able to command. Josephus seems to have understood it as "added"; he has Jonathan secretly going out into the countryside and "gathering a large force from among his supporters" (Ant. 13.28).

τύπτειν, used absolutely, is very rare, but see Ezek 7:6 LXX (where, however, the understood object, ὑμᾶς, is obvious). Therefore, attempts have been made to link it with ἐν ταῖς δυνάμεσι. In LXX, τύπτειν ἐν always translates ב להכות (see Judg 20:39; 2 Sam 24:17), "to smite <someone> in – i.e. a member of – <a specified group>." In some instances, ἀναβαίνειν ἐν translates ב עלה, meaning "to go up against," "to invade" (4 Kgs 17:5; cf. Jer 31:18 LXX = 48:18 MT; 2 Chr 21:17). See Goldstein, 1 Macc., p. 395. ἐν ταῖς δυνάμεσι seems to be an almost literal translation of בחיל. It may mean "with the troops" (so Abel, RSV, NEB, Tedesche-Zeitlin) or "against the troops" (so Goldstein, Grimm). Neither translation solves all problems, but the latter (admittedly taking the text to be faulty Greek) has the advantage of better fitting the verbal construction. The Vorlage of 1 Macc 9:66b may have read והחלו להכות ולעלות בחיל (similarly Kahana) which can be rendered "they began to smite and to go up against the armed forces." This appears to be a case of hysteron proteron and the logical sequence would be "they went up against the armed forces and started to smite (them)." Several MSS use the verbs in singular, with Jonathan as the (implied) subject, indicating that he continued solely with his small band of men. RSV, NEB, and Kahana, among others, follow that tradition, but it is more plausible that Jonathan secured reinforcements before daring to attack Bacchides' positions.

[23] 1 Macc 9:69. The seeming doublet with 9:61 has already been noted. Ant. 13.25, 31.

[24] 1 Macc 9:70-72; cf. 10:6; cf. Ant. 13.32, which mentions an exchange of prisoners.

offered in return we do not know. Perhaps he committed himself to respect the *status quo* of Jerusalem where the *Akra* remained a stronghold of his opponents.

This last campaign of Bacchides was decisive for the future of the Hasmoneans. If Bacchides had conquered Bethbasi and captured Jonathan and Simon, it would probably have meant the end of the Hasmonean movement. However, after the siege of Bethbasi failed, Bacchides, at least by his parting agreement, gave some form of recognition to Jonathan's leadership. On the other hand, Jonathan's opponents were weakened by the loss of many of their leaders and by the fact that the central government no longer supported them as fully as before. Jonathan was again able to stay in northern Judea and for the time being established himself in Machmas (Michmash).[25]

Reportedly, he began to "judge" the people. The language here as elsewhere in 1 Macc is intentionally echoing the Book of Judges.[26] Jonathan's role is depicted as one for all the people (λαός); he is said to have "removed the ungodly from Israel" (1 Macc 9:73). Thus, even though for the moment his activity was confined to a limited area, his mission is shown as one for all Israel. Also in this respect the Judges of ancient Israel are a model.[27]

It is evident that these stereotype expressions veil a much more complex reality. Jonathan did not in fact remove his "ungodly" opponents from the *Akra* or from Beth-zur and probably did not undertake any major raid because that would have been likely to trigger a military response.[28]

Jonathan seems to have had his headquarters at Michmash from 157 to 152 BCE, but we know next to nothing about his or his followers' activities during these years. It seems to have been a relatively peaceful period in which "the sword ceased from Israel" (1 Macc 9:73).

These unknown years undoubtedly were important for Jonathan and his supporters. At the beginning, their lawful existence was barely recognized, while at the end the contenders for the Seleucid empire vied for Jonathan's support. This was of course in part due to the desperate need of both Demetrius I and Alexander Balas to get every possible assistance. On the other hand, Jonathan must have become

---

[25]1 Macc 9:73; *Ant.* 13.34. Abel (*Macc.*, p. 178) and others have pointed out that it was another Jonathan, Saul's son, who had achieved an earlier victory at Michmash (1 Sam 13-14), but except for the names there is no similarity.

[26]Judg 10:1-3; 12:7-13; see also the affinity between 1 Macc 9:28-31 and Judg 10:18; 11:6-11.

[27]Cf. Judg 3:10; 4:4; 10:1.

[28]See J.C. Dancy, *1 Macc.*, p. 139.

influential enough to command attention and respect abroad so that in the end the support of his faction, and not that of his enemies, the traditional supporters of the Seleucids, seems to have been preferred. We are not told, however, what offers were made to the occupants of the *Akra*. It is not inconceivable that both Alexander Balas and Demetrius I tried to win the support of both sides.

Jonathan's Move to Jerusalem

When in 153/2 BCE Alexander Balas invaded Coele-Syria, Demetrius wrote a letter to Jonathan requesting[29] that he raise an army and become his ally. Demetrius also offered the return of the hostages who had been held in the *Akra* since Bacchides had taken them. Jonathan seized this opportunity and entered Jerusalem. We are not told if he had had access to the city previously, but the text suggests that there was no immediate armed opposition to his entering.[30] Demetrius' letter was read aloud in public "in the hearing of all the people and of those from the *Akra*."[31] Fear arose, however, because Jonathan had been authorized to raise an army. Josephus, perhaps interpreting 1 Macc correctly, specifies that only "the ungodly (ἀσεβεῖς) and the renegades (φυγάδες) from the *Akra* became very much afraid" (*Ant.* 13.40).

Not only did Jonathan achieve the release of the hostages, but he established himself in Jerusalem and initiated the restoration and strengthening of the city's fortifications; also, the gentile garrisons of the fortresses built by Bacchides are said to have abandoned their posts at this time.[32] After a short while, however, we find the same fortresses, or at least some of them, again occupied by enemies of Jonathan (1 Macc 11:41; 12:45). We hear nothing, however, of a reoccupation of abandoned fortresses, which would have been a major operation in the face of Jonathan's resistance. Perhaps, therefore, we should suppose that the fortresses were never completely abandoned by the Seleucid troops, though some men may have deserted when they became aware of Demetrius' shift in policy.[33]

---

[29] 1 Macc 10:6 has ἔδωκεν αὐτῷ ἐξουσίαν (authorized him), *Ant.* 13:38 instead has προσέταξεν αὐτῷ (ordered him). The authenticity of the letter cannot be proven, but its contents are plausible.
[30] 1 Macc 10:7-9; cf. *Ant.* 13.39-40.
[31] 1 Macc 10:7; cf. *Ant.* 13.39.
[32] 1 Macc 10:9-13; *Ant.* 13.40-42.
[33] Dancy (*1 Macc.*, p. 141) suggests that "presumably [the garrisons] were withdrawn to oppose Alexander at Ptolemais." But 1 Macc 10:12-13 indicates flight of the troops to their homes, not reassignment.

In any event, the people at Beth-zur and in the *Akra* held out. First Maccabees suggests and *Ant.* tells us that the garrisons there consisted in large part of Jews opposed to Jonathan.[34] Their tenacity is quite remarkable. It may be that they found it difficult to settle elsewhere. In fact, according to 1 Macc 10:14, of the places fortified by Bacchides, Beth-zur served as their "place of refuge" (φυγαδευτήριον). This does not exclude them from the *Akra,* which had been fortified before Bacchides came. They may have anticipated that if they settled elsewhere in Seleucid territory, the Seleucid government might eventually hand them over to Jonathan.[35] Egypt, which had welcomed Onias IV, was probably not favorably inclined toward the allies of the late Menelaus. On the other hand, however, a decade hereafter, Jews who had fled Hasmonean Judea lived in many areas around the Eastern Mediterranean.[36] Thus, there were positive reasons why people could decide to hold out in the *Akra* and in Beth-zur. At least some of them owned land in Judea which may have been threatened by confiscation if they left the country. Also, a genuine attachment to their native country cannot be excluded. As a matter of fact, Beth-zur was vacated only after a long siege by Simon (1 Macc 11:65-66). The *Akra* gave up only in 141 BCE after its communications with the outside world were completely blocked off and some of the occupants had starved to death (1 Macc 13:49-51). What made these people resist for so long may be impossible to ascertain, but their attachment to Jerusalem seems to have been based on more than military and economic factors. Religious motives, which 1 Macc would have suppressed, may have been involved as well.

Before the final blockade, and for several years at least after Jonathan had moved into Jerusalem, the people of the *Akra* were able to move outside their fortified area so that they could buy and sell. This is indicated by the fact that 1 Macc 13:49 reports the interruption of such trade as a new development (cf. also 12:36). To make this possible, in the long periods between the several Hasmonean attacks on the *Akra* some tacit or explicit agreement must have existed between the parties.[37]

---

[34]1 Macc 10:14; 11:20-21; *Ant.* 13.42.

[35]Cf. 2 Macc 4:33-34; 13:3-8.

[36]1 Macc 15:21-23. The authenticity of the documents referred to here has been denied by Willrich (*Urkundenfälschung,* pp. 58-69) and by Gauger (*Apologetik,* pp. 293-302), but the extent of Jewish settlements supposed is not inherently unlikely. Cf. *Sib. Or.* 3.271, which, however, may be dated as late as the mid-first century BCE.

[37]Cf. 1 Macc 4:41; 6:18-32; 11:20-23.

If they were able to sell as well as to buy, they may have had some domestic production, such as clothing, pottery, tools. Most raw materials and foodstuffs had to be brought into the *Akra*. Some items may have been imported by the *Akra* and then sold on the local market.[38] The inhabitants of the *Akra* may have controlled a substantial part of the food supply – for themselves and perhaps for others too – in the form of landownership or cooperative arrangements with other landowners. The Hasmoneans had confiscated some land, but substantial areas of Judea must have remained outside their reach, for they were unable to control food supplies at the source and had to build a wall around the *Akra* to starve its inhabitants (1 Macc 12:36; 13:49). We do not know where supplies and local support for the *Akra* came from, but southwest of Jerusalem the Hasmonean presence seems to have been weak at least until they recaptured Beth-zur in 144 BCE or later.[39] The gradual consolidation of Hasmonean power in the north and northwest will have adversely affected the *Akra* and may have contributed to its growing isolation and eventual demise.

If the economic activity of the *Akra* continued relatively unhampered for long periods of time, its inhabitants must have had substantial reserves. They could not have relied exclusively on payments by the Seleucid government or on income from the sale its own tangible products.

The *Akra's* chief source of support, however, was its role as a strategically important base, available, if needed, against the Hasmoneans or even against the Ptolemies. If the flow of supplies into the *Akra* had depended entirely on the Hasmoneans' good will, it would have been cut off much earlier. It continued because every serious threat to the *Akra* caused an intervention by the Seleucid government, as long as it had the power to intervene.[40]

Jonathan's High Priesthood

Jonathan's position had been drastically altered by his move to Jerusalem, but another even more important development was to come. Alexander Balas, Demetrius' rival, was interested in Jonathan's

---

[38]Cf. J. Jeremias, *Jerusalem in the Time of Jesus* (Philadelphia: Fortress, 1969), pp. 2-38.

[39]1 Macc 11:65-66. Beth-zur was captured under Antiochus VI (144-142/1 BCE); see 1 Macc 11:54.

[40]When Judah besieged the *Akra*, the main Seleucid army responded (1 Macc 6:18-32). Jonathan apparently paid his way out of the troubles caused by his attack on the *Akra* (1 Macc 11:20-24). Simon finally conquered it, not without Seleucid protests, when the power struggle between Tryphon and Demetrius II prevented any effective government intervention (1 Macc 13:49-52).

support too. Therefore he offered him not only the title and insignia of a "Friend" but also the high priesthood.[41] First Maccabees does not tell us how this offer came about. Presumably something was done to bring Jonathan's achievements to Alexander's attention and to suggest the advantages of an alliance, as well as the appropriate price. Since Jonathan benefited considerably from the arrangement we may reasonably conjecture that he instigated it, and, through his friends in Alexander's circle asked for the office, in return for loyalty to Alexander and perhaps some other inducements. For leverage, the applicants could use the earlier promises by Demetrius. On the other hand, according to *Ant.* 20.238, Jonathan was appointed high priest not by Alexander but by "the descendants of the sons of Asamonaios" who "had been entrusted" (i.e. by God) with the leadership of the nation, and had therefore fought the Macedonians. This statement is part of Josephus' list of high priests which probably is based on archival material reflecting Hasmonean family tradition. It suggests that despite the death of three of Mattathias' five sons his extended family was still at the core of the Hasmonean movement. How much influence they actually had in Alexander's decision to appoint Jonathan high priest we do not know.

Surprisingly, the decisive change in Jonathan's status receives no comment in 1 Macc. The author is singularly laconic about the event: "And Jonathan put on the sacred vestments in the seventh month of the one hundred and sixtieth year at the Feast of Tabernacles (October 152 BCE) and he gathered troops and prepared a large supply of arms. And Demetrius heard these things...."[42]

When one compares this statement with other texts that deal with the high priesthood, the difference is immediately evident. Of the

---

[41] 1 Macc 10:15-20; *Ant.* 13.43-45.

[42] 1 Macc 10:21. J. G. Bunge dates Jonathan's accession to the high priesthood in 150 BCE, after the death of Demetrius I ("Zur Geschichte und Chronologie des Untergangs der Oniaden und des Aufstiegs der Hasmonäer," *JSJ* 6 [1975] 33-46). His redating is based on the assumption that the Jewish sources of 1 Macc indicated only days and months but not years; for evidence to the contrary see 1 Macc 13:41-42; 14:27. Bunge further gives more credence to Josephus' statement that Jonathan was high priest for seven years (*Ant.* 20.238) than to the precise date in 1 Macc, despite the fact that Josephus is manifestly wrong on many items in his chronology of high priests (See Hölscher, *Hohenpriesterliste*, pp. 3-7). Bunge does address the problem of the differences between the letters of Demetrius I and Alexander Balas on one hand and the historical narrative on the other. But his reconstruction, which supposes that Jonathan actually did furnish a large army to Demetrius I and joined Alexander's side only after Demetrius' death, requires a rearrangement of the text which poses as many problems as it solves.

elaborate installation ceremonies described in the P sections of Exodus and Leviticus, nothing except the donning of the vestments is mentioned, nothing of the high priestly splendor described by Ben Sira.[43] Interesting too is the fact that Jonathan entered office a few days *after* Yom Kippur when the presence of a high priest would have been needed most.[44] There is not even a reference to the connection between the Hasmonean priesthood and Phinehas, so carefully pointed out earlier.[45]

Such taciturnity suggests that Jonathan's appointment as high priest was considered irregular or controversial. We hear nothing further of his high priestly office, except in connection with official diplomatic acts and correspondence where his title is confirmed (1 Macc 11:27, 57) or referred to.[46]

We are not told what personal, religious, or political considerations led Jonathan to aspire to the high priesthood. For many generations the office had been held by the Oniad family.[47] As noted above, Alcimus may or may not have been a member of that family; Menelaus certainly was not, in spite of Josephus, *Ant.* 12.239, 383 and 20.235. The Hasmoneans did not belong to the high priestly family, but did claim to be priests.

Jonathan's bid for the high priestly office was presumably prompted by the desire to become officially the political and religious leader of Judea. It is well known that since Ptolemaic and probably since later Persian times high priesthood and political leadership of Judea were commonly combined in one person.[48] We have no information as to when this amalgamation occurred, but it was probably some time after Nehemiah.[49] Thus, when Jonathan was given an opportunity to

---

[43]Exod 29:1-35; Lev 8:5-36; Sir 45:6-24; 50:1-21.

[44]Zeitlin's explanation that the letter of appointment did not arrive in time is possible, but not verifiable. S. Zeitlin, *The Rise and Fall of the Judaean State* (3 vols., 2d ed; Philadelphia: JPS, 1968-78), 1.125.

[45]1 Macc 2:26, 54. See pp. 30-31 above.

[46]1 Macc 10:69; 12:3, 6. It is impossible to establish whether or not Jonathan is meant in 10:32, 38; in any event, the references are primarily to every occupant of the office, not to the one who happened to hold it at the date of the grant. A posthumous reference to his high priesthood is found in the decree in honor of his brother Simon (1 Macc 14:30).

[47]See the partial reconstruction by F.M. Cross, *JBL* 94 (1975) 17; cf. *Ant.* 20.234.

[48]Nicanor was governor of Judea for a while (2 Macc 14:12), but this appears to have been an extraordinary assignment, designed primarily to restore order and return control to the high priest Alcimus (2 Macc 14:13).

[49]See Hecataeus of Abdera, in Stern, *Greek and Latin Authors* 1, no. 11 = Diodorus Siculus 40.3.5; *Ant.* 12.161. Josephus incorrectly puts this development immediately after the return from the Babylonian Exile (*Ant.* 11.111). Cf. A.

become Alexander Balas' representative in Judea, the outward expression of his new position was the awarding of the high priesthood. This is not to say that only political considerations were involved. Religious questions were generally very much intertwined with political ones. But the treatment of his high priesthood in 1 Macc indicates a preponderance of the political side.

The Jewish Sects in Jonathan's time?

Interrupting his account of Jonathan's foreign relations, Josephus inserts a reference to the three Jewish sects which, he tells us, existed at the time: Pharisees, Essenes, and Sadducees (*Ant.* 13.171-173). However, he records none of their activities, but instead gives only a free rewriting and expansion of a short passage from the conclusion (sections 162-165) of his description in *J.W.* 2.119-166, to which he here refers the reader, and which reflects the situation in the first century CE. Essentially, *Ant.* repeats the earlier statement in *J.W.* about how Pharisees and Sadducees view fate, adding an analogous sentence on the Essenes' view of the matter. Therefore, while the Dead Sea Scrolls may throw some light on the relations between the Hasmoneans and some Essenes, assumptions about relations with Pharisees and Sadducees are mere guesswork. Indeed, not even their existence at Jonathan's time can be confirmed from other sources. We next hear about them only in their relations to John Hyrcanus.

Domestic Opposition Against Jonathan

After Jonathan becomes high priest, all we learn about him is centered around his foreign policy, especially his relations with the various Seleucid rulers. His domestic opponents are mentioned several times, but, to judge from our pro-Hasmonean sources, they never had the strength or courage to confront him directly. Instead, they always turned, unsuccessfully, to the Seleucids (or Ptolemies) to accuse him; Josephus at times identifies these enemies as belonging to the *Akra*.[50] First Maccabees, on the other hand, never states explicitly that there were any Jews in the *Akra*, but acknowledges that Jews pleaded with various Seleucid rulers on behalf of the *Akra* (1 Macc 6:21-27; 11:21). Although both 1 Macc and Josephus use a variety of pejorative terms for Jonathan's opponents, they are hardly distinguished as belonging to separate groups. In the Greek text of 1 Macc they are most commonly

---

Cody, *A History of Old Testament Priesthood* (AnBib 35; Rome: Pont. Bibl. Inst., 1969) 175-180; M. Smith, *Palestinian Parties*, 109-112, 177.

[50] 1 Macc 10:61, 64; 11:4-5, 21, 25-26. *Ant.* 12.252, 364. *Ant.* 12.362 distinguishes between the (non-Jewish?) garrison and the Jewish renegades in the *Akra*.

characterized by their lawlessness,[51] but in most cases this may simply be a translation of the broader Hebrew term רשע. Perhaps their lawless behavior is stressed for apologetic purposes, in order to show Jonathan and implicitly the later Hasmoneans as defenders of the Torah. The reasons for their opposition to Jonathan are never stated clearly, except for stereotyped phrases such as "they hated their people" (1 Macc 11:21). It seems fairly evident that they cooperated or tried to cooperate with the Seleucid government(s) as much or more than Jonathan did. Thus, they stood in the tradition of Menelaus and Jason, with the important distinction that now Jonathan was a formidable competitor for Seleucid support.

If we identify this group of Jonathan's opponents as "Hellenizers," resistance against him surely came from a variety of other quarters too. For one, there probably were other candidates who considered themselves and were considered by pious Jews worthier of the high priesthood than Jonathan. Whether or not the Teacher of Righteousness was a rival of Jonathan for this office cannot be ascertained on the basis of the available evidence. The Qumran literature shows us however that there was intense animosity between different groups even though they maintained the same basic tenets of a religious outlook.

First Maccabees, and consequently Josephus, are completely silent about this type of opposition. If only the historical references of the Dead Sea Scrolls could be determined, they would permit a more detailed reconstruction of intergroup relations in Jonathan's time. However, these documents represent so many different viewpoints and are often – at least to modern readers – so obscure in their historical references that few safe conclusions about their authors' opponents can be drawn. The Qumran people were not on good terms with the Hasmoneans as representatives of the Jerusalem establishment, but it is impossible to trace the history of their relations in any detail. For instance, we do not know whether it was Jonathan or another Jerusalem priest who came to attack the community of the Teacher of Righteousness on their Yom Kippur (1QpHab 11.4-8). The following is an analysis of what we may learn about the Hasmoneans from the Dead Sea Scrolls.

---

[51]ἄνομοι: 1 Macc 9:23, 58, 69; 10:61 (Sinaiticus); 11:25; παράνομοι: 10:61 (most MSS); 11:21; "those who have abandoned the Law and the commandments": 10:14.

Excursus: The Dead Sea Scrolls and the Hasmoneans

The Dead Sea documents are generally thought to come from one or more sects hostile to the Hasmonean priests of Jerusalem and therefore useful in delimiting supporters and opposition of the Hasmoneans. In using them for this purpose, however, we must be careful not to combine indiscriminately evidence from all of them. As Hunzinger has shown for the War Scroll and Murphy-O'Connor for the Damascus Document, these writings went through several redactions in which different points of view can be discovered.[52] Similarly, the Dead Sea Scrolls seem to have been brought to Qumran and/or written or copied there during the course of more than a century. Thus we find considerable differences in outlook between 1QS, 1QSa, and CD. Terms can vary in meaning from text to text.[53] Hence we cannot be sure that the term "Wicked Priest" always means the same person, but many scholars now believe it usually refers to Jonathan.[54] If this opinion is correct, we can learn a great deal about otherwise unknown aspects of his life. It is also possible, however, that Simon is meant.[55]

At first the Wicked Priest "was called by the name of truth," i.e., he was considered at least *acceptable* by the sectarian author of 1QpHab 8.8-9.[56] The author of the Habakkuk Pesher rejected the Wicked Priest's later rule and presumably his high priesthood, but not because of his lack of qualification for the high priesthood. Allegedly it was avarice that led him to disregard biblical commands (1QpHab

---

[52]C.- H. Hunzinger, "Fragmente einer älteren Fassung des Buches Milhama aus Höhle 4 in Qumran," *ZAW* 69 (1957) 131-151. J. Murphy-O'Connor, "The *Damascus Document* Revisited," *RB* 92 (1985) 223-246, and earlier studies by the same author. See also Schürer-Vermes-Millar 3.401; 3.393-394.

[53]E.g., "Judah" usually refers to the author's group, but in 4QpPss^a 2.13 it includes the "Violators of the Covenant." "Israel" in parts of CD refers to all Jews (e.g., 1.14; 4.2, 4), in 4QpNah 3-4.iii.5 to members of the sect only.

[54]See J. Murphy-O'Connor, "The Essenes and Their History," *RB* 81 (1974) 216, 224; Stegemann, *Entstehung*, pp. 95-115; Schürer-Vermes-Millar 2. 586-587; cf. J.H. Charlesworth, "The Origin and Subsequent History of the Authors of the Dead Sea Scrolls: Four Transitional Phases Among the Qumran Essenes," *RevQ* 10 (1980) 218-222.

[55]See F.M. Cross, *The Ancient Library of Qumran and Modern Biblical Studies* (Rev. ed.; Garden City: Doubleday, 1961) 127-160.

[56]The exact meaning of this phrase is widely debated and therefore not narrowly determinable. Brownlee translates "was considered a member of the Truth Party" and offers eight alternate interpretations (*The Midrash Pesher Habakkuk* [SBL, 1979], 134-137), but he recognizes that in the early stages of the group's development "the Truth" may not yet have had its strictly sectarian character.

8.9-12). His financial resources were in part acquired through confiscations from internal enemies, in part collected from foreign peoples.[57]

At least once there was a (violent) confrontation between "the Wicked Priest" and "the Teacher of Righteousness." On a day which the Teacher held to be the Day of Atonement, the Wicked Priest came to the latter's residence in exile and (physically?) attacked him and his followers (1QpHab 11.4-8). We are not told why this was done, but the commentary on Habakkuk sees in the Priest's persecution (?) of the Teacher the cause for the punishment inflicted on the Priest – a painful death at the hands of his enemies (9.9-12). The critical word in line 10 stating the cause is uncertain. This incident may be reflected also in 4QpPss[a] 2.17-18, where, however, neither the Teacher of Righteousness nor the Wicked Priest is explicitly mentioned. This passage has led Stegemann to connect the Wicked Priest with "Manasseh,"[58] a name that recurs frequently among the enemies of the sect in the Nahum Pesher.[59] This fragmentary commentary makes clear reference to events in the reign of Alexander Jannaeus (3-4.i.2-8). Strugnell dated it to the end of the Hasmonean or the beginning of the Herodian period.[60] Even though we are unable to fully decipher the coded language, it is reasonable to recognize in it veiled allusions to the situation of the first half of the first century BCE.

Among the enemies mentioned, "Manasseh" serves to identify a group with political power (4QpNah 3-4.iii.9). The group seems to be structured with different ranks of membership (iii.9-iv.4). The Pesher identifies "[No-]Amon" of Nah 3:8 as Manasseh – possibly because of some tie between the Hasmoneans and the Ammonites.[61] We are told of the group's nobles, its warriors and heroes, and of its women and children who will go into captivity.[62] Furthermore, we are told that the House of Peleg joined Manasseh (iv.1) and that at the final end Manasseh's reign (מלכותו) over Israel will be brought down (iv.3).[63]

---

[57]Cf. 1 Macc 6:24; 10:84-89.

[58]*Entstehung* , pp. 100-103.

[59]4QpNah 3-4.iii.9 (2x); iv.1,3,6.

[60]J. Strugnell, "Notes en marge du Volume V des 'Discoveries in the Judaean Desert of Jordan,'" *RevQ* 7 (1969/71) 205.

[61]The Jewish refugees from Transjordan (1 Macc 5:45) who probably became Hasmonean supporters may have been disparaged in Judea as "Ammonites."

[62]4QpNah 3-4.iii.9-11; iv.3-4. Perhaps a reference to women and children of the Hasmonean family who were held captive first by their own relatives and later by the Romans?

[63]This may give a terminus ante quem for the Pesher because apparently it does not know of Herod's accession in 37 BCE.

Manasseh is sometimes identified as the Sadducees[64] and the House of Peleg as the Hasmonean family or one of its branches.[65] But this is problematic since, for instance, kingship belonged to the later Hasmoneans, not the Sadducees. Stegemann considers Manasseh the designation for the "representatives of the ruling class."[66] It seems that we have to go a step further. We are dealing with a group that accepts and perhaps recruits adherents. Its diverse membership as well as its juxtaposition to Ephraim, another segment of the Jewish population,[67] suggest that "Manasseh" is more than merely a restricted circle of grandees. We may here find confirmation for the existence of a coalition that supported Hasmonean leadership some time during the first century.

A similar impression is given by the people around the "Lion of Wrath," who, according to the most plausible explanation, is Alexander Jannaeus. Again, we hear of his nobles, his warrior bands, and the men of his counsel.[68]

Thus the Dead Sea Scrolls give us several (negative) assessments of the Hasmoneans and their supporters, showing them as one among several separate groups within the Jewish community, at least during the first century BCE. Again, however, we must be careful to point out that it is by no means certain that this opposition started already in the time of Jonathan and by no means likely that it continued unchanged until the composition of the various Pesharim, probably in the first century BCE. *A priori* we should expect that relations between the Hasmoneans and the Dead Sea sectarians changed in the course of about a century and that the later state of affairs would be reflected in the later compositions.

The Temple Scroll (11QTemple) presents many unique problems. Yadin dated it in the time of John Hyrcanus or shortly earlier and thought that it originated within the Qumran sect.[69] Wacholder stresses its exalted status and sectarian character. He calls it "the

---

[64]E.g., J.D. Amusin, "The Reflection of Historical Events of the First Century B.C. in Qumran Commentaries (4Q161; 4Q169; 4Q166)," *HUCA* 48 (1977) 144-145, 151.

[65]Stegemann (*Entstehung*, pp. 228-229) identifies the House of Peleg as the Pharisees.

[66]*Entstehung*, p. 92.

[67]4QpPss^a 2.17; 4QpNah 3-4.iv.5-6.

[68]4QpHos^b 2; 4QpNah 3-4.i.5, 10-11. Is אנשי עצתו perhaps the equivalent of οἱ τὰ αὐτοῦ φρονοῦντες or possibly οἱ φίλοι αὐτοῦ?

[69]*Temple Scroll*, vol. 1 pp. 390, 398.

Qumranic Torah" and dates it around 200 BCE.[70] Neither date is based on persuasive evidence. In a recent article by Hengel, Charlesworth, and Mendels strong arguments are set forth for dating at least the section on kingship (cols. 56.12-60.?) between 103 and 88 BCE.[71] If this dating is correct, the Temple Scroll presents constructive criticism for the Hasmonean king, not leaving him any priestly function, to be sure, but legitimating and regulating his royal office.

In contrast with the Pesher literature, the Temple Scroll is devoid of all open polemics. This may be due to its literary form and function as a new Torah, but it may also mean that its composition, or at least the part dealing with kingship, was shaped prior to the intense conflict between Qumranites and Hasmoneans. Another possible scenario is suggested by the Damascus Document. It offers a hint that at least at one point a rapprochement between the Hasmoneans and Qumran was attempted (CD 19.15-17), when the princes of Judah "entered a [the?] covenant of repentance" (CD 19.16). The Temple Scroll may reflect that situation, but of course no lasting reconciliation took place.

The Damascus Document contains numerous references to groups of opponents, who differ mostly on ill-defined doctrinal grounds.[72] The few references to the "Princes of Judah" (CD 8.3; 19.15) may mean the Hasmonean rulers. If this is so, also the term "movers of the boundary" may sometimes apply to them (CD 19.15-16; 5.20) Still, it is not clear whether this refers to Hasmonean territorial expansion or appropriation of their opponents' lands, or whether it has to do with the interpretation of Torah, or all three (cf. CD 20.25). God's punishment for the offenses of these princes is predicted because (1) in spite of having entered a covenant of "repentance," they have not left their evil ways, but have continued in their adulterous practices, their unjust wealth, and hatred of their brothers;[73] (2) they have chosen the way of life of the Gentiles. However, the kings of Yavan (= the Seleucids) will come to take revenge (CD 19.22-24).

There are no indications that any one Hasmonean ruler is meant in particular. Thus, this may be a criticism of the dynasty and its supporters down to the author's time, or the princes may be the entourage of any Hasmonean from Jonathan on.

---

[70]B.Z. Wacholder, *The Dawn of Qumran. The Sectarian Torah and the Teacher of Righteousness* (Cincinnati: Hebrew Union College Press, 1983), p. 211.

[71]M. Hengel, J.H. Charlesworth, D. Mendels, "The Polemical Character of 'On Kingship' in the Temple Scroll: An Attempt at Dating 11QTemple," *JJS* 37 (1986) 28-38.

[72]See Stegemann (*Entstehung*, pp. 128-185) for an exhaustive examination.

[73]CD 19.15-19; cf. 1QpHab 8.11-12; 9.3-7.

Of the other sectarian literature from Qumran the Hodayot frequently speak in terms of friends and enemies of the author(s) (e.g. 1QH 5.20-7.5). Most of the struggle appears to have been against former adherents of the sect. No clear evidence can be gained concerning the Hasmoneans. The other published sectarian literature either does not address the question of outside groups or is too fragmentary to yield any reliable information concerning the Hasmoneans.

Sometimes the "Man of Lies" who appears in the Damascus Document and also in several other Dead Sea Scrolls, surrounded by a "schismatic" community, has been identified with the "Wicked Priest." Both Jeremias and Stegemann, however, have shown that the identification is unlikely.[74] Consequently, the identification of the "Man of Lies" with any known historical figure has thus far not been generally accepted. Other opponents mentioned in the Dead Sea Scrolls include (a person named) Zab, "the Wall Builders," "the Community of Apostates," "the Seekers-After-Smooth-Things," "the Violators of the Covenant," "the House of Absalom and the Men of Their Council," and Ephraim. Some of these groups may be identical or overlapping or successors to each other, but the various terms convey a sense of the great variety of expressions of Judaism in the second and first centuries.

Despite their complexity, fragmentary state, and partial publication, the Qumran documents round out our view of the Hasmoneans. They show that they constituted one of many groups. Pious opposition against Hasmonean high priests was strong, but not necessarily based on unchanging principles. Thus, attempts at reconciliation were undertaken, even though they failed. The scrolls further indicate that the Hasmoneans had a considerable following. "Manasseh" was a coalition from several segments of society. Hence we may suppose that while they had no political party in the modern sense, nevertheless various groups were known to be adherents or supporters of a central clan, the Hasmonean family. The Qumran documents however do not permit us to detect the historical development of this coalition which certainly underwent significant changes in composition and outlook.

Jonathan's Foreign Policy

The treatment in 1 Macc (and *Ant.*) of Jonathan's leadership differs markedly from what we learn about his brothers Judah and Simon. First of all, coverage of his activities is very sporadic. We know next to nothing about the years 156-153, 151, 149-146 BCE. Furthermore, from

---

[74]G. Jeremias, *Der Lehrer der Gerechtigkeit* (Göttingen: Vandenhoeck & Ruprecht, 1963), pp. 77-78; Stegemann, *Entstehung*, pp. 99-100.

the time he becomes high priest the focus is exclusively on his relations with outside powers. We hear nothing about the internal affairs of Judea, let alone about his exercise of high priestly functions.

This difference between the accounts of Jonathan and those of his brothers is too clear to be accidental. Perhaps Jonathan did concentrate on external affairs, while entrusting the internal affairs of Judea to his brother Simon; perhaps, also, 1 Macc relied on a chronicle of Judea's foreign affairs for most of chapters 10-12. Nothing in these chapters seems to be based on local oral traditions, though the author, writing about 50 years after the events, could still have consulted eyewitnesses.

We cannot be sure of the author's motives for his reticence on Judean affairs, but apparently he wishes to make Jonathan's achievements in foreign relations more conspicuous than his dealings with his countrymen. We may guess that a description of internal affairs would have been unpleasant to the dynasty or to the intended audience or would have caused controversy. In any event, the author chose to emphasize the undisputed achievements of Jonathan's foreign policy.

Relations with Demetrius I

The agreement with Bacchides after Bethbasi had stabilized relations between Jonathan and the government of Demetrius I. It was with the advent of Alexander Balas that Demetrius needed Jonathan's loyalty and support more than ever. The consequent release of the hostages from the *Akra* and permission for Jonathan to raise an army were gladly accepted (1 Macc 10:1-9), but these concessions were not sufficient to bind Jonathan to Demetrius. After Jonathan had received the high priesthood from Alexander Balas, Demetrius allegedly made an even more sweeping offer in a letter to the Jews of Judea (not to Jonathan personally). It included generous tax exemptions, rebates, and subsidies favoring the Temple and its personnel; territorial expansion of the high priest's jurisdiction, release of captives, respect for Jewish holidays, and other favors (1 Macc 10:22-45; *Ant.* 13.47-57).

The reliability of this letter has frequently been doubted, reportedly even by Jonathan himself (1 Macc 10:46).[75] If the letter is basically genuine, and the omission of Jonathan's name is a strong indication of this, it provides some pieces of information that are of interest here. The omission of Jonathan's name suggests that Demetrius

---

[75]Scholars are divided between considering it a forgery (Willrich, *Urkundenfälschung*, pp. 37-41) and describing it as "one of our most valuable sources for the fiscal and political structure of the Seleucid empire at this time" (Goldstein, *1 Macc.* p. 405). Schürer-Vermes-Millar presents a middle-of-the road approach (1, pp. 178-179 n. 14).

believed he could influence the Jews of Judea aside from or against the Hasmoneans, indicating that Jonathan still had powerful opponents in Judea.[76] That the letter glosses over insubordination in Judea, offers tax exemptions where no taxes could be expected, offers the territory of Ptolemais as a gift, although it was no longer under Demetrius' control, and makes unrealistic promises of subsidies for the Temple priesthood – all this can be attributed to "diplomacy," if we think Demetrius may have believed the Jews would be taken in by it. Perhaps he thought it worth trying. Letters cost little. On the other hand, the likelihood that such offers would discredit the writer may also discredit the letter. Thus, no decisive case can be made for or against the authenticity of the letter. It may be reliable only as evidence for the objectives of potential beneficiaries. In this sense it may contain useful information, but not necessarily for Jonathan's time.

According to this letter, three districts of Samaria "have been added" to Judea.[77] It is generally agreed that the districts named in a letter of Demetrius II are meant: Aphairema, Lydda, and Ramathaim (1 Macc 11:34). Demetrius II, writing about seven years later, says "we confirm" the Jewish possession of these districts, but it is unclear when they were added to Judea.[78] Actually there may have been a gradual process in which southern Samaria, part of the original Hasmonean power base and undoubtedly home of a considerable Jewish population, gravitated more and more toward Jerusalem. Only the final step in this process would have officially attached the districts to the fiscal domain of Judea.

Reportedly, "Jonathan and the people" immediately rejected the offers of Demetrius I as insincere and remained loyal to Alexander Balas (1 Macc 10:46-47). As 1 Macc also reports, a realistic assessment of Demetrius' past policies may have led to this conclusion.

Jonathan and Alexander Balas

Accordingly, Jonathan developed cordial and lasting ties to Demetrius' opponent Alexander Balas, although the latter passed himself off as a son of the hated Antiochus IV Epiphanes. Balas named Jonathan high priest and at the same time appointed him "Friend of the King" (1 Macc 10:20). Two years later, in 150 BCE, on the occasion of

---

[76]Cf. Abel, *Macc.*, pp. 184-185.

[77]1 Macc 10:38; cf. 10:30. The differences in Josephus (*Ant.* 13.50) do not seem to be based on independent information.

[78]Abel may be right in concluding that the shift was finalized only under Demetrius II, whereas the unification with Judea may well have been envisaged since the beginnings of the Hasmonean revolt (*Macc.*,p. 189).

Balas' wedding with the Ptolemaic princess Cleopatra Thea, Jonathan was promoted to the rank of the "First Friends"; he was also appointed στρατηγός and μεριδάρχης (1 Macc 10:65). We do not know how these new titles affected his real position, but it is generally understood that he officially became the civil and military authority for Judea.[79] As a problem for Jonathan and for modern commentators, however, there remained strongholds in Jerusalem and throughout the country, that were still held by his enemies.[80]

Jonathan was supported by Alexander Balas against vociferous internal opposition.[81] We learn that he endeared himself through lavish gifts not only to the kings Alexander Balas and Ptolemy Philometor, but also to their entourage (1 Macc 10:60). More important, he remained loyal to Balas throughout his struggles with Demetrius I and Demetrius II.

In or shortly after 148 BCE, Jonathan's position was challenged by Apollonius, Demetrius II's governor of Coele-Syria (1 Macc 10:67-73). Instead of surrendering, Jonathan reportedly selected 10,000 men and went down to attack Joppa, which had a garrison of Apollonius' troops. The town surrendered, but Apollonius moved on to Azotus (Ashdod) with his main force. Despite an attempted ambush by Apollonius, Jonathan was victorious, with the help of his brother Simon. To make the victory complete, Jonathan burnt down (parts of) Azotus and the surrounding towns, in particular the temple of Dagon where many people had taken refuge. Reportedly, 8,000 of Jonathan's enemies were killed by the sword or by fire (1 Macc 10:74-85).

After a brief excursion to Ascalon, where he was received with great honors (perhaps the fate of Azotus had been a lesson), Jonathan returned to Jerusalem loaded with spoils (1 Macc 10:86-87). Balas appropriately rewarded Jonathan for this successful campaign, because at least temporarily it had assured him control over Joppa and Ascalon in the southern coastal region of Palestine. Jonathan was now treated as a "Relative of the King" and received the town of Ekron and its territory as a personal gift (1 Macc 10:88-89). In 145 BCE, when King Ptolemy Philometor passed through the country on his way to Syria, the people of Azotus complained to him about Jonathan. They showed him the burned temple of Dagon and piled up along the king's road the remains of those who had been killed – evidently Jonathan's victory

---

[79] Abel, *Macc.*, p. 196; Goldstein, *1 Macc.*, p. 417; Schürer- Vermes-Millar, 1, p. 180, n. 16.
[80] Cf. 1 Macc 11:20-22, 41; *Ant.* 13.121, 133. Josephus again stresses that the *Akra* had a Macedonian garrison as well as Jewish residents.
[81] 1 Macc 10:61, 63-64.

had not given him control of the city. Ptolemy listened to their complaints, but preferred to remain on good terms with Jonathan who met him in Joppa and accompanied him as far north as the river Eleutherus (1 Macc 11:4-7).

Though numbers of troops and casualties may be somewhat exaggerated, it is clear that Jonathan had provided himself with a powerful army. For the time being, he did not use it to gain complete independence or for territorial expansion, but in effect he had become an almost independent power of regional importance.

Jonathan and Demetrius II

Shortly after the death of Alexander Balas in the summer of 145 BCE, Jonathan decided to remove one of the last and most conspicuous signs of Seleucid sovereignty in Judea: the *Akra* in Jerusalem (1 Macc 11:16-20). This attempt, however, did not meet the approval of certain Jews, called "violators of the law, enemies of their people" (1 Macc 11:21), who took the trouble to denounce it at the court of the new king, Demetrius II. Jonathan was ordered to give up the siege of the *Akra* and to appear before the king in Ptolemais. He decided to continue the siege, but also to take the risk and go, accompanied by some of the "elders of Israel" and of the priests, taking along substantial gifts too (1 Macc 11:21-24). Although some of the "lawless" Jews appeared at Ptolemais to oppose him, he was able to soothe the king's anger and even received substantial concessions from him: confirmation of his high priesthood and the other positions he had held under Balas, plus remission of taxes on Judea and on the three districts of Aphairema, Lydda, and Ramathaim in return for a relatively moderate lump sum payment of 300 talents.[82] But the status of the *Akra* remained unchanged.

Some time later, Jonathan made another attempt to get control over it. This time he formally requested the removal of the garrisons from Jerusalem and from the other fortresses (1 Macc 11:41). Demetrius promised to comply with the request because he found himself in dire need of support. He had discharged all but his mercenary troops, without giving them satisfactory compensation. The discontent of the veterans led to an upheaval in the city of Antioch. Upon Demetrius' request, Jonathan sent three thousand men who apparently were instrumental in restoring Demetrius' control over the city.[83] Jonathan's men did bring back much booty from this mission, but the promised reward, removal of the Seleucid garrisons from Judea, did not

---

[82] 1 Macc 11:25-28, 34; cf. 2 Macc 4:8-9, 24.
[83] 1 Macc 11:42-53; cf. Diodorus 33.4.2.

materialize. This spelled the end of Jonathan's collaboration with Demetrius II.

When, probably early in 144 BCE, Antiochus VI was proclaimed a rival king by Tryphon, Jonathan joined their side. Consequently, he confronted Demetrius' armies several times. Once he almost lost a battle due to an ambush, in the Plain of Hazor. When the situation appeared hopeless, most of his men took to flight, with the exception of two units under the command of Mattathias, son of Absalom, and Judah, son of Chalphi.[84]

Another time, Jonathan almost clashed with Demetrius' troops near Hamath (Epiphania) on the Orontes, not far from Apamea. But Demetrius' men are said to have fled by night before any engagement took place (1 Macc 12:24-30).

We thus can see that Jonathan's range of operation had been widened tremendously. It is hard, however, to discern to what extent Jonathan undertook raids for economic reasons and for his own advancement, or to what extent he was acting under orders from the Seleucids he supported. Spoils were an important, if sometimes secondary, consideration.

Jonathan and Antiochus VI

It appears that under Antiochus VI (that is, under the guardianship of Tryphon) Jonathan got more power than ever before. He was confirmed as high priest, made one of the "Friends of the King" with special privileges and confirmed in his control of "the four districts" – evidently the previous "three" of southern Samaria plus (probably) the adjacent Acrabatene.[85] His brother Simon was named governor of the coastal area "from the Ladder of Tyre to the borders of Egypt" (1 Macc 11:59). At one point, Jonathan allegedly commanded the entire Syrian army (1 Macc 11:60, but see *Ant.* 13.148). Simon besieged Beth-zur, conquered it and placed his own soldiers or settlers there (1 Macc 11:65-66). Significantly, the city was reduced to surrender only after a long siege, and then had to be given terms – the former

---

[84]1 Macc 11:70. No other information about these men is available, but it is possible that Mattathias was related to the Absalom who had been Judah's envoy to Lysias (2 Macc 11:17) and to Jonathan, son of Absalom who occupied Joppa on behalf of Simon (1 Macc 13:11). Perhaps, these men were somehow related to their Hasmonean namesakes; 1 Macc is very sparing in its praise for non-Hasmonean heroes (cf. 1 Macc 5:62). For a Hasmonean named Absalom, see *Ant.* 14.71. It is uncertain whether the phrase "the House of Absalom and the Men of Their Council" (1QpHab V.9-10) refers to a contemporary individual bearing that name or to King David's rebellious son.

[85]1 Macc 11:57-58; see Abel, *Macc.*, p. 216; Goldstein, *1 Macc.*, p. 439.

inhabitants went free.[86] We do not know where they went, presumably to their friends and relatives in other "fortresses" or in the cities in the Negev, along the coast and in the Decapolis. The growth of Hasmonean power resulted not only in admiration, but also in anti-Hasmonean sentiment, which may have been spread also through people who were expelled from Judea.

Simon secured his control of Joppa by putting a garrison there. Allegedly, this was to forestall a plot to hand the city over to Demetrius' forces (1 Macc 12:33-34). He also fortified Adida at the edge of the Shephelah (1 Macc 12:38).

These were not isolated instances, but part of a planned and coordinated effort to secure and perhaps enlarge the area of Judea, with Jerusalem as the central concern: Jonathan convened "the elders of the people" and held counsel with them about, among other things, building fortresses in Judea and strengthening the walls of Jerusalem (1 Macc 12:35-37). Some remains of the Hasmonean walls of Jerusalem, not necessarily of Jonathan's time, have recently been excavated.

Relations with Rome and Sparta

Jonathan's security needs were also addressed by an embassy he sent to Rome. Since no Roman response is preserved, we do not know the outcome of this mission beyond the fact that the envoys were given letters of safe conduct for their return to Judea.[87] Josephus, who is here independent of 1 Macc, states that Jonathan "strengthened his authority by friendship with Rome"; the implication that he did so at least partly as a safeguard against his countrymen (*J.W.* 1.48) may be an inference of Nicholas of Damascus or of Josephus, but since it contradicts both the picture given by 1 Macc and Josephus' own bias in favor of the Hasmoneans, it is possibly correct. Rome had intervened decisively in the affairs of Antioch and Egypt, it could do so again, it could also intervene in those of Judea – why not? – and its prestige was great. Alliance with Rome would presumably strengthen Jonathan's position at home and also serve as a deterrent for any Seleucid pretender who might want to infringe upon Judean autonomy.

Allegedly the ambassadors also carried a letter to Sparta (1 Macc 12:5-18). The authenticity of this document is dubious.[88] In any event,

---

[86]Some authors see a reference to this in *Megillat Taanit*, 14 (17) Sivan. Cf. Lichtenstein, Fastenrolle, pp. 281-282, 319, 327.
[87]1 Macc 12:1-4. For discussion and bibliography on the embassy see Gauger, *Apologetik*, pp. 179-182.
[88]See Willrich, *Urkundenfälschung*, p. 24; Cardauns, "Juden und Spartaner," *Hermes* 95 (1967) 320-321; Abel (*Macc.*, pp. 231- 233), and Goldstein (*1 Macc.*,

relations with that city had to be on a different level. No immediate payoff in terms of Judea's security could be expected. The correspondence shows above all that at the time the letter was written, not necessarily during Jonathan's time, the Hasmoneans did not intend to separate from the Gentiles, but to stress an existing or assumed common heritage. In this zeal they were not unlike other powers of the Hellenistic world.[89] The fact that Sparta was on good terms with Rome may have been a consideration, but the evidence suggests that to have a powerful advocate in Rome was not the primary aim of the contact with Sparta.[90]

Jonathan's Final Days

After a career that showed his military and diplomatic acumen, Jonathan succumbed to a ruse by the parvenu Tryphon. Summoned to Beth-shan, Jonathan went with a large army, reportedly 40,000 men (1 Macc 12:41), to encounter Tryphon. Even if the number is exaggerated, Jonathan's military strength was acknowledged by Tryphon (1 Macc 12:40-44), who persuaded him to dismiss most of these troops. Jonathan was apparently taken in by Tryphon's promise to give him Ptolemais, plus the other fortresses, and command over his army (1 Macc 12:45). With only 1,000 men, Jonathan came with Tryphon to Ptolemais where he was promptly arrested while his men were slain (1 Macc 12:46-48). Another 2,000 men, whom Jonathan had left behind in Galilee, managed to make their way back safely to Judea, though they were pursued for a while by Tryphon's troops (1 Macc 12:47, 49-52) – fairly good evidence that Galilee at this time was not predominantly, nor even largely, Jewish.

The news of these unexpected reverses caused "all Israel" to be in "great mourning."[91] Reportedly, the news of Jonathan's capture also triggered Gentile attempts to destroy "them," since "they" had lost their leader (1 Macc 12:53; *Ant.* 13.195-196). Such attempts would have been adequately motivated by desires for plunder and for revenge for the raids conducted by Jonathan. That they were directed against "the Jews" as a particular ethnic or religious group is unlikely; even those

---

pp. 447-462) defend its authenticity. Full bibliography in R. Katzoff, "Jonathan and Late Sparta," *AJP* 106 (1985) 485.

[89]Tyre/Delphi: *Supplementum Epigraphicum Graecum* 2.330; cf. *Ant.* 14.255. Katzoff suggests that the main feature shared by Sparta and Judea was the non-Hellenic character of their educational systems (*AJP* 106 [1985] 488-489).

[90]1 Macc 12:14-15; See Cardauns, *Hermes* 95 (1967) 320; differently Goldstein, *1 Macc.*, pp. 447-452.

[91]1 Macc 12:52; Josephus (*Ant.* 13.194) speaks of the inhabitants of Jerusalem instead.

Jews who lived in neighboring cities (e.g. those Hellenizers who had fled to coastal cities) were probably not attacked.[92]

Jonathan was kept a prisoner for a while, according to Tryphon for non-payment of taxes. But when his brother Simon sent the required sum of 100 talents of silver and two of Jonathan's sons as hostages, Jonathan was not released. Instead, Tryphon attempted to regain Judea by force and had Jonathan killed in Gilead (?) after his advance was stopped by a heavy snowfall.[93] Jonathan's remains were brought to Modein and splendidly buried in a new family tomb.

The Achievements of Jonathan and His Supporters

We have followed Jonathan's independent career from his beginning as the leader of a band of outlaws. It has been noted that there are extended periods about which 1 Macc and consequently Josephus are nearly silent, but, more importantly, the record concerns mostly military and foreign affairs and cannot possibly be complete.

The Dead Sea Scrolls unfortunately are almost always ambiguous in their historical references. But whether or not Jonathan is spoken about as "the Wicked Priest," the scrolls suggest that during the second and first centuries BCE the social, religious, and political situation in Judea was complex and that more than two or three sects or parties existed. Furthermore, whenever the Dead Sea documents address the question of the current establishment in Jerusalem, they express strong opposition.

After Jonathan established himself in Jerusalem and became high priest he was opposed by several forces: (1) The garrisons in the *Akra* and in fortresses in other parts of the country, probably consisting of Jews and non-Jews. (2) The Jews in these garrisons and many Jews elsewhere (probably some in Judea, but more in the Decapolis region and in cities along the coast) together constituted a class of opponents with enough power, resources, and persistence to appeal repeatedly to the Seleucid government in Antioch for Jonathan's removal. These people probably came mostly from those circles of Hellenizers who had supported Jason or Menelaus. (3) Opposition from more traditionally religious groups of priests and laypeople who may have rejected Jonathan's high priesthood on formal or practical grounds. Their eschatology or other teachings may also have caused them to reject Jonathan. (4) Jonathan's rule was opposed by Gentile cities on the

---

[92]Abel's description of the attacks as "antisemitic" (*Macc.*, p. 231) is inappropriate.

[93]1 Macc 13:12-24. The date of Jonathan's death is uncertain, but the winter of 143/2 BCE is the most probable time.

borders of Judea and was threatened several times by Seleucid armies. The internal opposition was so strong that reportedly Demetrius I could appeal to the Jewish people over Jonathan's head.

Against these opponents Jonathan relied on various resources. His brother Simon was his right-hand man. During Jonathan's leadership Simon is shown in several instances not only assisting Jonathan, but also acting independently. In particular, he fortified Adida and installed a garrison in Joppa. More importantly, Simon replaced the inhabitants of Beth-zur by soldiers or settlers of his choice (1 Macc 11:66). Apparently this became his standard policy toward conquered towns whenever feasible; it was later followed in Joppa, Gezer, and the *Akra* (1 Macc 13:11, 47-48, 50).

One basis of the power of Jonathan and Simon were the men who would fight for them. These were at first volunteers. Jonathan began with the remains of Judah's army, no more than a few hundred men. When captured by Tryphon, he allegedly had at least 40,000 men under his command. These troops, presumably paid for in part by the booty from Jonathan's campaigns, differed considerably from the band that had initially gathered around Mattathias and Judah in response to the persecution. At the core must have been a well-trained standing army, capable of being dispatched to distant places on short notice (cf. 1 Macc 11:44). It is not clear whether Jonathan commanded also non-Jewish troops. 1 Macc 11:60 states that he was supported by "the entire force of Syria," whereas Josephus says that he was authorized by Antiochus VI (i.e. Antiochus' viceroy Tryphon) to fight the generals of Demetrius, but that the cities gave him no troops (*Ant.* 13.148). Josephus' text is ambiguous as to whether he actually raised, or merely was authorized to raise, a large force from Syria, Phoenicia, and elsewhere. The cities' refusal to cooperate would not have prevented his recruiting from the countryside and the adjacent deserts.

In any event, the Hasmoneans' power did not and could not rest on troops alone. The troops had to be and were backed up by an extensive body of rural supporters, the original core of the movement, whose lands in and north of Judea provided economic support and presumably many recruits.

Beyond this, it was important for Jonathan to be accepted by the remaining priestly and lay aristocracy in Jerusalem. Apparently he was successful and gained the cooperation, if not the wholehearted allegiance, of at least part of those influential circles. Bacchides had taken the sons of the leading men of (rural ?) Judea as hostages (1 Macc 9:53), presumably because he feared their fathers might further the Hasmonean cause. The rural aristocracy will have had marital connections with the important families of Jerusalem, so their support probably facilitated Jonathan's acceptance. It is stressed that Jonathan consulted the "elders of the people" about building fortifications in Judea and Jerusalem (1 Macc 12:35-37) and took some of them and of the priests along for important negotiations with Demetrius II (1 Macc 11:23). Thus Jonathan seems to have had a good, if perhaps delicate, working relationship with the "Council of Elders" (1 Macc 12:6). We do not know its composition. It may have been an element of conservative continuity or of latent hellenizing sympathies, but its members, if not chosen by Jonathan, at least do not seem to have been disloyal to him.

Besides "the elders," the Temple authorities played an important role in Jerusalem, and the Hasmoneans had to gain their support. In this Jonathan was not wholly successful, as the decree giving Simon control over the Temple more than two and a half years after Jonathan's death suggests (1 Macc 14:42-43). The bitter complaints of dissident priests are found in the Dead Sea Scrolls. Part of the difficulty was due to the compromises between religious law and practical considerations, dictated by the realities of rule. In terms of religious developments, Jonathan is the first who is reported to have actually broken the Sabbath rest for the purpose of self-defense.[94] Another important break with traditions based on biblical law was his assumption of the high priesthood, which had far-reaching consequences for the Hasmonean dynasty as well as for the structure of Jerusalem society. The fact that 1 Macc tells us so little about it suggests that it was controversial. Jonathan's relations with priests and other Temple personnel are very obscure. As high priest, one of his principal functions would have been to direct the affairs of the Temple, but outside of documents (some of dubious authenticity) we hear of priests only when Jonathan asks some of them to accompany him to see Demetrius II in Ptolemais.[95] The importance of the priests becomes more evident in several documents of Simon's time. Levites are never mentioned in connection with Jonathan. Later, it was made explicit that Simon was to have full authority over the Temple personnel, including all appointments (1 Macc 14:42). The fact that this had to be made explicit by public decree confirms our expectation that the hereditary Temple staff had hitherto been a semi-independent center of some power, whose members had doubtless cooperated with Jonathan, but not much farther than they themselves saw fit.

---

[94] 1 Macc 9:43-49; cf. 2:40-41.

[95] 1 Macc 11:23; Codex Sinaiticus lacks the reference to priests and has ιουδαιων instead. It may be right. See the use of היהודים in Neh 2:16; 5:1, 17 and the comments by Smith, *Palestinian Parties*, pp. 152 and 264, n. 17.

With the support thus secured (and in the process of securing it), Jonathan achieved remarkable accomplishments. Chief among them was the creation of a solid territorial base. Whereas in the beginning he had to flee to the desert and did not even have a safe place for his baggage, he gradually gained control over Judea, to which he was able to add the districts of Aphairema, Lydda, Ramathaim, Ekron, and perhaps Akrabatene, all through concessions from various Seleucid rulers with whom he managed to maintain more or less friendly relations. His brother Simon is even said to have been made governor of the coastal district from the Ladder of Tyre to the borders of Egypt. While he never governed *de facto* the whole area, Hasmonean influence spread to the coastal plain where the port cities of Joppa and Ascalon opened their gates.

With both Jonathan and Simon in official government positions, with an established territory, they must have created or absorbed the structures of a regular government: besides a standing army, an at least rudimentary bureaucracy for the civil and fiscal administration of the country. To give only one example: the extensive defense construction, begun under Jonathan and completed under Simon, must have been planned, financed, supplied, supervised and executed through the cooperation and coordination of a fairly complex staff of military planners, engineers, skilled craftsmen, accountants, supervisors, and construction and transportation crews. Our sources are completely silent on this administrative consolidation that must have taken place or at least begun under Jonathan.

In 1 Macc, Jonathan is the least prominent of the three brothers who succeeded each other in a position of leadership. In contrast to his brothers Judah and Simon, no poetic passage is devoted to his praise, and he is not even mentioned in Mattathias' programmatic farewell speech (1 Macc 2:65-66). Yet, in many ways he was the decisive person, who laid the foundations for the future of the dynasty and of important facets of Jewish society. The silence of 1 Macc may express silent disapproval for the extent of cooperation with Seleucid rulers which was necessary for this accomplishment.

4

Simon

Accession and Early Successes

As we have seen, Simon had assumed increasing responsibilities while Jonathan was still in power. When his brother was arrested, Simon seems to have taken over without delay. A quick and smooth transition was crucial because Tryphon was trying to regain effective control over Judea (1 Macc 13:1). Besides, unspecified hellenistic towns of the area wanted to take advantage of the lack of leadership due to Jonathan's removal and planned to attack Judea with impunity (1 Macc 12:53). Their plan apparently never materialized because of Simon's swift takeover.

Tryphon was a more menacing power. In order to effect Jonathan's release, Simon gave in to Tryphon's demands for arrears in tribute or taxes and sent two of Jonathan's sons as hostages, although he reportedly was aware that this might not help to free Jonathan: 1 Macc states that he complied with these demands "lest he arouse great hostility among the people" and be accused of having been remiss in his efforts to get Jonathan released (1 Macc 13:15-19). What happened to Jonathan's sons when their father was murdered at Baskama, we do not know; the Vulgate's report that they too were killed is probably an inference, but a probable one.[1] Perhaps Simon was not entirely displeased by this removal of possible rivals for his and his sons' aspirations to high priesthood and leadership.[2]

We are not informed when and how Simon became high priest. We may be sure he was not nominated by Tryphon: he was only *confirmed* by Demetrius II (1 Macc 14:38; cf. 13:36). According to 1 Macc 14:35 it was

---

[1] 1 Macc 13:23 (V); see Abel, *Macc.* p. 239; Goldstein, *1 Macc.* p. 76 n. 65.
[2] See Geiger, *Urschrift*, pp. 209-210; Goldstein, *1 Macc.*, p. 76n. 65.

the people (ὁ λαός) who made him high priest. But this cannot have happened at a "great assembly" reported by 1 Macc 14:27-49, since that assembly is dated in the "third year under Simon the High Priest" (1 Macc 14:27; cf. 13:42), a fact often neglected in the literature.[3] It may be that shortly after Jonathan's capture and before his death an assembly that designated Simon "leader" (ἡγούμενος) also made him high priest. In fact, both offices are described as given to him by "the people."[4] The necessarily provisional character of his assuming office before Jonathan's death may in part account for the lengthy process of confirmation.

As one of his first concerns Simon finished the rebuilding of the walls of Jerusalem begun by Jonathan. In order not to delay, this was accomplished through the employment of all available soldiers (1 Macc 13:10). Also, Simon soon sent a sizable detachment to Joppa under Jonathan, the son of Absalom, perhaps a relative of the Hasmoneans.[5] Joppa had been attacked by Hasmonean troops several times before; they even had left behind a garrison.[6] Now, however, (some of ?) the residents were expelled and replaced by the force under Absalom. Joppa remained in Hasmonean hands with only a brief interruption in the time of John Hyrcanus.

Simon may have found it important to hold Joppa for several reasons: (1) As before, he was afraid that it would become an enemy base. (2) It was the best port for Judea's overseas contacts, commercial and otherwise, "a gateway to the islands of the sea" (1 Macc 14:5). A source hostile to the Hasmoneans describes it as a base for piracy.[7] (3) With Joppa at the sea and Adida (already taken, 1 Macc 12:38) at the edge of the mountains as Hasmonean army outposts it would be easier to watch troop movements in the coastal plain and to guard the access to

---

[3]E.g. E. Rivkin, *A Hidden Revolution* (Nashville: Abingdon, 1978), pp. 12, 217; J. VanderKam, *Textual and Historical Studies in the Book of Jubilees.* (Missoula: Scholars Press, 1977), p. 248 (reviewing earlier studies without approving their conclusions).

[4]1 Macc 13:8; cf. 14:35. "The people" (ὁ λαός) are distinguished here from the ἔθνος (13:6) as well as from the "warriors" (13:10: ἄνδρας πολεμιστάς) and it is impossible to know the composition of the assembly, although from the context it is likely that many of the participants were members of the Hasmonean armed forces. An earlier version of my discussion of Simon's high priesthood appeared as "The High Priesthood of Simon Maccabeus: An Analysis of 1 Macc 14:25-49" in *SBL 1981 Seminar Papers* ed. K.H. Richards (Chico, CA: Scholars Press, 1981) pp. 309-318. I am indebted to James VanderKam for his response to that paper.

[5]1 Macc 13:11. See chap. III n. 84 above.

[6]1 Macc 10:76; 12:33-34; cf. 2 Macc 12:5-7.

[7]Strabo 16.2.28.

Judea from the northwest and southwest, where all major invasions since Antiochus IV had originated.

After the immediate danger from Tryphon had ceased, Simon arranged a solemn funeral for Jonathan at the Hasmonean ancestral grave in Modein, *not* Jerusalem (1 Mac 13:25-30). Reportedly, all Israel mourned for him for many days. Simon took this opportunity to erect a monument over the tombs of his parents and four brothers, thus stressing the importance of his family and of its place of origin. A similar emphasis on the importance and the achievements of the Hasmonean family is found in the speech attributed to Simon after Jonathan's capture (1 Macc 13:3-5) and in the decree in his honor (14:29-30).

The monument, as described in 1 Macc 13:27-29, was quite large and probably took considerable time and expense to build. The layout is not clear to us, and lacking archaeological evidence, cannot be reconstructed with confidence. We do not know whence Simon and/or his architect got the ideas for the design. However, we can discern elements it has in common with other monuments and some of these suggest foreign influences (which had been at work in Palestine long before Simon's time).

Pyramids were used for the burial of prominent persons not only in Egypt, but also in Italy.[8] The famous tomb of Mausolus (died 353 BCE) in Halicarnassus included a pyramid-like structure on a high base, with columns around it,[9] apparently somewhat similar to Simon's monument. Pyramids were also part of several later tombs on the outskirts of Jerusalem and at Petra.[10]

Suits of armor were set up as trophies by the Greeks in the sixth century BCE at the latest. During the Hellenistic period, trophies were frequently used. Most of our evidence comes from the Seleucids. Several coins of Seleucus I show Nike crowning a trophy.[11] Numenius, a general of Antiochus III or Antiochus IV, set up trophies on the Persian Gulf after a double victory (Pliny, *NH* 6.152). Antiochus VII set up a trophy after a victory over the Parthians at the River Zab.[12] By the mid-second century BCE the Romans had adopted the Greek custom of setting

---

[8]Porsenna's tomb at Chiusi (late 6th/early 5th century BCE): Pliny, *NH* 36.13; Pyramid of C. Cestius in Rome (c. 12 BCE): E. Nash, *Pictorial Dictionary of Ancient Rome* (Tübingen: Wasmuth), 2 (1962), 321-324.

[9]Pliny, *NH* 36.30-31.

[10]Queen Helena of Adiabene (mid-first century CE): *Ant.* 20.95; for tombs in the Kidron Valley see N. Avigad, *Ancient Monuments in the Kidron Valley* (Jerusalem: Bialik Institute, 1954 (in Hebrew); on pp. 131-132 Avigad discusses evidence for the use of pyramids in tomb structures in Palestine and Syria.

[11]Gardner, *Syria*, nos. 36-40.

[12]*Ant.* 13.251 = Stern, *Greek and Latin Authors*, no. 88.

up trophies, as Picard has shown.[13] He is wrong, however, in asserting that only Greeks and Romans used trophies – Simon and later Herod did so, too. What religious meaning, if any, Simon and the planners of the Modein monument attached to trophies is uncertain.

The columns with suits of armor and also with carved ships find their closest parallel in the Roman *columnae rostratae* (See Pliny, *NH* 34.11.20; cf. Livy 42.20.1). A fragmentary copy of one commemorating the naval victory of C. Duilius (260 BCE) is extant.[14] What the μεχανήματα of 1 Macc 13:29 were is uncertain.[15]

While the layout of the monument is unclear, the structure of hewn stones *over* and in front and back of the tombs, with pairs of pyramids[16] and columns around (the pyramids?) suggests a large platform. Such platform structures were rare in Greek cities, but were often used for temple or palace districts in the Middle East, for example in Nimrud, Persepolis, and Baalbek.

Simon seems to have planned the site as a demonstration of his power not only to Jews, but to Gentiles as well. The monument was to be seen "by *all* the seafarers" (along the coast) (1 Macc 13:29), as the statue of Athena Promachos on the Akropolis in Athens could be seen all over the north of the Saronic gulf. Specification of seafarers without mention of travelers on land *might* indicate Simon's interest in the potentialities of Joppa, but more probably results simply from the situation of the monument on a relatively low hill near Modein, where it would be visible to ships at sea, but not to nearer travelers on land (because of intervening trees, etc.).

Josephus' description of the monument differs considerably from that in 1 Macc. He omits the trophies and the carved ships and speaks of roofed colonnades instead (*Ant.* 13.211). This may be an imaginative rendering of the information supplied by 1 Macc, but it may also reflect changes made in the intervening period. Trophies, which generally had pagan religious connotations and could be considered images of human beings, were found objectionable by many Jews who may have

---

[13]G. Charles-Picard, *Les Trophées Romains* (Paris: Boccard, 1957) p. 137; for Seleucid trophies see *ibid.* pp. 68-75.

[14]See drawing in Daremberg-Saglio, I.^{2} p. 1351 fig. 1787. E. Nash, *Pictorial Dictionary of Ancient Rome* 1 (1961), 282.

[15]The word often means "siege engines." Abel - Starcky (p. 192 note a) think them elaborate structures not compatible with the Roman model of a *columna rostrata*. Other conjectural translations are "elaborate setting" (RSV); "socles" Abel, *Macc.* p. 240; "Kunstwerke" Grimm, *1 Macc.*, p. 199.

[16]1 Macc 13:28. How *seven* pyramids could be arranged μίαν κατέναντι τῆς μιᾶς for *six* people (two parents plus four brothers) is a minor mystery.

altered the monument accordingly.[17] The monument was still being shown in the time of Eusebius,[18] but its exact location is no longer known.

Relations with Demetrius II

Simon took further measures to protect Judea from Tryphon, "because all Tryphon did was to plunder" (1 Macc 13:34). He continued to fortify the strongholds in Judea, providing them with high walls and towers and storing provisions in them (1 Macc 13:33). He also made contact again with Demetrius II, whom Jonathan had abandoned for Antiochus VI. In answer to Simon's request, Demetrius responded with a letter (1 Macc 13:36-40), recognizing Simon as high priest and "Friend" of kings, granting full amnesty, plus exemption from general taxes and from the duties and other levies until then collected in Jerusalem.[19] He also granted remission of the king's claim for crown money and confirmed the *status quo,* including Simon's possession of fortresses in Judea. It is not clear what Simon offered in return besides a golden crown and a palm branch sent to Demetrius as a gift.[20] Perhaps Simon had also offered him manpower (13:40), like the troops Jonathan had earlier sent to Demetrius' assistance. In any event, Demetrius was now very weak and had no means to govern Palestine. Therefore, Simon will not have had to offer much in return for the confirmation of what he already had.

It is surprising that 1 Macc 13:41-42 marks this moment as the point at which "the yoke of the Gentiles was removed from Israel." Demetrius II was not a present danger, and his concessions meant little. Furthermore, as far as taxes are concerned, Demetrius' letter to Simon only repeats the exemptions he is said to have earlier granted Jonathan in perpetuity.[21] Either the letter of 1 Macc 11:30-36 is in whole or in part a forgery[22] – and the extension of the grant "to all those who sacrifice in Jerusalem" is extremely suspicious – or its provisions were

---

[17]Herod encountered violent opposition when he put up trophies around his newly built theater (*Ant.* 15. 272-291, especially 276-279).

[18]Eusebius, *Onomasticon* (ed. Klostermann), p. 132. See also Watzinger, *Denkmäler,* II (1935) 22-23; Goldstein, *1 Macc.,* pp. 474-475.

[19]Probably this meant the allegedly long promised exemption for all of Judea. See 1 Macc 10:30-31; 11:28-29, 34-36; cf. 13:41. The precise meaning of ἀφέματα (13:37) is unknown. See Abel, *Macc.,* p. 243.

[20]1 Macc 13:37. These gifts were standard practice at the accession of a new king and on other occasions. Cf. 2 Macc 14:4; Welles, *Royal Correspondence* 22.11. See Bickerman, *Institutions,* p. 112.

[21]Cf. 1 Macc 13:37,39 with 1 Macc 11:34-36.

[22]So Willrich, *Urkundenfälschung,* p. 42.

not honored by Demetrius when he felt himself secure. The latter seems to be indicated by 11:53 and also by various details: The delegation to Demetrius "to secure remission (of taxes)" (13:34) would not have been necessary if he had already granted it, unless the grant had been annulled. The second letter refers to the crown money as "owed" (13:39), but the first explicitly abolishes the obligation to pay it (11:34-35). Confidence in these matters is unjustified, but it seems likely (a) that the first letter has been interpolated by someone who wanted to extend its provisions from the residents of Hasmonean territories to all Jews who had made pilgrimages to Jerusalem, (b) that whatever grants it originally contained had been effectively abrogated by Demetrius after he thought himself securely in power.

In any case, Demetrius' letter to Simon was perceived by Jews – or presented by Simon's propaganda – as the decisive event with which "the yoke of the Gentiles was lifted from Israel" (1 Macc 13:41). Thus, Simon appeared as the liberator of his people, ushering in a new era.

Josephus conveys the same impression when he states that "Simon...liberated the people from servitude to the Macedonians, so that they no longer paid tribute to them (*Ant.* 13.213). Kippenberg rightly stresses the economic concerns that dominated the idea of "liberation," but this fact does not prove his assertion that the Hasmonean revolution was primarily a struggle against economic exploitation.[23]

"The Yoke of the Gentiles Lifted from Israel"

This event may be commemorated by *Megillat Taanit*, either under 27 Iyyar or, more probably, 3 Tishri.[24] The change was considered of such importance that the method of dating contracts and other documents was altered. Prescripts were to read Έους πρώτου ἐπὶ Σίμωνος ἀρχιερέως μεγάλου καὶ στρατηγοῦ καὶ ἡγουμένου Ἰουδαίων, roughly to be translated "In the first year of/under Simon the great high priest and commander and leader of the Judeans" (1 Macc 13:42). This may be interpreted in three different ways: (1) ἔτους πρώτου refers to the first year of a new era (of the freedom of the Jews); the ἐπὶ phrase merely indicates that Simon was high priest at this time. (2) ἔτους πρώτου refers to Simon's first year in office; thus the dating is

---

[23]H.G. Kippenberg, *Religion und Klassenbildung im antiken Judentum. Eine religionsgeschichtliche Studie zum Verhältnis von Tradition und gesellschaftlicher Entwicklung* (Göttingen: Vandenhoeck & Ruprecht, 1978) pp. 92-93.

[24]See Goldstein, *1 Macc.*, pp. 478-479. Lichtenstein's suggestion (Fastenrolle, pp. 282-286) to assign both dates to this event is impossible.

similar to that by regnal years, a common practice. (3) ἔτους πρώτου refers to the first year of a new era of Simon, in contrast to that "of the kingdom of the Greeks" (1 Macc 1:10).

The idea of an "era of freedom" has the following points to commend itself:[25] (a) several cities used eras that began with their liberation from Seleucid rule (Aradus 259 BCE; Tyre 126 BCE; Ascalon 104/3 BCE);[26] (b) the practice of mentioning (high) priests and priestesses in contracts and other documents is well attested in Seleucid as well as Ptolemaic inscriptions.[27] However, the events referred to in these documents were *not* dated by the priestly officials named, the date was established by regnal or era years; (c) many weight inscriptions have a Seleucid date followed by ἐπί with the name of the *agoranomos*. Obviously the year number is independent of that official;[28] (d) many inscriptions are dated by eponymous officials such as the *stephanephoroi* in Miletus,[29] priests,[30] or high priests,[31] but these generally are annual offices. Thus, we do not find regnal year dates "in the first (or whatever) year in the priesthood of" (ἐπί) – plus the name of the priest. The dating in 1 Macc 13:42 and 14:27 is quite different.

Thus, the epigraphic evidence makes the idea quite attractive that the new era, if there was one, was not based on Simon's term of office, but on the liberation from Seleucid rule and taxes. Another element should be added: Simon had been high priest and *strategos* before he received Demetrius' letter.[32] That he was made Ethnarch on this occasion is possible, but cannot be proven. Thus, the link with Simon's accession is rather tenuous.

On the other hand, the dating formula in 1 Macc 13:42 and 14:27 does follow the pattern of royal dates in several of the later books of the Septuagint.[33] By analogy to these, 1 Macc 13:42 should mean "In

---

[25]See also Goldstein, *1 Macc.*, p. 479.

[26]Bickerman, *Chronology*, p. 73.

[27]See Welles, *Royal Correspondence*, pp. 183-184.

[28]Inscriptions grecques et latines de la Syrie 1071 f-g; 1213 a-m.

[29]T. Wiegand, *Didyma*. Part 2: *Die Inschriften* by A. Rehm (Berlin: Mann, 1958), nos. 424-475 and passim.

[30]L. Robert, *Etudes Epigraphiques et Philologiques* (Paris, 1938), pp. 293-296; *Orientis Graeci Inscriptiones Selectae* 338.

[31]The inscriptions from the temple tomb of Opramoas at Rhodiapolis in Lycia give an almost complete list of eponymous high priests from 116 to 152 CE (*Tituli Asiae Minoris* II.905).

[32]1 Macc 14:38; 11:59; cf. perhaps also *Ant.* 12.419.

[33]Hag 1:1, 15; 2:10; Sach 1:1, 7; 7:1; Dan (LXX) 1:1; 9:1; cf. Sirach, *Prologue*; R. Cagnat et al., *Inscriptiones Graecae ad Res Romanas Pertinentes* III.128.

the first year *of* Simon....″[34] This is the way Josephus' paraphrase of it would normally be interpreted (*Ant.* 13.214) and both the paraphrase and the interpretation may well be correct. As Abel-Starcky point out,[35] there is no documentary evidence for an era of Simon. The dated coins of Alexander Jannaeus bear regnal, not era years.[36] Goldstein, however, suggests that a date "under the high priest Hyrcanus...in the ninth year," is based on an era of 142 BCE which had as its starting point the letter of Demetrius to Simon, but the text of this passage is corrupt and, as it stands, may equally well refer to the ninth year of Hyrcanus.[37] Thus, the new dating system in 1 Macc most probably refers to Simon's years in office.

The Capture of Gezer and the Surrender of the Akra

After having gained recognition, Simon moved to secure his power by attacking what seem to have been the principal remaining pro-Seleucid strongholds in the country. He first attacked Gezer, probably because it could serve the enemy for expeditions into Judea and because he could use it as a base for operations in the coastal plain.[38] Gezer was a town with a Seleucid garrison (1 Macc 9:52) and a predominantly non-Jewish population. Since the recent extensions of Judean territory, its surroundings had come under Hasmonean rule. Simon's men were able to make a breach in a tower[39] and to enter the city which surrendered without further fighting. Simon reportedly did not enslave the inhabitants, but expelled them, cleansed the houses which contained

---

[34]Against Goldstein, *1 Macc.*, p. 479. For an analogous dating formula in the Babylonian Talmud see *b. Rosh Hashanah* 18b: "In the year so and so of Yohanan the high priest of the Most High God."

[35]pp. 194-195.

[36]J. Naveh, "Dated Coins of Alexander Janneus," *IEJ* 18 (1968) 20-26, plate 2.

[37]*Ant.* 14.148. Goldstein, *1 Macc.*, pp. 479-480; Broughton (*Magistrates* 1, pp. 491-492) and Stern (*Documents* pp. 158-159) point out the difficulties with Josephus' dating of the document.

[38]1 Macc 13:43. The Greek MSS have Gaza, but this is surely mistaken. Cf. *Ant.* 13.215; *J.W.* 1.50; Abel, *Macc.* p. 245.

[39]Simon's use of a siege engine (ἐλέπολις 1 Macc 13:43) may indicate Hasmonean adoption of hellenistic technology; invention of the machine is commonly attributed to Demetrius Poliorcetes (died 283 BCE). See references in Liddell - Scott, s.v. However, similar devices appear on Assyrian monuments and may have been in use in the Near East ever since. See R. Barnett, *Assyrian Palace Reliefs* (London: Batchworth, n.d.) plates 23, 35, 38, 40. For bibliography, see K. Galling, *Biblisches Reallexikon* (Tübingen, 1937) 91-92.

idols, and settled in the city "men who do the law";[40] he also strengthened the fortifications and built himself a residence in the city (1 Macc 13:46-48).[41] Remains of a housing complex, dated by coins and pottery around the time of Antiochus VII (138-129 BCE), have been assigned by the excavators to the Hasmonean reconstruction.[42]

A Greek inscription discovered in the debris of that area is taken by Macalister to mean "Says Pampra[s]: may fire pursue Simon's palace."[43] If the inscription was put in a visible place, the writer no doubt intended to leave town before it was discovered. But he may also have built his curse into a wall so that none of his contemporaries could read it. Pampras may have been one of Simon's numerous prisoners of war, whom he probably used extensively in his ambitious building projects.[44] Simon not only resettled Gezer with observant Jews, but also stationed there his son and future successor, John Hyrcanus, whom he made commander of all his forces (1 Macc 13:53). This was certainly in recognition of Gezer's strategic position on a hill surveying the coastal plain to the north, west, and east. Furthermore, Gezer had a good water supply and very fertile land surrounding it. Thus, it was not only a military asset, but an economic one as well.

Once Gezer was taken, Simon then closed in on the *Akra*, which was now left without any substantial nearby support. In spite of the brevity of 1 Macc's account, the surrender of the *Akra* is treated as one of Simon's most important achievements, being commemorated by an annual celebration.[45] Simon's policy regarding Gezer and the *Akra* was somewhat similar. But instead of conquering the *Akra* by military means, he forced it to surrender by continuing the economic blockade started by Jonathan. It lasted approximately two years, from 143 to 141

---

[40]R. Reich identifies seven water reservoirs, excavated by Macalister, as *miqvaot* ("Archaeological Evidence of the Jewish Population at Hasmonean Gezer," *IEJ* 31 [1981] 52).

[41]The report in 2 Macc 10:32-38 about an earlier capture of "Gazara" by Judah is either fictionalized or refers to a different town by a similar name. See Abel, *Macc.* p. 415.

[42]J.D. Seger, "The Search for Maccabean Gezer," BA 39 (1976) 142-144. A jar handle with the inscription Σιμιου is interpreted as a reference to Simon himself. The name of the jar's owner was Simias instead. What Macalister believed to be Simon's palace has been identified as belonging to the time of Solomon. Y. Yadin, "Solomon's City Wall and Gate at Gezer," *IEJ* 8 (1958) 80-86. R.A.S. Macalister, *The Excavation of Gezer*, 1 (1912), pp. 209-223.

[43]*Gezer* 1, pp. 211-212. E. Gabba, *Iscrizioni greche e latine per lo studio della Bibbia* (Turin, 1958) 31-32.

[44]See 1 Macc 14:7, where reference is presumably not to liberated Jews, but to conquered Gentiles; cf. Goldstein, *1 Macc.*, pp. 490-491; *pace* Abel, *Macc.* p. 251.

[45]1 Macc 13:49-52; 14:7, 36.

BCE,[46] until the starving inhabitants asked for terms. Simon did not make them prisoners, but expelled them and had the *Akra* "purified from the things that defiled it" (1 Macc 13:50). We do not know what this purification entailed. *Megillat Taanit* tells us that the people of the *Akra* withdrew from Jerusalem on 23 Iyyar,[47] while 1 Macc speaks of the formal triumphal entry of Simon's people on the same day, thus leaving little or no time for cleansing in between. This point should not be pressed, because both reports are probably inferences from the festival that celebrated both events.[48]

The cleansing of the *Akra* parallels the cleansing of the Temple by Judah. 1 Macc shows Simon in more than one way completing the work that Judah had started, as is apparent from the synopsis below.

1 Macc 4		1 Macc 13	
41	Judah orders his men to fight those in the *Akra* so that he can cleanse the Temple.	50	Simon overcomes the Akra,
43	Priests cleanse the Temple, remove the stones of pollution (τοὺς λίθους τοῦ μιασμοῦ).	50	cleanses the *Akra* of all pollutants (ἀπὸ τῶν μιασμάτων).
52-54	On 25 Kislev 148 the Temple is rededicated with songs, stringed instruments (κιθάραις) and lyres and cymbals.	51	On 23 Iyyar 171 they enter the *Akra* with songs and hymns, stringed instruments (νάβλαις), lyres and cymbals, praise and palm branches.
58	Great rejoicing among the people, the reproach of the Gentiles is removed.	51	A great enemy is crushed.
59	Judah, his brothers, and the whole assembly of Israel decree (ἔστησεν) every year eight days of celebration with merriment.	52	Simon (on his own authority) decrees (ἔστησε): every year this day should be celebrated with merriment.
60	They build strong walls around Mount Zion.		Simon strengthens fortifications of the Temple Mount

---

[46]Cf. 1 Macc 12:36-37; 13:49-51.

[47]Lichtenstein, *Fastenrolle*, pp. 319, 286-287.

[48]Similarly, 25 Kislev is remembered as the day of the purification of the Temple in 2 Macc 10:5, whereas 1 Macc 4:52 and *Megillat Taanit* recall it as the day of the rededication.

61	Judah stations a garrison there,		and starts living there with his entourage,
	fortifies Beth-zur, for the people to have a stronghold against Idumea.	48, 53	has fortified Gezer, stations his own son there.

Some analogies between the cleansing of the Temple and the taking of the *Akra* are inherent in the events. But it seems that 1 Macc goes beyond that and purposefully shows Simon as the worthy successor of his brother; he does as Judah did, and his achievements repeat, confirm, and surpass Judah's.

Sometimes Simon's removal of idols is connected with Josiah's destruction of pagan altars and cult objects. But it should not be overlooked that their actions are quite different. Josiah *defiled* the places of worship outside Jerusalem,[49] Simon *cleansed* Gezer as well as the *Akra*. Simon's acts undoubtedly reflect the emphasis on purity that had gained importance since the Babylonian Exile and became even more central in Qumran and in rabbinic Judaism.[50] It is noteworthy that excavations have uncovered numerous *miqvaot*, most of them dating to the Hasmonean period, and many located in places under the direct control of the Hasmoneans, such as their winter palace in Jericho.[51] What distinguishes Simon and his successors is their willingness and ability to translate concern for purity into political as well as military action. We are given the impression that Torah observance was mandatory and that Gentiles were not allowed to live in Judean territory.[52]

---

[49]2 Kgs 23:4-20. 2 Chr 34:3-7 speaks of defiling as well as cleansing.

[50]See M. Smith, *Palestinian Parties*, pp. 110-112, 133-134, 179-180; J. Neusner, *The Idea of Purity in Ancient Judaism. The 1972-73 Haskell Lectures* (Leiden: Brill, 1973); id., *A History of the Mishnaic Law of Purities*, vol. 22: *The Mishnaic System of Uncleanness: Its Context and History* (Leiden: Brill, 1977).

[51]E. Netzer, "Ancient Ritual Baths (Miqvaot) in Jericho," *Jerusalem Cathedra* 2 (1982) 106-119; D. Small, "Late Hellenistic Baths in Palestine," *BASOR* 266 (1987) 59-74; For Gezer see n. 40 above.

[52]1 Macc 14:36; see Arenhoevel, *Theokratie* pp. 17-20. The policy of forced circumcision adopted by Hyrcanus and his successors may be in part an extension of Simon's policy: Simon had enough adherents so that he could expel people from Gezer, the *Akra*, and Joppa and replace them with his supporters. Later, when the conquered territory became too large, Simon's successors decided to Judaize the gentiles. The conquered population would be more useful as Jewish subjects than as foreign enemies or slaves. A shortage in men loyal to Hyrcanus may be indicated by the fact that he had to recruit a

Beyond its military and economic benefits, Simon's policy was certainly also intended to prove to pious Jews his dedication to the observance of the Torah.[53] With the conquest of Gezer and the *Akra*, Simon had removed what appear to have been the last remaining centers of foreign domination. It was no accident that he established residences for himself, his family, and his entourage in those two locations.[54] On one hand, possession of the conquered territory naturally fell to him. On the other hand, the area adjacent to the Temple was particularly suited as a (fortified) residence for the high priest. Gezer's strategic importance has been pointed out. In Jerusalem Simon seems to have kept an at least rudimentary government staff and a substantial military force.[55] Command of the military, however, was given to Hyrcanus who resided in Gezer (1 Macc 13:53). Having thus secured territorial control, Simon could reach for further goals: internal consolidation and external recognition and possible protection of his position.

Simon's Relations with Rome

First Maccabees on several occasions refers to Simon's relations with Rome and Sparta: Reportedly, the news of Jonathan's death caused mourning in both cities; the text further implies that the Romans on their own initiative sent a document renewing with Simon the alliance they had established with Judah and Jonathan (1 Macc 14:16-18). The document is not quoted; instead, a letter of the Spartans to Simon and to the Jewish people follows. It mentions the names of Jewish ambassadors, Numenius son of Antiochus and Antipatros son of Jason (1 Macc 14:20-23). Next we hear that Simon dispatched Numenius to Rome to confirm the alliance with a golden shield worth one thousand minas (14:24). In the subsequent document honoring Simon it is stated that Demetrius treated Simon well because he heard that the Romans had received his envoys with respect and considered the Jews their friends and allies (14:38-40). Later, interrupting the description of Antiochus VII's siege of Dora, Numenius' return from Rome is reported. Allegedly, he and his entourage brought back a copy of a circular letter that a Roman consul Lucius had addressed to at least

---

costly mercenary army (*J.W.* 1.61; *Ant.* 13.249). See also M. Smith, Maccabean Conversions, pp. 5-7.

[53]Cf. Exod 23:31-33; Deut 7:1-6; 12:29-30.

[54]Josephus' account of the leveling of the *Akra* seems to be wrong; at least it hardly belongs to Simon's time. *J.W.* 1.50; *Ant.* 13.215-217; see 1 Macc 15:28; Abel, *Macc.* p. 247; Goldstein, *1 Macc*, p. 483.

[55]1 Macc 13:52: οἱ παρ' αὐτοῦ; 14:37.

twenty-four governments of the Eastern Mediterranean. It said that Rome had asked kings and countries to maintain friendly relations with the Jews and to turn over to Simon escapees from Judea (15:15-23).

Josephus makes only a passing reference to Simon's alliance with Rome (*Ant.* 13.227), but quotes a *senatus consultum* (*Ant.* 14.145-148) which is in many ways related to the letter of the consul Lucius.

The difficulties of these texts with regard to their chronology, authenticity, and meaning have caused a long series of scholarly discussions. There is a general consensus that Rome would not have taken the initiative to establish friendly relations with Simon, that there was at least one embassy to Rome that included Numenius, and that the *senatus consultum* of L. Valerius (*Ant.* 14.145-148) is basically genuine. There is also a growing consensus that such an embassy took place probably in 142/1 BCE.[56]

In spite of Bickerman's and many others' defense of the letter of the consul Lucius,[57] the arguments against its authenticity are rather strong.[58] Some of those who reject the letter of Lucius as a forgery argue that the *senatus consultum* of the praetor L. Valerius was the only Roman response to Simon's embassy (of 142 BCE) and that the letter of Lucius is a wishful creation based on it. However, L. Valerius Flaccus, the presumed sponsor of the *senatus consultum* was not consul until 131 BCE and his praetorship would usually be not much earlier than 134 BCE, the last possible year.[59] But, though unusual, it would not be impossible that he was praetor as early as 143 BCE.[60]

---

[56]Based on the reference to Simon's successful embassy to Rome in the decree in his honor (1 Macc 14:27, 40: 140 BCE) and (wrongly?) on the consulship of L. Caecilius Metellus Calvus (142 BCE). A date in 139 BCE is unfounded, *pace*, Fischer, *Partherkrieg*, p. 101.

[57]E. Bickerman, *Gnomon* 6 (1930) 357-360; Goldstein, *1 Macc.*, pp. 492-500 (with some earlier bibliography).

[58]Succinctly stated by A. Giovannini - H. Müller, "Die Beziehungen zwischen Rom und den Juden im 2. Jh. v. Chr.," *Museum Helveticum* 28 (1971) 160-165 (including bibliography); see also J.D. Gauger, *Beiträge zur jüdischen Apologetik* (1977) pp. 285-302. Cf. A. Momigliano, "Ricerche sull'organizzazione della Giudea sotto il dominio romano (63 a.C. 70 d.C.)," *Annali della R. Scuola Normale Superiore di Pisa*, Ser. 2, Vol. 3 (1934) 215-217. Following Bickerman, Momigliano accepts a genuine base for the letter, but considers the extradition clause and at least part of the list of addressees unauthentic (1 Macc 15:21-23).

[59]See Broughton, *Magistrates* 1.491 n. 2.

[60]Intervals between the two offices often exceeded the minimum of two years. See for example Cn. Baebius Tamphilus (praetor 199, consul 182 BCE), M. Iunius Brutus (pr. 191, cos. 178), A. Hostilius Mancinus (pr. 180, cos. 170), L. Cornelius Lentulus (pr. 140 or 137, cos. 130), C. Marius (pr. 115, cos. 107). For these dates see Broughton, *Magistrates* vol. 1, passim. It should be added that after 167 BCE, when Livy's account breaks off, we know less than half of the

Furthermore, Demetrius' recognition of Simon's high priesthood[61] took place probably by the fall of 142. If this was, as 1 Macc 14:40 declares, a reaction to the favorable outcome of the Jewish embassy to Rome, the embassy can hardly have received the *senatus consultum* as late as December 13 of 142 (cf. *Ant.* 14.145), even if this Roman date actually corresponded to early fall of that year. The probable date would be December of 143 – but this would require that the embassy was originally not Simon's but Jonathan's.

Other scholars, especially many of those who accept the letter of Lucius as genuine, date the *senatus consultum* of L. Valerius under Hyrcanus I, either in 127/6 BCE (the ninth year of Hyrcanus I) or in 134.[62] But with such a view it is hard to account for the similarities between the *senatus consultum* and the situation under Simon.[63] In sum, the texts under consideration present too many inconsistencies and contradictions to admit of assured interpretations.

At least, however, it seems reasonable to accept the report that an embassy was sent, and to take the letter, whenever produced, as evidence of the Hasmoneans' concerns. If we do so, it becomes clear that the Hasmoneans wanted to strengthen their international position by friendly relations with Rome, and this appears also *a priori* probable. Roman guarantees for the recently won harbor of Joppa were considered a high priority (*Ant.* 14.147). Rome's positive response was seen as a cause for national pride (1 Macc 14:40) – and for concessions by Demetrius II. Stronger outside recognition could also be expected to give the Hasmoneans added strength in dealing with internal opponents. Moreover, it appears from the letter that enemies of the Hasmoneans had fled in sizable numbers to foreign shores and were a source of concern to Simon and his government. The list of addressees may in part represent recipients of letters based on the *senatus consultum* of L. Valerius. Other names may have been added later, so that it is unsafe to assume that anti-Hasmonean refugees could be found in, let alone extradited from all the indicated territories. However, expulsions of anti-Hasmoneans had often taken place.[64]

---

praetors and even fewer dates of office. Thus, there may even have been another otherwise unknown praetor L. Valerius.

[61]1 Macc 13:36, 41; 14:38-40.

[62]So Broughton, *Magistrates* 1, 491-492 n. 2, because 134 is the latest possible time at which the consul of 131 could have been praetor. Goldstein, *1 Macc*, p. 479, comes to the same conclusion by the ingenious assumption that "the ninth year" (*Ant.* 14.148) is counted according to the era of 142/1 BCE.

[63]See Giovannini-Müller, p. 165.

[64]See 1 Macc 2:44; 11:65-66; 13:50; 2 Macc 10:15.

As a final note we may add that the ambassadors all had Greek names (Numenius, Alexander, and perhaps Antipater). Their fathers bore either Greek or Grecized Hebrew names (Antiochus, Jason = Jeshua, Dorotheus = Nathanyah).[65] This is another indication of how at least superficial hellenistic influence permeated Judean society in general and the Hasmonean movement in particular.

The "Great Assembly" of 140 BCE

A central, yet highly problematic part of 1 Macc is a document honoring Simon (14:27-49). It is introduced as a spontaneous expression of thanks to Simon and his sons by the people (ὁ δῆμος), because Simon and his family had fought off the enemies of Israel.[66]

The document, as we have it, is structured as follows:

A. Preface (14:27-28)

B. Account of Hasmonean achievements (vv 29-40)

   I. Simon's family

     1. Genealogy and general goals (v 29)

     2. Jonathan's achievements and demise (v 30)

   II. Simon's achievements (including those before Jonathan's death)

     1. Response to aggression (vv 31-32)

     2. Fortifications (vv 33-34)

     3. *The people* reward Simon with the high priesthood (v 35)

---

[65]*Ant.* 14. 146; cf. 1 Macc 12:16; 14:22, 24; 15:15.

[66]1 Macc 14:25-26. The following phrase καὶ ἔστησαν αὐτῷ ἐλευθερίαν would normally mean "they (Israel) established freedom for him (i.e. Simon)." In fact, the Lucianic MSS and the Syriac versions add his name here. But since this interpretation does not agree with the context, translators generally assume *constructio ad sensum* and posit that "they (Simon and his family) established freedom for it (i.e. Israel)." See Abel, *Macc.*, p. 255; Goldstein, *1 Macc.*, p. 486. This rendering makes sense, but is grammatically implausible, since the earlier verbs referring to Simon and his family are in the singular, whereas Israel is here, as usual in 1 Macc, construed with the plural (cf. 1:25, 53; 2:70; 9:20; 13:26; exceptions: 12:52; 14:11). A possible solution would be to read ἐλευθέρια (neuter plural; Liddell-Scott: "thanksgiving for liberty") instead of ἐλευθερίαν. Then the phrase may be rendered: "They (Israel) established a thanksgiving to him (Simon) for (their) freedom." Liberty was an ideal frequently appealed to in the hellenistic period. The liberation of cities as well as of individuals was commemorated in festivals and inscriptions. For the *Eleutheria* celebrated at Plataeae see Plutarch, *Aristides* 21. For private thanksgiving see *Inscriptiones Graecae* vol. 9, fasc. 2, 1034.

    4. Crowning internal achievement: expulsion of Gentiles, cleansing and fortification of Jerusalem (vv 36-37)

    5. *King Demetrius* rewards Simon with the high priesthood because he heard of his success with Rome (vv 38-40)

C. I. *The Ioudaioi and the priests* reward Simon with the high priesthood and other functions and privileges (vv 41-43)

  II. Acts of this document made binding on the people (vv 44-45)

D. Final resolutions (vv 46-49).

The preface and dispositions about the publication of the decree (vv 48-49) correspond generally to the style of contemporary inscriptions.[67] The distinction of social classes in v 28 – priests, people, rulers of the ἔθνος, and elders of the land – raises questions to be dealt with later.

Part B lists achievements of the Hasmoneans, primarily the military and political accomplishments of Simon. In addition to what we know from the narrative we find out that Simon was wealthy enough to furnish and pay his soldiers (v 32; cf. 16:11-12). We are also told that Simon was *first* made high priest by the people (v 35 ὁ λαός). The sequence of events differs in several instances from that in the narrative of 1 Macc. With the exception of relations with Demetrius and with Rome (discussed above), these differences may be explained by the topical arrangement of the material in the document, though it is not certain that this explanation is the correct one. For our purposes the most important part is the definition of Simon's position (vv 41-45), but before we discuss that we must put the whole process in proper perspective.

The assembly as described in 1 Macc has some antecedents in Jewish history[68] and the record of it is in many ways similar to honorary decrees in fashion in the hellenistic world. Yet, the purported document poses many problems that have led some scholars to doubt its authenticity.[69] Whereas the account of past achievements follows familiar patterns, the powers granted to Simon are almost

---

[67]See especially *Orientis Graeci Inscriptiones Selectae* 737. The curious dating formula in v 27 has already been discussed above. The meaning of the attribute given Simon "great in the *asaram* of God" (ἐν ασαραμελ) has been lost by corruption of the transcribed Hebrew. For conjectures see A. Schalit, *König Herodes* (Berlin: De Gruyter, 1969), pp. 781-787.

[68]See Goldstein, *1 Macc.*, p. 503.

[69]See Willrich, *Urkundenfälschung*, pp. 69-72.

unparalleled because, as a rule, a polis would not grant such powers to any individual, and a king would not need them. A situation like Simon's arose only when someone came to power by unusual means *and* wanted his authority legitimized. The case of Vespasian is quite instructive, as we shall see below.

Extended discussion[70] has shown that 1 Macc 14:27-49 is a report – probably in the main accurate, but certainly far from verbatim – of an honorific decree set up in the Temple as a testimonial to Simon. One reason for thinking there was an actual text of the sort described is that the report of its contents contradicts in some points the story told in the rest of 1 Macc.[71] Because of these differences, we are justified in assuming that the author of 1 Macc was using a source. On the other hand, many details show that the source has not been followed exactly,[72] and others suggest that the source did not exactly follow the hellenistic model. At the beginning, this decree seems not to have been "proposed," but "announced" (v 28). We are not told by whom.[73] At the end, the pretense of recording a text is dropped and we are told that "the people approved" (v 46) and "said" (v 48) what are normally parts of a proposed decree (the provisions of publication etc.). Hence scholars are divided between those who think that the source stopped at v 45, because the decree form is abandoned, and those who think it continued to v 49 because it is resumed.[74] Goldstein has an ingenious solution which I interpret as follows and think may be correct, namely that vv 29-45 were a proclamation drawn up by "the leaders of the nation" and announced to the people by a herald and that the whole transaction, including the subsequent action taken by the assembly, was

---

[70]See Abel, *Macc.*, pp. 254-262; F.M. Cross, *The Ancient Library of Qumran and Modern Biblical Studies* (Rev. ed.; Garden City: Doubleday, 1961) 137-141; Goldstein, *1 Macc.*, pp. 501-509.

[71]In particular, the chronology and causal connection of Simon's relations with Rome and Demetrius II (v 38-40) differs from that in the narrative.

[72]Later additions and changes: topography of conquered towns (vv 33-34) added by translator (?) (Momigliano, *Prime linee* p. 169); καὶ ὅπως μέλη αὐτῷ περὶ τῶν ἁγίων (vv 42, 43) dittography (Goldstein, *1 Macc.*, p. 508). Only according to this document (v 40) were the Jews ever called "brothers" by the Romans. Abel (*Macc.*, pp. 259-260) and Goldstein (*1 Macc.*, pp. 506-507) consider this an intrusion from the Spartan correspondence into an otherwise authentic document. Geiger (*Urschrift* p. 212 note) conjectured that in v 29 Simon's name may have been substituted for that of Judah in order to emphasize Simon's role.

[73]Goldstein conjectures that the decree was drawn up by "the leaders of the nation" and announced by herald (*1 Macc.*, p. 503.)

[74]Ended at v 45: Bévenot, *Makkabäerbücher*, p. 160; Schürer-Vermes-Millar 1.194 n. 15. Continued to v 49: Abel, *Macc.*, p. 261.

then recorded in a document (vv 27-49) which was the source of vv 25-49.[75]

At both beginning and end – legally the most important parts – the hellenistic decree form is not followed precisely. But it is unlikely that the holding of a large assembly in the third year of Simon is a later invention, because a forger would have been inclined to put the definition of Simon's powers at the beginning of his independent career and would have avoided reference to a conspicuous record of it in the Temple, if no such record existed.

Perhaps a later situation may be helpful in understanding how Simon gained power in Jerusalem. Vespasian was proclaimed emperor by his troops in Egypt on July 1, 69 CE. Late in December of that year, the Roman Senate recognized him and formulated his extensive powers in a *senatus consultum* which was soon afterwards transformed into law by a popular assembly. The wording of this law, the latter part of which is extant, still bears the characteristics of the *senatus consultum*.[76] Similar stages of acceptance may be detected in the decree for Simon:

(1) He was proclaimed leader and high priest first by "the people."[77] It is plausible that Simon was designated high priest soon after (or perhaps even before) Jonathan's death, but since at first he lacked confirmation by the temple aristocracy and did not have full control over the temple, the exact date of his accession as high priest is never given in 1 Macc. Josephus too suggests that Simon was first appointed high priest not by the Seleucid authorities, as at least his four immediate predecessors had been, but reached the post by some other means. Whether it was by "popular" decision or by his own initiative or a combination of both is impossible for us to know, but the confused and fragmentary accounts in 1 Macc and Josephus suggest some irregularity.[78]

---

[75]1 *Macc.*, pp. 503, 509. Goldstein plausibly conjectures that ἐγνώρισεν is a mistranslation of Hebrew הודע which here should have been understood "was brought to our attention," but can also mean "he informed"; cf. Vulgate: *nota facta sunt haec*. Abel comes to a similar conclusion by a different route (*Macc.*, p. 257).

[76]H. Dessau, *Inscriptiones Latinae Selectae* 244.

[77]1 Macc 14:35; cf. 13:2.7-8. See p. 106 above.

[78]Josephus' accounts about Simon's accession are contradictory. According to *J.W.* 1.53, Simon was appointed high priest (by whom?) in 170 Sel. (143/2 BCE [autumn era] or, perhaps, 142/1 BCE [spring era]), confirming 1 Macc 13:41-42. But the purported occasion for his accession, a victory over Cendebeus, did not occur until several years later. Perhaps Josephus or his source confused it with the successes of Simon alluded to in 1 Macc 14:36. In *Ant.* 13.213 Josephus indicates that Simon was appointed high priest by the multitude (πλῆθος) and

(2) Some time afterwards, his position was recognized by Demetrius II (1 Macc 14:38).

(3) Only in his third year did Simon gain official approval by the priests and other leaders of the country. Such a stage seems to be reflected in the body of the decree (vv 29-45).[79]

(4) The decree as we have it would then represent a fourth and last stage: a large assembly of the entire people, including priests and (lay) leaders,[80] received and approved an announcement of the honors and powers awarded Simon by the leaders of (3). Also common folk (perhaps Simon's most ardent supporters) were allowed to participate. The assembly was informed of the decree and accepted it without major changes. Thus, while the decree proper ends at 14:45, the acceptance by the assembly and provisions for publication were appended and made part of the permanently inscribed record (1 Macc 14:46-49).

By assuming these different stages, we are able to account for the repetition of the approval formula (vv 41, 46), for the several awards and final acceptance of Simon's high priesthood (vv 35, 38, 41, 46, 47), and for the fact that "the people" (ὁ λαός) started to use Simon's name in documents from his first year on (1 Macc 13:42), whereas only from his third year on, by order of the *Ioudaioi* and priests, no contract was allowed to omit it (14:41, 43). We can see, then, that after starting from a limited power base of Hasmonean supporters, Simon had won

---

that in the first year of his high priesthood, 170 Sel., he liberated the people from Macedonian rule. Josephus may here have tried to harmonize his material from 1 Macc and other sources.

[79]At v 41 the Greek text seems to be corrupted by the intrusion of ὅτι. This is recognized as a scribal error by a large majority of commentators, because otherwise the document, instead of recording substantive decisions would only repeat what Demetrius heard (Goldstein, *1 Macc.*, p. 507; Stern, *Documents*, p. 138; Abel, *Macc* p. 260). An indication that there was a third intermediate stage is the fact that the formula of approval (v 41) does not mention the members of the assembly as in v 28, but only priests and Ἰουδαῖοι which here clearly does not mean all Jews or Judeans, since at least the clergy is shown as a separate group (again v 47). In postexilic literature the term "Israel" similar to the term "people" (λαός), often refers to lay people only and excludes priests and Levites (Neh 11:3; 1 Chr 9:2; 1QS 9.11). Ἰουδαῖοι may here be used in that sense (cf. 1 Macc 14:44: τοῦ λαοῦ καὶ τῶν ἱερέων), but it more likely means a restricted influential group with some official standing, as in several instances in Nehemia (2:16; 5:1, 17). See M. Smith, *Palestinian Parties*, pp. 152 and 264 n. 17.In other occurrences of Ἰουδαῖος in the decree (vv 34, 37, 40), Jews or Judeans seem to be meant, but with reference to the garrison of Beth-zur, the term clearly refers to law-abiding (pro-Hasmonean) Jews as opposed to apostate (former?) Jews (14:33; cf. 10:14).

[80]Cf. Neh 10:15 and 3:12-19 respectively. See M. Smith, *Palestinian Parties*, pp. 153-154.

acceptance and support from wider segments of Judean society, which are here specified as "the people" and "the *Ioudaioi* and the priests." Significantly, Seleucid acceptance had come before that by "the *Ioudaioi* and the priests." The old guard dies, but it does not surrender until it has to.

Simon's Powers

The powers Simon was granted were extensive: He was confirmed as high priest, political leader and military commander,[81] given charge over the Temple and control over the countryside, the armories and the fortresses (vv 41-42). Also, he alone was to wear purple and gold. Any form of opposition, including verbal criticism and assembly without his approval, was put under heavy penalty. Thus, his powers were almost unlimited.

If we ask why Simon wanted these powers officially granted him, and the grants publicly recorded, the evidence suggests this display of support was intended to counter some opposition. From the provisions of the decree we may infer that his opponents had included influential priests, because even in his third year as high priest Simon had to be assured that he was in charge of the Temple and that he could make necessary appointments "on his own authority" (14:42). Furthermore, since the wearing of purple and gold had to be forbidden, opposition to Simon would seem to have included aristocrats or would-be aristocrats. The ban on speaking against Simon and on meeting "without him" (v 44) – i.e. without his approval – suggests fear that opponents, by public meetings and speeches, might win popular following. Also, the opponents were evidently thought able to organize such meetings. Finally, the specific authorization to appoint deputies in charge of the countryside, the armories, and the fortresses, suggests that Simon's control of these was not as secure as the narrative of 1 Macc would make us believe.

Opposition to Simon certainly included the Qumran community or its antecedents in which dissident priests played a prominent role.[82]

---

[81]Simon's titulature in 1 Macc is unfortunately rather inconsistent. He is called high priest fifteen times, leader (ἡγούμενος) four times (the latter perhaps synonymous with ἐθνάρχης which occurs three times; cf. 1 Macc 13:42 with *Ant.* 13.214), and στρατηγός three times. All these terms occur in our document as well as in other documents incorporated in 1 Macc and seem to fairly represent his various official functions. The high priesthood was the most important or, perhaps, the most controversial of these offices. Josephus uses similar terminology. See further Goldstein, *1 Macc.*, p. 479.

[82]Cross (*Ancient Library*, p. 141) considers the early years of Simon's high priesthood "the appropriate occasion for the crystallization of the Essene sect."

This, however, was not the only opposing faction. Not to mention the former Hellenizers and Seleucid supporters, other members of the established priestly and lay aristocracy in Jerusalem and in the countryside must have felt threatened by Simon. Where the Sadducees stood – if at this time they existed at all as an organized group – cannot be ascertained, but those who considered Zadokite ancestry essential for the high priesthood probably had difficulty in accepting Simon.[83]

Given the existence of such an opposition, it would seem that in spite of the extensive powers granted Simon, the document recording the grants is, in its final form, the fruit of a compromise. The fact that Simon had been in office for two years before these powers were officially bestowed on him by a general assembly means that negotiations could have taken place earlier. We shall try to define the segments of the population which supported him.

From the beginning Simon had troops which gave him his initial success (1 Macc 14:32). They will have consisted largely of Jonathan's forces. Presumably few held out for Jonathan's sons or were irreconcilably alienated by their disposal.

After his early successes, according to the document as well as according to the narrative of 1 Macc, Simon was first proclaimed successor of Jonathan by "the people" (ὁ λαός 14:35; cf. 13:2, 7). This term normally means common people, sometimes common soldiers (e.g. 1 Macc 5:30; 12:44), but in 1 Macc it specifically excludes not only priests, but also opponents of the Hasmoneans (7:6) and is therein similar to the usage of the term "Israel."[84]

In 1 Macc 14, "the people" are distinguished on the one hand from Simon's original followers and his warriors (v 32), on the other from "the priests" and "rulers of the nation (ἀρχόντων ἔθνους) and "the elders of the countryside" (τῶν πρεσβυτέρων τῆς χώρας) (14:28).[85] No dignitaries bearing exactly these titles are mentioned elsewhere in 1 Macc, but Jonathan is said to have relied on the assistance of "elders of the people" (12:35; cf. 11:23), and the sons of "the leaders of the countryside" (τῶν ἡγουμένων τῆς χώρας) had been held hostages by Bacchides (9:53), evidently in order to prevent their fathers from assisting the Hasmoneans. These local leaders may be the "elders" of

---

[83]Yet even according to the pro-Pharisaic account in *Ant.* 13.293, John Hyrcanus had a close friend among the Sadducees *before* he broke with the Pharisees.
[84]Cf. Arenhoevel, *Theokratie*, p. 6 n. 15.
[85]The usage in Nehemiah is similar. "People" are differentiated from the clergy (Neh 10:35) and from the ruling (lay?) aristocracy (Neh 7:5). See also *Orientis Graeci Inscriptiones Selectae* 90.12, ὁ τε λαὸς καὶ οἱ ἄλλοι πάντες with Dittenberger's note 48.

cur document (v 28). We should not, however, deduce that the rural population was solidly in support of Simon. We have seen that the long survival of the pro-Seleucid forces in the *Akra* indicated that they had considerable support in the countryside. It is plausible to suppose that other local notables were, or tried to seem, neutral. Accordingly, the document's specific grant to Simon of control of "the countryside" (v 42) may be understood as directed against local centers of resistance.

Many of the priests who concurred in the approval of the document (vv 28, 41, 47) may have been long-standing supporters of the Hasmoneans.[86] Others may have joined Simon's side only reluctantly, because his high priesthood put a seal of near permanence on the Hasmonean tenure of the office, thereby further weakening the position of the former priestly aristocracy, already shaken up by the unconventional accessions of Jason, Menelaus, Jonathan, and perhaps Alcimus.[87]

This supposition is supported by the facts that, although the people are said to have made Simon high priest and (political) leader without reservation, the approval given by "the *Ioudaioi* and the priests" stipulated that he should hold those offices "in perpetuity until a trustworthy prophet should arise" (v 41). "In perpetuity" (εἰς

---

[86]Cf. 1 Macc 4:42.

[87]Rivkin has tried to show that the Pharisees were the moving force that gave Simon the high priesthood, contrary to Pentateuchal law (*A Hidden Revolution* [Nashville: Abingdon, 1978], pp. 215-251, especially pp. 217-223, 239, 249). His argument depends on equation of the "great assembly" of 1 Macc 14:28 with the "great assembly" of tannaitic literature. Since the Pharisees claimed descent from the men of the latter assembly, he argues the assembly must have been a creation of *Soferim*/Pharisees, and since the former assembly gave Simon the high priesthood, it was the Pharisees who did so (pp. 220-221). However, (1) there is no mention of Pharisees in connection with the assembly of 1 Macc 14; (2) this assembly did not give Simon the high priesthood – in fact it took place in Simon's third year as high priest; (3) the gift is represented by 1 Macc as in accord with Pentateuchal law – the author points out that the (high) priesthood belongs to the descendants of Mattathias as heirs of Phinehas (2:26, 54). In addition, the Hasmoneans themselves were willing and able to reinterpret biblical law for new situations and did not need the assistance of the Pharisees for this. See 1 Macc 2:40-41 (Sabbath observance); *b. Sanh.* 82a; *b. Abod. Zar.* 36b (intercourse with a heathen woman); *m. Maaser sheni* 5:15 (tithe). If we accept Josephus' claim that at Jonathan's time the Pharisees existed (*Ant.* 13.171), we should suppose that in Simon's time they also existed. However, the claim is suspect, though not necessarily false, because it carries no indication of its significance, and it tells us nothing of any influence the Pharisees may have had in the political and religious life of the country. The "great assembly" of tannaitic literature (*m. Abot* 1:1) may, indeed, be a literary reflection of that of 1 Macc 14:28, but to use such a literary reminiscence as evidence for Pharisaic domination of the Hasmonean assembly is improper.

τὸν αἰῶνα) has been understood as a reference to the hereditary character of his position,[88] but the Greek says nothing of this and Abel pointed out that it may be a hebraized rendering of the common hellenistic formula for granting an office or honor "for life" (διὰ βίου).[89] In fact, εἰς τὸν αἰῶνα like its Hebrew equivalent לעולם is sometimes used in connection with a person's lifelong activity or condition.[90] Thus it does not necessarily suggest the institution of a new dynasty, and in fact, its failure to mention Simon's descendants suggests that Abel's conjecture may be right.

It is difficult to gauge how serious the limitation "until a trustworthy prophet shall arise" was considered. For one thing, it indicates that Simon's reign *might* someday, before his death, have to be terminated – the prophet *might* designate another ruler.[91] On the other hand, expectation of a future prophet is mentioned in connection with Judah Maccabee as well (1 Macc 4:46). Here too the matter in question – the disposition of the polluted stones of the altar – was one in which the conservative Jerusalem priesthood, that here may have sided with Judah, would have had much to say. So the postponement of the question until the arrival of a true prophet, found in both cases, may reflect a consistency in the policy of the same group. At all events, "the *Ioudaioi* and the priests" were not willing to grant Simon unqualified perpetual authority, and Simon was willing to accept the high priesthood on these terms.[92]

Other limitations of Simon's power may be inferred from what is omitted in the document. He is not declared king, and this may be due to consideration for Jewish as well as Seleucid sensitivities. Other arguments from the document's silence have suggested to scholars additional compromises or limitations of Simon's power and some of those conjectured may perhaps have been intended.[93]

---

[88]Schürer-Vermes-Millar 1, p. 193 without evidence; Goldstein, *1 Macc.*, p. 508, referring to Exod 32:13, 2 Sam 7:12-13, where, however, the promises are made explicitly for dynasties, not individuals.

[89]*Macc.*, p. 260; cf. *Orientis Graeci Inscriptiones Selectae* 737.

[90]E.g. Exod 21:6; Deut 15:17.

[91]Not necessarily an eschatological messiah – all anointed kings and high priests were "messiahs." See M. Smith, "What Is Implied by the Variety of Messianic Figures," *JBL* 78 (1959) 66-72.

[92]At least in some circles, one or more prophets were expected with one or more messiahs. See 1QS 9.11; John 1:21 and passim. For the gift of prophecy attributed to John Hyrcanus, see below, pp. 149-150.

[93]Goldstein sees the following omissions as indications of compromise: Jonathan's political title (*1 Macc.*, p. 504), Judah (*ibid.*), liberation of Israel (p. 500), liberation from taxation (p. 505), contacts with Sparta (p.493). Against Zeitlin (*Rise and Fall* 1, pp. 149), there is no evidence that the "privilege of legal

Simon and Antiochus VII Sidetes

Our sources do not offer much information about Simon's rule after his position was approved by the great assembly of 140 BCE. We are informed only about his relations with Antiochus VII and about the events leading to his own death and Hyrcanus' succession.

Antiochus VII Sidetes decided to reach for the Seleucid throne after his brother Demetrius II had become a captive of the Parthians (c. 139 BCE), while Tryphon held large parts of the Seleucid empire and was trying to secure royal power for himself. Before acting, Antiochus of course tried to enlist support. The letter[94] in 1 Macc 15:2-9 is probably one of many letters to local leaders whom he approached. It confirms, "for all time," the exemptions, rights and privileges previously granted to Simon and reiterates that Jerusalem shall be "free."[95] It also generously grants Simon possession of all weapons and fortified sites he held already, remits all royal claims for past taxes and abolishes those for future taxes, and promises that as soon as the kingdom will be firmly in Antiochus's hands, he will greatly honor Simon, Simon's people, and the Temple. New is the authorization for Simon to strike his own coins as currency for his country (15:6). Whether or not Simon ever took advantage of this permission we do not know, but no extant coins can be attributed to him.[96] Reportedly, Antiochus VII nullified all concessions to Simon soon after they were made (1 Macc 15:27). 1 Macc does not state any reason for Antiochus' change of policy.

When besieging Dora, where Tryphon had taken refuge, Antiochus reportedly refused assistance in manpower and money generously offered by Simon (1 Macc 15:26).[97] Instead, he is said to have dispatched a certain Athenobius to Simon, in order to demand

---

interpretation was taken from Simon and his descendants" and given to an independent *Bet Din*. Against Rivkin (*Hidden Revolution*, p. 249), there is no evidence that the great assembly of 140 BCE established such a *Bet Din* "to exercise ultimate authority over the twofold Law."

[94]ἐπιστολή is often used in the plural, as here, even when referring to one letter. For examples see Liddell-Scott.

[95]15:7. On this see Goldstein, *1 Macc.* p. 514.

[96]So U. Rappaport, "The Emergence of Hasmonean Coinage," *AJS review* 1 (1976) 172-173; Goldstein, *1 Macc.*, p. 514; *pace* W. Wirgin, *On Charismatic Leadership from Simon Maccabaeus until Simon Bar-Kochba*, Leeds University Oriental Society Monograph Series No. 5, Leeds 1964, pp. 36-37.

[97]Abel (*Macc.*, p. 266) may be correct in positing that the successful outcome of Numenius' embassy to Rome was inserted at this point (1 Macc 15:15-24) in order to contrast Roman fidelity with Seleucid fickleness. It might also be that 1 Macc wants the reader to understand that Dora was besieged twice (15:13; 15:25 ἐν τῇ δευτέρᾳ).

restitution of Joppa, Gezer, of the *Akra* in Jerusalem, and of many other places, or compensation for lost property and revenues in the amount of 1,000 talents (1 Macc 15:28-31). Simon replied that the land taken over was ancestral territory of the Jews. In the case of Joppa and Gezer however, Simon justified their conquest not as recovery of ancestral land, but as a punitive and preventive measure, because "they had done great harm to the people" (1 Macc 15:35). Therefore for these places, and these alone, he offered King Antiochus compensation, in the amount of one hundred talents. It is worth noting that territorial claims were not based on biblical precedent,[98] but apparently on recent settlement patterns. Unfortunately it seems impossible to ascertain whether this was done because of a pragmatic view of Jewish territory or as a tactical maneuver in order to show flexibility. In a very perceptive and timely book, Mendels has collected the evidence for Hasmonean territorial policy.[99] He correctly notes a shift of emphasis from defense of a way of life to territorial conquest, but this shift seems to have been gradual, dictated more by the circumstances than by a one-time decision to conquer the entire land.[100]

Antiochus did not accept Simon's offer. While he himself was still pursuing Tryphon, he made his general Cendebeus governor of the coastal area, with a sizable army at his disposal. His mandate was allegedly (a) to encamp "opposite" Judea, (b) to fortify the village or town named Kedron, and (c) to "wage war against the people" (1 Macc 15:39). Cendebeus entered Jamnia – apparently without a fight.[101] His troops then allegedly started raids into Judean territory, taking some prisoners (1 Macc 15:40-41), but he does not seem to have tried to reconquer all of Judea. His raids probably helped to finance his troops, and so to maintain Seleucid prestige and a Seleucid military power in the area.

John Hyrcanus, stationed at Gezer, is said to have gone to Jerusalem to alert his father Simon of the danger from Cendebeus' troops. Simon then charged his two eldest sons, John and Judah, with the war against Cendebeus. It is not sure whether Gezer had fallen into the latter's hands, but the gathering of the Hasmonean troops in Modein (1 Macc

---

[98]Cf. Josh 21:21; 1 Kgs 9:15-17.

[99]D. Mendels, *The Land of Israel as a Political Concept in Hasmonean Literature* (Tübingen: Mohr, 1987) pp. 47-49.

[100]For a territorial concern retrojected to Mattathias' time, see 1 Macc 2:46 (cf. p. 35 above), against Mendels, *Land*, p. 47.

[101]1 Macc 15:40. Josephus reports, however, probably wrongly, that Simon had conquered Jamnia (*J.W.* 1.50; *Ant.* 13.215).

16:4), northeast of Gezer, suggests that Hyrcanus may have been driven out of his fortress.[102]

In any event, the onslaught of Cendebeus was taken very seriously. An army of as many as 20,000 men was gathered, for the first time cavalry are mentioned in Hasmonean forces (1 Macc 16:4). Bartlett sees the cavalry as proof of aristocrats finally joining the Hasmoneans.[103] Cendebeus' troops were defeated and allegedly 2000 of them were killed in the coastal plain between Modein and Kedron. Judah was wounded in a battle. First Maccabees emphasizes the role of John Hyrcanus who alone led the pursuit of the enemy troops and occupied and burned Kedron.[104] The enemy fled to "the forts in the fields of Azotus" (16:9-10).

Here we see for the last time 1 Macc's characteristic depiction of Hasmonean courage and leadership in the face of a powerful enemy – the third generation, represented by Hyrcanus, is true to the earlier ones.

Josephus' account of events differs. He indicates that Simon sent his sons in command of the more powerful troops, but also himself led another force in a guerilla campaign in the hills, where he successfully ambushed various detachments of Cendebeus' men.[105] Here Josephus is evidently independent of 1 Macc, but whether his source is more reliable than 1 Macc is uncertain. Doubts about *J.W.*'s reliability arise from the inherent unlikelihood of the aged Simon leading a guerilla campaign. Furthermore, we have seen that *J.W.* mistakenly links Simon's accession to the high priesthood to his victories over Cendebeus.[106]

We may therefore tentatively assume that the separate source of *J.W.* here was a romantic but inaccurate "Story of the Hasmoneans," and this will make us cautious of relying on it hereafter when 1 Macc

---

[102]Differently Goldstein, *1 Macc.*, p. 520.

[103]*Macc.*, p. 210.

[104]Goldstein appears to contradict himself when he considers Simon the grammatical subject of 1 Macc 16:4, 6-7 (*1 Macc.*, pp. 518, 520-521) and at the same time claims that he did not lead the army in combat (*1 Macc.*, p. 172). The traditional solution, to take Hyrcanus as the implied subject at least of vv 6-7 seems more plausible. See Abel, *Macc.*, pp. 278-279. Yet another possibility is to suppose that the subject in vv 6-7 is Cendebeus, the last single commander previously mentioned. The attention given to the location of his cavalry would then be explained by the author's parenthetical comment in the second half of v 7 ("and the cavalry of the opponents was very numerous"). For *J.W.* 1.52-53; *Ant.* 13.226-227 see below.

[105]*J.W.* 1.52-53; *Ant.* 13.226-227.

[106]See note 78 above.

ceases. It probably incorporated popular oral traditions. How Josephus received this material we do not know, but it is unlikely that it was transmitted by Nicholas of Damascus. Nicholas' romances are of a more "literary" and traditional sort.

Simon's Death

After these struggles, according to Josephus, Simon lived the rest of his life in peace,[107] until his murder in the month of Shebat 177 Sel. Bab. (January/February 134 BCE).[108] At that time Simon was making a tour to inspect various towns of his realm. With his wife, two sons, and a number of servants, he visited his son-inlaw Ptolemy, son of Abubus, in the fortress of Dok near Jericho.[109] Ptolemy was his *strategos* for the plain of Jericho and was rich – he may have become so through his relation with Simon, or his wealth may have secured his appointment. In either case he probably came from a family of some social standing. His father's name seems to have been Habub, a Semitic name identifiable also in an inscription from Palmyra,[110] but he had given his son the name carried by the Macedonian rulers of Egypt, enemies of the Seleucids. Unfortunately we have no means of determining this Ptolemy's family background further. He seems to have had good connections in Transjordan, because after killing Simon and his sons, he found refuge in Philadelphia at the court of the tyrant Zenon who was nicknamed (in Greek) "of half a pint" (*Kotylas*).[111]

The popular following of the Hasmoneans is indicated by the fact that Ptolemy evidently did not hope for a general rising to support him once Simon was killed. Instead, according to 1 Macc 16:16-20, he killed two of Simon's sons along with their father, sent messengers to Gezer to murder the third (John), and wrote to Antiochus for help, offering to surrender the country to him. Josephus in *J.W.* 1.54-60 had a different source which he still preferred when writing *Ant.* 13.228-235 although by that time he knew and had used 1 Macc. According to this source (a "Story of the Hasmoneans"?) only Simon was killed at first, his wife and two sons were taken hostages. Nothing is said of a letter to

---

[107]*Ant.* 13.277, probably intended to replace the mistaken statement in *J.W.* 1.53 that Simon became high priest at this point.

[108]1 Macc 16:14. The year 134 is accepted by Bickerman, *Gott*, p. 157, n. 2; Abel, *Macc.*, p. 281. Goldstein, *1 Macc.*, p. 524; 135 BCE is still preferred by Bunge, *Untersuchungen* pp. 681-683, n. 85.

[109]1 Macc 16:14-15; *J.W.* 1.54; *Ant.* 12.228. Josephus calls the fortress Dagon (*J.W.* 1.56; *Ant.* 13.230). For bibliography see Möller-Schmitt, *Siedlungen*, pp. 77-78.

[110]*Inventaire des inscriptions de Palmyre* VIII.152.

[111]*J.W.* 1.60; *Ant.* 13.235.

Antiochus. 1 Macc 16:18-20 says Ptolemy also wrote to the Judean military commanders, offering them rewards if they would join his side, and sent men to seize both Jerusalem and the Temple mount.[112] Josephus again says nothing of a letter to the commanders, and has Ptolemy himself lead the attempt to take the city.[113] Both sources agree that Hyrcanus learned of the impending danger, and 1 Macc concludes its detailed account with the report that he liquidated the would-be assassins.

For the rest it mentions Hyrcanus' "wars," "deeds of valor," "building of the walls," and "accomplishments," indicating the interests that still dominated the dynasty's propaganda around the end of his reign (approximately the writer's time). From here on we depend mainly on Josephus' two accounts, which here are almost identical. According to him, both Ptolemy and Simon's surviving son, John (later Hyrcanus) raced for Jerusalem. John got there first and was supported by the common people[114] because of their memory of his father's "achievements" (*J.W.*) or "good deeds" (*Ant.*) and their hatred "of Ptolemy's crimes" (*J.W.*) or just "of Ptolemy" (*Ant.*). Such slight differences tell us more of Josephus' literary technique than of the events reported. As things turned out, Ptolemy tried to enter the city, but was driven back by Hyrcanus' lower-class supporters.[115]

Antiochus Sidetes failed to offer Ptolemy timely assistance, and the Hasmonean army seems to have remained by and large on Hyrcanus' side, since we hear nothing of any extensive support for Ptolemy. This state of affairs suggests that Simon and his family had a fairly broad and loyal base of support.

---

[112]See F.M. Cross, *Ancient Library* pp. 145-146.

[113]*J.W.* 1.54-55; *Ant.* 13.228-229.

[114]*J.W.* 1.55: ὁ λαός, ὁ δῆμος; *Ant.* 13.229: τὸ πλῆθος, ὁ δῆμος.

[115]That the Hasmoneans' opposition in Qumran interpreted the demise of Simon and two of his sons as the fulfillment of the curse of Joshua (Josh 6:26 according to LXX and 4QTestim 22-23; cf. 1 Kgs 16:34) is a dubious conjecture. 4QTestim 21-30 undoubtedly alludes to contemporary events, but reference to Simon is not as clear as Cross thinks. We hear nothing of Simon's rebuilding Jericho. "The fortress in Jericho" was built by Bacchides (1 Macc 9:50). Bacchides and Alcimus may be the two who "*returned* and fortified" Jericho according to 4QTestim 25 and did great evil throughout the land. If so, the preceding man of Belial who was a snare to *his people* (line 23) was Alcimus. Ptolemy, Simon's assassin, built the fortress of Dok *near* Jericho (1 Macc 16:15). Cross (*Ancient Library* pp. 148-152) identifies Simon not only as the "cursed man," but also as the "Wicked Priest." Evidence for the latter assertion is inconclusive. See also H. Burgmann, "Der Josuafluch zur Zeit des Makkabäers Simon," *BZ* 19 (1975) 26-40.

Conclusion

Simon, the last surviving son of Mattathias, had a long career and was in many respects able to bring to completion the work started by his father and brothers. Among his first achievements was the strengthening of defenses through an extensive building program. He also improved his strategic position by conquering Joppa, Gezer, and the *Akra*. Joppa gave the Hasmoneans access to the sea. The importance Simon attributed to this is evidenced by the family tomb he built.

He not only conquered, but also purified these places, showing himself a worthy successor of Judah who had purified the Temple. Such concern for purity had become prevalent among some Jewish groups during the Babylonian Exile if not before and was to remain so among Essenes and Pharisees. Nothing reported of his reign indicated indifference to purity laws.

Because of Seleucid rivalries and weaknesses, Simon achieved virtual autonomy and exemption from all or most Seleucid taxes for Judea. Complete independence was reached by his son and successor John Hyrcanus, after the death of Antiochus VII.[116]

More important, Simon was able to broaden the base of support that his brothers had created. Besides a paid and loyal army he had broad popular support, strengthened by the elimination of Seleucid taxation. He also gained more support from the priestly and lay aristocracy, which belatedly accepted him as high priest. It is not clear whether the powers given to Simon were intended to be hereditary, but they clearly set a precedent for his descendants and thus could serve as a basis for dynastic claims.

Besides thus increasing his support in the Judean population, he created further bases outside Judea. Some of these, the places he conquered and settled with Judeans, will have rewarded and confirmed the closest and neediest of his Judean supporters. Hasmonean expansion probably also attracted allies, as Roman expansion did. Some of the neighboring towns/tribes may have been anxious to ally themselves with the growing Hasmonean power because they did not like Seleucid taxation any more than the Judeans did, and they had more reason to fear the Judeans than the Seleucids.

Opposition against Simon was of various kinds, though his enemies are simply called "lawless and evil" (1 Macc 14:14). With *external*

---

[116]The attribution of coins of Antiochus VIII to a Jerusalem mint is very doubtful and therefore does not prove continued Seleucid sovereignty over Judea. See U. Rappaport, "The Emergence of Hasmonean Coinage," *AJSreview* 1 (1976) 181.

opposition he dealt primarily by military action and colonization, replacing potential enemies in newly conquered towns with loyal followers. Treaties with Rome and Sparta enhanced his prestige in dealing with opposition forces. *Internal* opponents fled the country (cf. 1 Macc 15:21) or went into internal exile, as the Qumran community did. Objections against Simon as high priest probably lingered on even in some priestly circles in Jerusalem. The opposition that finally caused his downfall came from the most unexpected quarter – his own son-in-law. But Simon had laid the groundwork solidly enough so that his son Hyrcanus could take over with relative ease.

The time of Simon's rule is described in the most glowing terms in 1 Macc 14:4-15. Peace and prosperity through strength is the main theme of this hymn which recapitulates many of Simon's achievements, but is silent about his high priesthood[117] and contains no substantial evidence of messianic identification.

While traditional values and concepts were stressed by the Hasmoneans and their supporters, we find that under Simon there was an increasing openness to Hellenistic and other foreign influences. We can see this in particular in the funerary monument for his family, in the form of the document drawn up in his honor, in the correspondence with Sparta, and in his exclusive use of purple and gold.

---

[117]Abel, *Macc.*, p. 252 considers v 15 an allusion to his high priesthood.

5

John Hyrcanus I

When his father was murdered, John Hyrcanus, the first or second son of Simon (1 Macc 16:2), was still a fairly young man, born during or after the persecution of Antiochus IV.[1] For several years he had been stationed in Gezer as commander of his father's troops (1 Macc 13:53) and had had some military success (1 Macc 16:1-10). Thus, he had an army at his disposal and was not unprepared to succeed his father. This he did without apparent hesitation. Upon being admitted to Jerusalem, he assumed the office of high priest and offered sacrifice in the Temple before starting to pursue his brother-in-law, Ptolemy (*J.W.* 1.56; *Ant.* 13.230). His accession as high priest was certainly quick. We hear nothing of the presumable opposition (adherents of Ptolemy, perhaps of his late brothers, anti-Hasmonean elements, etc.). John proceeded to besiege Ptolemy in the fortress of Dok (Dagon) near Jericho.[2]

The siege was complicated by the fact that Ptolemy held John's mother and brothers as hostages. The mother's courage in exhorting John to continue the siege despite her tortures is described in dramatic and dubious detail. After some time, John desisted from the siege, reportedly because of the advent of the sabbatical year, and Ptolemy killed the hostages and fled to Philadelphia. The relationship between the coming of the sabbatical year and the end of the siege remains uncertain.[3] Hence it is unsafe to draw conclusions about Hyrcanus' religious or political leanings from this incident.

---

[1]This is, at least, supposed by the (false ?) allegation that his mother was taken captive under Antiochus IV. *Ant.* 13.292; cf. *b. Qidd.* 66a, where the story is told of "King Yannai" who is usually Alexander Janneus.

[2]*J.W.* 1.57-60; *Ant.* 13.230-235.

[3]Josephus in both *J.W.* 1.60 and *Ant.* 13.234 supposed that in a sabbatical year *all* work was prohibited "as on the Sabbath days." Hence he concluded that the advent of the sabbatical year prevented Hyrcanus from continuing the siege.

Hyrcanus and Antiochus VII Sidetes

Not too long after Hyrcanus' accession, probably in his first year, Antiochus marched against Judea and besieged Jerusalem.[4] It may be that he had set out in response to, or in collusion with Ptolemy, son of Abubus. In any event, he plundered the country and shut up Hyrcanus in the city which, thanks to its new strong walls, was difficult to take.

The siege lasted, at least, for almost a year[5] and led to severe shortages in the city. Hence Hyrcanus expelled from the city all those who could not help in its defense (*Ant.* 13.240). These were not permitted by Antiochus to pass his circumvallation and thus were trapped between the walls. Such dramatic developments of the consequences of sieges were common in Greek historiography and

---

But no such prohibition is known to biblical or rabbinic law. Furthermore, there is no evidence that fighting was ever suspended during the sabbatical year. Judah fought during the supposedly sabbatical year of 164/3 or 163/2 BCE. (1 Macc 6:49, 53) and Simon made some of his conquests during a sabbatical year (143/2 or 142/1 BCE). According to 1QM 2.6-9, the eschatological war is to be interrupted during sabbatical years; this does *not* prove that in other wars Essenes would have refrained from fighting during sabbatical years (and the list of forbidden activities in *Jub.* 50:12, which has been cited as a parallel, applies to Sabbath *days* only). Hence there is little basis for Goldstein's suggestion (1 *Macc.*, p. 541) that Hyrcanus refrained from fighting in accordance with Qumran halakah, because he "probably tried to win and keep the loyalty of as many Jewish sects as possible." Further, what we have hitherto glimpsed of Qumran opinion of the Hasmoneans makes it unlikely that Hyrcanus would have tried to win their approval. Finally, scholars who think they can date the sabbatical years of the second century BCE, commonly locate one in 136/5 (Tishri to Elul) or 135/4, and another in 129/8 or 128/7 BCE (Goldstein, 1 *Macc.*, p. 541; B.Z Wacholder, "The Calendar of Sabbatical Cycles During the Second Temple and the Early Rabbinic Period," *HUCA* [1973] 153-196). But Simon's death is most plausibly dated in 134 BCE (see above chap. IV n.108), hence the siege following his death could not have been interrupted by the advent of a sabbatical year until fall of 129 at the *earliest* – some five years later. To suppose that Hyrcanus tried for five years to capture a fortress near Jericho without being able to take it is unjustified, and contradicts Josephus' implicit chronology. Hence several scholars have suggested that Josephus wrote carelessly and that the siege was raised because of food shortages *after* the sabbatical year of 136/5. See, for example, Schaumberger, *Biblica* 36 (1955) 430-431. Other conjectures are equally easy, for instance the reference to the sabbatical year may be a conjectured excuse for Hyrcanus' failure to rescue his mother. In sum, it seems wise to share Bickerman's skepticism concerning the role of the sabbatical year in these events (*Gott*, p. 157 n. 2). On the whole question see also Schürer-Vermes-Millar 1, pp. 202-203 n. 5.

[4]For the chronology see Jacoby, *Fragmente* vol. 2D p. 874; Schürer-Vermes-Millar 1, pp. 202-203 n. 5.

[5]From the Pleiades' setting to Sukkot: *Ant.* 13.237, 241.

probably sometimes did occur in Greek history. Here the excluded Jerusalemites are said to have survived until the coming of Sukkot. Then Hyrcanus readmitted them and asked Antiochus for a seven-day truce. Antiochus granted the request and reportedly even sent animals for sacrifice.[6]

Shortly thereafter, Hyrcanus sent representatives to Antiochus asking, evidently as a condition of surrender, that "their ancestral form of government be given back [or allowed] to them."[7] What this request meant, we do not know. Perhaps the request was for a guarantee of their right to observe their ancestral laws, but Hyrcanus may also have asked for the continuation of the traditional form of government, with the high priest, not a governor, at its head. We are not told explicitly that the request was granted, but nothing is said of any change of observances, and Antiochus offered a peace on substantially the same conditions that he had earlier demanded of Simon (1 Macc 15:28-31). Surrender of arms, tribute for Joppa and other communities outside of Judea, and a garrison, i.e. the partial restoration of the *Akra*, in Jerusalem. The Jewish envoys agreed to everything but a garrison – a source of pollution – in Jerusalem. They offered hostages and 500 talents, the same amount earlier demanded (in addition to tribute) from Simon in case he intended to keep the conquered areas (1 Macc 15:31). Antiochus VII accepted this offer, raised the siege, and withdrew (*Ant.* 13.248).

Allegedly, the advisers of Antiochus Sidetes pointed out the Jews' unsociable customs and counselled that the king either totally destroy the city and the Jewish people or that he abolish their laws and force them to change their ways; but the king did not follow their advice. Instead, his moderation is praised and contrasted with the harshness of Antiochus Epiphanes.[8]

Before leaving Jerusalem, Antiochus had the city walls dismantled. Whereas reports by Diodorus, Josephus, and Pseudo-Plutarch in somewhat legendary guise emphasize Antiochus' restrained attitude and the relatively mild peace settlement,

---

[6]*Ant.* 13.242-243; Stern, *Greek and Latin Authors* no. 260 (Ps.-Plutarch, *Moralia* 184 E-F). Both Josephus and Ps.-Plutarch seem to rely on the same source.

[7]τὴν πάτριον αὐτοῖς πολιτείαν ἀποδοῦναι, *Ant.* 13.245.

[8]Diodorus 34/35.1; *Ant.* 13.244-246. The accusation of ἀμιξία (*Ant.* 13.245) may be semantically related to פרישות, because both terms refer to separateness, but it is unwarranted to see the Pharisees as its main target. The separateness of the Jews is a *topos* among Greek and Latin authors at least since Hecataeus of Abdera (ca. 300 BCE); Diodorus 40.3.4 = Stern, *Greek and Latin Authors* no. 11. See E. Bickerman, "Ritualmord und Eselskult," *Studies* 2, pp. 225-255.

Porphyry says that he killed the noblest of the Jews.[9] This statement does not inspire confidence, since Hyrcanus survived the siege. On the other hand, the source for the former accounts tries to show Antiochus in the best possible light and may have suppressed mention of harsh measures.[10]

Rome's role in these events is disputed and depends largely on how one dates two *senatus consulta* preserved by Josephus (*Ant.* 13.260-264; 14.249-250), both expressing Roman concern over the activity of a King Antiochus in Palestine. The first decree was in response to requests by envoys of the Jewish people. They had asked that Rome intervene to force Antiochus to surrender Joppa and its harbors as well as Gezer and Pegae and other territories taken in war, contrary to a decree of the senate. Also, the senate was asked to forbid further passage of royal troops through the Jews' land "and that of their subjects" (!) and to invalidate the decrees issued by Antiochus during the war, to require the return of the spoils he had taken, and to assess the damage caused by the war (*Ant.* 13.261-263). The Romans renewed their alliance with the Jews, but indefinitely deferred action about their requests. The second *senatus consultum*, embedded in a Pergamenian decree, actually resolves that a King Antiochus, son of Antiochus, "shall not wrong the Jews" and that the fortresses, harbors, territory, and everything else he may have taken from them shall be given back. Also, the garrison is to be expelled from Joppa "as they requested" and the Jews shall have the right to export goods from their harbors, but any other exporters except King Ptolemy, must pay export duties (*Ant.* 14.250).

Because of chronological and textual difficulties, one or both of these decrees have been assigned by some scholars to dates after the death of Antiochus VII, but others have argued that only in the war between Antiochus VII and John Hyrcanus can a Seleucid king have reconquered Joppa and Gezer, and have therefore dated both documents during that war.[11] The second decree, known only from a Pergamene

---

[9]Diodorus 34/35.1.5 = Stern, *Greek and Latin Authors* 1, no. 63; Porphyry, *ibid.* 2, no. 457b. In *Ant.* 13.247 καθεῖλε δὲ καὶ τὴν στεφάνην τῆς πόλεως may mean that he pulled down the entire wall or just its top, so that it would be less useful for defense purposes.

[10]Posidonius is often considered to have been the source for Diodorus, Josephus, and Pseudo-Plutarch. For a note of caution see Stern, *Greek and Latin Authors* 1, pp. 142-144. Posidonius is quoted elsewhere as giving an obviously exaggerated account of Antiochus VII's extravagance (Jacoby, *Fragmente* 87 F 9, 11).

[11]See the detailed discussion in Schürer-Vermes-Millar 1, pp. 204-206, with earlier bibliography. The argument there supposes that Antiochus VII returned Joppa and the other cities in question to the Jews, but in the passage

report in which it seems out of place, looks like an expression of wishful thinking based on the requests reported by the first, with some adjustments (to later problems?). Finally, even if both decrees were genuine, we could not conclude that the second was obeyed by the Seleucids. Sidetes would hardly have complied at once and in the confusion following his debacle much was left undone. We are not told what arrangements Sidetes made, after the city's surrender, for the government of Judea and adjacent territories. Josephus' silence on this point may reflect his dislike of what was done.

Both *J.W.* 1.61 and *Ant.* 13.249 report that before Antiochus left Jerusalem, Hyrcanus took about 3000 talents of silver from the tomb of David, and also that Hyrcanus gave Antiochus 300 talents. According to *J.W.*, this was bribe money coming from David's tomb. *Ant.*, probably in order to remove an embarrassing detail, calls it tribute and does not state its provenance. Both say that with the remainder of the funds from David's tomb Hyrcanus hired mercenaries. Josephus says he was the first independent Jewish ruler (since the fall of the monarchy) to employ foreign troops, but some of the Jewish Persian governors – among them Nehemiah – presumably had foreign troops in their garrisons (see Neh 2:9). The mention of mercenaries at this point is particularly unexpected because after a defeat restrictions on the size and composition of an army might be expected instead.[12] Perhaps casualties and the need to restore the country's economy after the war (*Ant.* 13.237) made the Judean population inadequate for Hyrcanus' army. Further, while he was shut up in Jerusalem, support for him in the countryside may have dwindled. Moreover, his handling of the siege, especially his decision to drive out of the city all those unable to fight (*Ant.* 13.240-241) – if this was carried out – probably caused widespread disaffection. Only *J.W.* closely connects the opening of the tomb and hiring of the mercenaries with Antiochus' departure; *Ant.* 13.248-250 writes first of Antiochus' departure, then of the opening of the tomb, and only then of Antiochus' entry in Jerusalem. Even if the 300 talents paid to satisfy Antiochus did come from the tomb, the rest of the money may not have been taken out at once, and the mercenary force may have

---

used as evidence (*Ant.* 13.246) this is not said. Antiochus required a tribute for "Joppa and the other cities around Judea" as one of his *peace conditions*, but this probably refers to the tribute in arrears since the Jewish seizure. It says nothing of the arrangements to be made for the future. This vitiates much of the argument.

[12]In the Treaty of Apamea it was specified that Antiochus the Great may not recruit mercenaries from the lands under Roman rule (Polybius 21.42.15 [LCL]).

been raised only some years later. Josephus' chronology is notoriously unreliable.[13]

According to *Ant.* 13.250, Hyrcanus became a friend and ally of Antiochus, admitted him into the city and provided his army lavishly with everything they needed – incredible at the end of a long siege, when the city's resources were exhausted. Antiochus' departure from Jerusalem was certainly an occasion for relief, perhaps commemorated on 28 Shebat.[14] He may have taken Hyrcanus with him as an "ally" or subordinate commander of a Jewish company – in effect a helpful hostage. Not long afterward, probably in the spring of 130 BCE, Hyrcanus accompanied Antiochus during the first part of his eastern campaign. Nicholas of Damascus records that the whole army remained for two days in one place, because of a Sabbath and a Jewish holiday, which Josephus identifies as Pentecost.[15]

Ever since Eusebius' time it has been claimed that John Hyrcanus got his surname after a victory over the Hyrcanians, but even Sidetes hardly reached Hyrcania – he met his death in battle probably in Media, and *Ant.* 13.254 supposes that Hyrcanus had returned to Judea before the abrupt end of the campaign.[16]

The medieval *Josippon* gives us two alternate explanations of these events. One version has Hyrcanus and his troops rest for two days because of Sabbath and holiday, while Antiochus moves on and meets defeat and death in battle.[17] A later manuscript tradition excludes any religious reason for Hyrcanus' delay. Rather it speaks of collusion between Arsaces and Hyrcanus and a pact between them. Pucci has tried

---

[13]See Cohen, *Josephus* pp. 32-33, 40-41. B. Bar-Kochva thinks that after the territorial expansion of John Hyrcanus there may have been a shortage of local manpower ("Manpower, Economics, and Internal Strife in the Hasmonean State," *Colloques Nationaux du Centre National de la Recherche Scientifique*, No. 936, *Armées et fiscalité dans le monde antique* [Paris, 1977] pp. 173-185, especially 175-177). On the funds from David's tomb see *ibid.*, pp. 182-185.

[14]*Megillat Taanit;* see Lichtenstein, *HUCA* 8-9 (1931-32) 287-288.

[15]*Ant.* 13.250-252 = Stern, *Greek and Latin Authors* 1 no. 88. It is unlikely that the army rested every Sabbath.

[16]Derivation of name: Eusebius, *Chron.* ed. Schoene, vol. 2, pp. 130-131; defended by T. Fischer, *Untersuchungen zum Partherkrieg Antiochos' VII. im Rahmen der Seleukidengeschichte* (diss., Tübingen, 1970) pp. 40-41. Campaign and death in Media: see Posidonius, Jacoby, *Fragmente* 87 F 9, 11; Aelian, *De natura animalium* 10.34. The name Hyrcanus had been in use in Palestine at least several decades earlier: *Ant.* 12.186-236; 2 Macc 3:11. See discussion in Schürer-Vermes- Millar 1, pp. 201-202 n. 2.

[17]D. Flusser, *The Josippon* [Josephus Gorionides] (Jerusalem: Bialik Institute, 1980-81), Vol. 1, p. 115.

to establish the historical probability of this account.[18] The facts that after the capture of Jerusalem by Sidetes, Hyrcanus was either left in power or was able to regain power shortly after Sidetes' death, and that he was soon able to expand his territory, are remarkable and may have had one or more of several reasons. It is possible that real or anticipated pressure from Rome prevented Sidetes from deposing Hyrcanus. It is also possible and somewhat more likely that Sidetes thought Hyrcanus was the most acceptable and reliable ruler of Judea that he could find. Again, he may have removed Hyrcanus, who may have returned to Jerusalem either after Sidetes' death or, if he escaped, even before it, and then, in Sidetes' absence regained power. Either of these possibilities (that he was left in power because most suitable, or regained power in spite of the Seleucids) would suggest that there was no comparable candidate for the high priesthood and no substantial aristocratic opposition to Hasmonean rule – at least none capable of keeping Hyrcanus out. Had there been any extended civil war we should probably have heard of it. This would indicate that Ptolemy, Hyrcanus' brother-in-law, had no great following and that Simon had eliminated from power or co-opted the earlier priestly opposition. Admittedly, the weight of Roman influence and the personal preferences of Sidetes are not known, so the political make-up of Judean society at this point cannot be reconstructed with complete confidence. However, it does seem likely that the Romans said little and did nothing, and that Sidetes' personal preference would have been to get rid of a dangerous local leader. Thus the suppositions that Hyrcanus had strong support from the Judean population, and that his opponents could muster nothing comparable, are hard to avoid. The certain things are that Sidetes conquered both the country and the city, but after his debacle Hyrcanus was again, or still, in power.

Hyrcanus' Conquests

After the death of Antiochus VII, Demetrius II became king for the second time, but was too weak to reassert his rule over Judea (*Ant.* 13.267). Hyrcanus used the lack of Seleucid power for a series of conquests beyond the borders of Judea. The chronology of these events is doubtful because the evidence is imprecise, implausible, and sometimes contradictory.[19] For most of these conquests no motives are stated and

---

[18]M. Pucci, "An Unknown Source on a Possible Treaty Between Hyrcanus I and the Parthians," *Zion* 46 (1981) 331-338 (in Hebrew); *idem*, "Jewish-Parthian Relations in Josephus," *Jerusalem Cathedra* 3 (1983) 13-25.

[19]*J.W.* 1.62 is not precise, but would normally be read as putting these conquests *during* the eastern campaign of Antiochus Sidetes. However, the

conjectures based on national, historical, religious, military, political, or economic considerations are possible but hazardous. According to Josephus (*J.W.* 1.63; *Ant.* 13.255), Hyrcanus first besieged Medaba, in Transjordan, and conquered it after a difficult six-month siege. This account is dubious because *Ant.* 14.18 reports that Alexander Janneus took Medaba from the Arabs. Furthermore, it is strange that Hyrcanus early in his reign should have spent so much time and energy at a relatively distant place.[20] The next town Hyrcanus allegedly captured, Samaga, is unknown.[21] The following Σικιμά τε πρὸς τούτοις in *Ant.* 13.255 may indicate that both it and "Medaba" were near Shechem.

Josephus goes on to say that Hyrcanus conquered Shechem and Mount Gerizim, subdued the "Cutheans" and laid waste their temple (*J.W.* 1.63; *Ant.* 13.255-256). Josephus dates these conquests during or immediately after the failure of Antiochus VII's eastern campaign (129 BCE). But the final destruction of Shechem is dated by the excavators not earlier than 112/1 BCE on the basis of a coin of that year found in context.[22]

Again we do not know for sure what caused this action, but the results are clear. Shechem was reduced to a village, the temple on Mt. Gerizim remained in ruins until it was replaced by a temple of Zeus Hypsistos in the time of Hadrian. The destruction of their temple may have persuaded some Samaritans to transfer their worship to Jerusalem, but most of them seem to have continued their cult on Mt. Gerizim, and intensified their hatred of Judeans. Many scholars think

---

supposition that they occurred then is hard to reconcile with the above-cited statement of Nicholas of Damascus (*Ant.* 13.250), and is ruled out by *Ant.* 13.254, which looks like a revision of *J.W.* 1.62.

[20]The problems have correctly been pointed out by Möller-Schmitt, *Siedlungen,* pp. 136-137. Avi-Yonah, (*Carta's Atlas,* p. 38) suggests that by conquering Medaba and nearby towns the Hasmoneans gained control over a section of the "Royal Road" from Eilat to Damascus. Relations between the earlier Hasmoneans and the residents of Medaba had not been good (see 1 Macc 9:36-42). If the name Medaba is corrupt, the town may have been the place now called Marda (Israel Archaeological Survey Map, Benjamin and Ephraim, 169 169). The survey has uncovered no hellenistic remains in the area and the name Marda is not attested in antiquity, but the geographic location, on the way from Jerusalem to Samaria, is suitable.

[21]*AJ* 13.255; *J.W.* 1.63. For different attempts to identify Samaga see Möller-Schmitt, *Siedlungen,* p. 164. G. Foerster, "The Conquests of John Hyrcanus I in Moab and the Identification of Samaga-Samoge," *Eretz Israel* 15 (1981) 353-355.

[22]G.E. Wright, *Shechem: The Biography of a Biblical City* (New York: McGraw-Hill, 1965) p. 172; *BASOR* 148, p. 27; see R.J. Bull and G.E. Wright, "Newly Discovered Temples on Mt. Gerizim in Jordan," *HTR* 58 (1965) 234-237; also *BA* 31 (1968) 58-72.

that the destruction of the temple made the split between the two cult communities final.

Hyrcanus next marched into Idumea in the South, captured Adora, Marisa and other towns, and made all Idumeans his subjects (*J.W.* 1.63; *Ant.* 13.257). As a condition of remaining in the country, they accepted circumcision and observance of the "laws of the Jews" (*Ant.* 13.257-258). This policy (not mentioned in the shorter account in *J.W.*) had an enduring effect. Idumea later became part of the Roman province of Judea (*J.W.* 2.96, 117) and Idumeans participated in the Great Revolt on the side of the Zealots (*Ant.* 17.254; *J.W.* 4.233-353).

A similar policy of conversion of non-Israelites as a prerequisite for their remaining in the country is attested for Aristobulus I, where Josephus cites Timagenes,[23] and for Alexander Janneus (*Ant.* 13.397). It is also ascribed, anachronistically, to Mattathias (1 Macc 2:46), who supposedly with his friends "circumcised by force all uncircumcised boys they found within the borders of Israel." This policy may have been intended to unify the country and strengthen Hasmonean power,[24] but it may also have expressed beliefs about the nature and importance of purity, of which the basic premise was that all inhabitants of the Holy Land should be Jewish.[25] It is noteworthy that this policy appeared – with the possible exception of Mattathias – only in the reigns of those Hasmoneans who maintained a numerous force of mercenaries, probably uncircumcised. Whether there were theological reasons for this different treatment, or whether it was a matter of convenience is uncertain.

The middle years of Hyrcanus' rule are almost completely unknown. Josephus says that after the death of Demetrius II (126/5 BCE), Alexander Zabinas (died 123 BCE), another Seleucid pretender, made an alliance (φιλία) with Hyrcanus. He adds that after the death of Antiochus VII Hyrcanus did not furnish the Seleucids any assistance, either as a subject or as a friend.[26] At the time of Alexander and especially during the fratricidal wars of Antiochus VIII Grypus and Antiochus IX Cyzicenus, Hyrcanus "lived in peace" (*Ant.* 13.272). Seleucid weakness and internecine warfare now permitted what amounted to total independence for Judea.

---

[23] *Ant.* 13. 318-319; Stern, *Greek and Latin Authors* 1, no. 81.
[24] See M. Smith, Maccabean Conversions, pp. 5-7.
[25] See E. Will - C. Orrieux, *Ioudaïsmos - Hellènismos*, pp. 191-193, 196. The question was raised again at the time of the war with Rome. See Josephus, *Life* 112, 149.
[26] *Ant.* 13.269, 273.

Between 113 and 107 BCE Hyrcanus started a major military expedition aimed mainly at the city of Samaria.[27] Allegedly he hated the Samarians "because of the injuries they had inflicted, in obedience to the Syrian kings, on the people of Marisa (Μαρισηνους) who were colonists and allies of the Judeans" (*Ant.* 13.275). It has frequently been pointed out that Μαρισηνους is probably corrupt. Marisa in Idumea, recently conquered by Hyrcanus, was about forty miles from Samaria, and south of Judea, where the Samaritans could not possibly get at it. Moreover, the people of Marisa were not, as far as we know, colonists from Judea. Therefore, several conjectures have been suggested.[28] Perhaps Marcus points in the right direction when he thinks of Jewish colonists in the territory of Samaria conquered by Hyrcanus.[29] An intriguing possibility is that ΜΑΡΙΣΗΝΟΥΣ is a corruption of ΓΑΡΙΖΕΙΝΟΥΣ/ΓΑΡΙΣΗΝΟΥΣ, i.e. the people around Mt. Gerizim. These represented the old, largely Israelite, population of "the hill-country of Ephraim," continued the old cult of Yahweh on their holy mountain, were commonly thought to be Jews, and sometimes claimed to be so.[30] They probably included a good many descendants of refugees escaped from Samaria when that city was destroyed and resettled by Macedonians.[31] Accordingly, there was probably even more than the usual neighborly hostility between the two towns and grounds for Hyrcanus' claim of injuries were probably plentiful. By taking up the cause of the *"Garizeinoi"* Hyrcanus was not only continuing Judah Maccabee's policy of intervention on behalf of Jewish – now, rather, Israelite – populations in the north, but was also bidding for their support. In his (earlier) conquest of Shechem and destruction of the Gerizim temple (*Ant.* 13. 255-256) he may have attempted to induce the

---

[27]*J.W.* 1.64-66; *Ant.* 13.275-281. The date is indicated by the references to Ptolemy Lathyrus (*Ant.* 13.278) who was coregent with his mother Cleopatra (III) 116-107 BCE and to Antiochus Cyzicenus (*Ant.* 13.276), whose dated coins start in 113 BCE See E. Will, *Histoire* 2.369-376. The fact that Cleopatra almost deposed her son when she found out he had furnished troops to Cyzicenus does not date this event toward the end of their coregency as is frequently assumed. Mother and son had trouble with each other from its beginning. *J.W.* 2.65 mentions Antiochus Aspendius (i.e., VIII Grypus) instead of Cyzicenus. The later version in *Ant.* seems to be a correction of this, confirmed by the course of events. See Schürer-Vermes-Millar 1, p. 210 n. 22.

[28]See Möller-Schmitt, *Siedlungen*, p. 134.

[29]In a note on *Ant.* 13.275 (LCL). Avi-Yonah, *Carta's Atlas*, p. 39, along similar lines, suggests Gerasa (Γερασηνους?), which he identifies with Guris (location 180 167).

[30]See Smith, *Palestinian Parties*, 188-192.

[31]Evidence for Macedonian settlement is cited and discussed by R. Marcus, *Josephus* (LCL), vol. 6, Appendix C, pp. 523-524.

"Garizeinoi" to worship in Jerusalem, but if such an attempt was made, it had not been wholly successful. Now, by action against the Macedonians, the ancestral enemies of the *"Garizeinoi,"* he may have hoped to conciliate many of the hold-outs and also to put himself at the head of the general native resistance to foreign rule. In this he may have been partly successful. The extraordinary speed with which Hasmonean power now spread across Palestine may be explicable in part on ethnic grounds, by the friendliness of the Israelite element in the rural population toward a power that could and did claim to represent the Israelite tradition. That the dynastic propaganda of 1 Macc chose the Book of Judges for its model was surely no accident.

In the first step to the conquest of the north (the attack on Samaria) the country population seems to have cooperated with the Hasmoneans or at least done nothing to hinder them. Hyrcanus was able to construct a ditch and a double wall around the city and put his two older sons Antigonus and Aristobulus in charge of the siege. The besieged called for and received assistance from Antiochus Cyzicenus, but his relief effort was unsuccessful. He was defeated and pursued as far as Scythopolis (Beth-shan). The siege was resumed. After a second call for help, Cyzicenus managed to get 6000 men from Ptolemy Lathyrus, against the wishes of Cleopatra, who had Jews among her staunchest supporters.[32] Cyzicenus did not dare to engage Hyrcanus in open battle, but ravaged his territory, thereby hoping to force an end to the siege of Samaria. Hyrcanus, however, had sufficient resources to continue the siege and inflict heavy casualties on Cyzicenus' mercenaries. Cyzicenus finally made his way to Tripolis, leaving two of his commanders in charge of operations in Palestine. One of them, Callimandrus, was killed in action, the other allegedly betrayed Scythopolis and other nearby places to the Judeans, but was unable to relieve Samaria.[33] The

---

[32] *Ant.* 13.284-287, including a quote from Strabo. It may be noted that Hyrcanus found himself on the same side of the conflict as his potential rivals, the descendants of Onias IV. We cannot be sure that this meant a rapprochement between Hasmoneans and Oniads because too many unknown factors are involved in the struggles between Ptolemaic and Seleucid factions. A rapprochement is suggested by Josephus who later has Ananias, a son of Onias IV, say to Cleopatra: "An injustice done to this man [Alexander Janneus] will make all of us Jews your enemies" (*Ant.* 13.354).

[33] *Ant.* 13.280. *J.W.* 1.66 says that the region of Scythopolis was overrun by Hyrcanus' troops *after* the fall of Samaria and knows nothing of betrayal. *Megillat Taanit* forbids fasting on 15 and 16 Sivan (June) because on those days "the men of Beth-shan and the men of the valley went into exile." M. Avi-Yonah ("Scythopolis," *IEJ* 12 [1962] 123-134) thinks that *Megillat Taanit* refers to voluntary emigration in the first century BCE. Lichtenstein (Fastenrolle, pp. 288-289) attributes this event to the time of Hyrcanus. Did the people of Scythopolis

date the wall of Samaria was taken is recorded as 25 Marheshvan (November or early December) in *Megillat Taanit*. Josephus says that the city was totally destroyed. Evidence of destruction attributable to the time of Hyrcanus has been found during excavation.[34]

In *J.W.* 1.65-66, Josephus adds that the inhabitants of Samaria were enslaved and that Hyrcanus' troops overran the whole country as far as Mount Carmel, but gives no details of these additional conquests. Several coastal cities south of Mount Carmel, including Straton's Tower, were not conquered until the time of Alexander Janneus (*Ant.* 13.324, 396).

Internal Affairs of John Hyrcanus

Several aspects of the internal life of the country are touched upon in a variety of sources. An important piece of information is a letter to Egyptian Jews, dated in or shortly before Kislev 188 Sel. (124 BCE).[35] It contains an effusive prayer for divine assistance to the recipients, a quote from an earlier letter, and an exhortation to celebrate "the days of Tabernacles in the month of Kislev" (2 Macc 1:9).

Two striking facts emerge: (1) Neither the high priest John Hyrcanus nor any other official appears as sender in what should be two official communications,[36] and (2) the feast of the month of Kislev is not explicitly connected here with the rededication of the Temple as it is in 1 Macc 4:59 and in *Megillat Taanit*.[37] This suggests that the memory of the events of Kislev 164 BCE was alive, but not necessarily closely connected with Judah and the Hasmoneans. The senders of the letter are identified as "the brethren, the Jews in Jerusalem and those in the countryside of Judea" (v 1). Who they were or if they had any official status we do not know. At least it appears that there were people independent and ambitious enough to send such a letter without express involvement of the high priest.[38]

---

perhaps suffer the fate that the Idumeans had avoided by undergoing circumcision (*Ant.* 13.257-258)?

[34]J.W. Crowfoot, K.M. Kenyon and E.L. Sukenik, *Samaria Sebaste*, vol. 1, *The Buildings at Samaria* (London, 1942), pp. 28-31, 121; G.A. Reisner et al., *Harvard Excavations at Samaria* 1908-1910 , vol. 1 (Cambridge, MA, 1924), pp. 50-58.

[35]2 Macc 1:1-10a. See Bickerman, Festbrief (= *Studies* 2.136-158).

[36]This omission distinguishes these two letters from Christian encyclical letters cited as parallels by Bickerman (*Studies* 2.145).

[37]Cf. 2 Macc 1:18; 10:6.

[38]Bunge (*Untersuchungen* p. 91) suggests that the letter was composed by Pharisees and that the omission of John Hyrcanus' name is evidence for a break between Pharisees and Hasmoneans before 124 BCE. These suggestions go beyond the evidence which does indicate, however, that the letter came

The economic condition of the country seems to have improved, beginning with the recovery after the invasion of Antiochus VII. We know of no further foreign interference during the time of Hyrcanus, except for the raids of Cyzicenus during the siege of Samaria. His 6000 men could have done considerable damage, but apparently they did not cause any major disruption in the life of the country. Presumably Judea paid no taxes or tribute to any Seleucid after Antiochus VII Sidetes, so that revenues remained in the country and a substantial portion accrued to Hyrcanus.[39]

Hyrcanus and the Pharisees

Josephus states: "Envy toward the good fortune of John and his children roused a στάσις ("sedition" or "faction") among his countrymen and a numerous opposition gathered and did not acquiesce until, after having been stirred up to open war, they were defeated" (*J.W.* 1.67). This cryptic statement is all that *J.W.* tells us about popular opposition to Hyrcanus. It may simply be a *topos* to explain opposition against a successful ruler. *Ant.*, on the other hand, is even more enigmatic. According to *Ant.* 13.288, Hyrcanus' good fortune caused envy among the Jews and according to 13.299 he brought the *stasis* to an end. What is described in between, however, is not civil war, but a banquet that ended in a rift between Hyrcanus and the Pharisees, as a result of which Hyrcanus went over to the Sadducees and annulled the laws the Pharisees had imposed on the people. The entire story of banquet, dispute, Pharisees, Sadducees, and legal consequences is known to *Ant.*, not to *J.W.*, and in *Ant.* comes as an interruption of the *J.W.* story.[40] Josephus has certainly taken it from a peculiar source. The

---

from a religious group in Judea not connected with Hyrcanus. Since the legend in *Ant.* 13.288-298 reports that Hyrcanus went over from the Pharisees to the Sadducees, it is tempting to suppose that the letter came either from the Sadducees before, or from the Pharisees after his change of sides. But there may have been other groups as well. One may think of the חבר היהודים or its representatives; but neither the character of this governmental body nor its possible relation to the senders of the letter can be ascertained. See D. Jeselsohn, "Hever Yehudim – A New Jewish Coin," *PEQ* 112 [1980] 14, for discussion and bibliography.

[39]*Ant.* 13.273: During the fratricidal wars of the Seleucids Hyrcanus was able "to exploit Judea undisturbed (!), with the result that he accumulated an unlimited amount of money."

[40]Both *J.W.* 1.67 and *Ant.* 13.288 say that Hyrcanus' good fortune caused envy. *J.W.* immediately continues to say that *stasis* arose, and was put down by Hyrcanus, who lived happily ever after. *Ant.* instead inserts the banquet story (13.288-298) before rejoining *J.W.* in mentioning the *stasis* that was put down by Hyrcanus, who lived happily ever after (13.299).

same source is evident in a close parallel in the Babylonian Talmud (*b. Qidd.* 66a).[41]

Both Josephus and the Talmud speak of a banquet given by a high priest Hyrcanus (*Ant.*)/King Yannai (*b. Qidd.*) for the Pharisees/all the Sages of Israel. At table, one Eleazar/Judah ben Gedidiah suggested that Hyrcanus/Yannai renounce the high priesthood and be content with secular rule, allegedly because his mother had been a captive, making him ineligible for the high priesthood. The allegation was false and all the Pharisees/Sages were indignant. However, a certain Jonathan/Eleazar ben Poirah told the host that all the Pharisees were against him. Consequently Hyrcanus/Yannai took measures against them and abandoned their teachings. The archvillain in both accounts is Eleazar, although in *Ant.* he is associated with the Pharisees, whereas in the Talmud he takes the place of Josephus' Sadducee Jonathan.

These common elements suffice to prove that there is a literary or traditional relationship between the two stories, though we are unable to determine its nature.[42] There are also, however, important differences: The names of the principals involved change, a frequent occurrence in legend.[43]

The Talmud adds several details not in Josephus: King Yannai had gone to Kohalit in the desert and conquered sixty towns there.[44] Furthermore, Eleazar ben Poirah asked the king to test the Pharisees and thereby caused the whole controversy. At the end, all the Sages were massacred[45] at the instigation of Eleazar – "and the world was

---

[41]For detailed comparisons of the banquet stories in Josephus and in the Talmud see J. Neusner, *The Rabbinic Traditions About the Pharisees Before 70* (Leiden: Brill, 1971) Part I, pp. 173-176; J. Efron, *Studies on the Hasmonean Period* (SJLA 39, Leiden: Brill, 1987) pp. 161-189. Both Neusner and Efron consider Josephus' rendition more trustworthy.

[42]Le Moyne (*Sadducéens.* pp. 54-55) gives a translation of yet a third account from a late medieval Samaritan text. As far as I can see, it used no ancient source other than Josephus.

[43]Abbaye, who transmitted the talmudic account, thought Yohanan (John Hyrcanus) and Yannai (Alexander Janneus) were the same person. See *b. Ber.* 29a. Thus no weight can be attributed to the name Yannai here, although the tradition *may* have referred originally to Alexander Janneus.

[44]The location of Kohalit is unknown, but the same name occurs four times in the Copper Scroll of Qumran, 3Q15 i.9; ii.13; iv.11-12; xii.10. See J.T. Milik, *DJD* 3, pp. 274-275.

[45]This trait reappears in a different story in which the sages were killed by the angel Gabriel when they failed to support Simeon ben Shetach in a court case against King Yannai and his servant (*b. Sanh.*19a-b).

desolate until Simeon ben Shetach restored the Torah." None of these details is historically reliable.

Josephus' account is fuller, but presents additional problems. He explains why the Pharisees were accused of being in agreement with the slanderer: they suggested a lenient sentence for him (*Ant.* 13.294). He also adds that Hyrcanus asked the Pharisees to tell him of any wrong he had inadvertently done. The Pharisees found no fault with him.[46]

Beyond this, Josephus mentions the Sadducees and is more specific about the roles of Pharisees and Sadducees and their relations to Hyrcanus and to each other. He states that among all the Jews, the Pharisees were most hostile to Hyrcanus and stresses their power and influence with the masses (13.288). He then goes on to say that Hyrcanus was (or: had been)[47] a pupil (μαθητής) of theirs and was (imperfect) greatly loved by them. Later on, he speaks of "the hatred of the masses" for Hyrcanus (13.296), who "lived happily thereafter" (299).[48] Some of these inconsistencies may have been caused by later copyists, but others are certainly due to Josephus' carelessness.

These contradictions and the omission of the Pharisees in *J.W.*[49] make us doubt Josephus' statements about their importance at the time of Hyrcanus, and about Hyrcanus' Pharisaism. Similarly, Josephus and several rabbinic texts report that Hyrcanus, while officiating in the Temple, heard a voice saying that his sons had just defeated Antiochus.[50] Such a story would hardly have been transmitted by his enemies.

After relating briefly that Hyrcanus died after having governed excellently for thirty-one years, Josephus ends both of his accounts of Hyrcanus by referring to the three extraordinary gifts he received: rule of the nation, high priesthood, and prophecy.[51] This accords with

---

[46]*Ant.* 13.289-290. For a king questioning sages at a banquet see *Letter of Aristeas* 187-292.

[47]The text is uncertain at this point. One group of manuscripts, preferred by Niese, uses the imperfect ἦν, the other group, preferred by Naber, has the pluperfect ἐγεγόνει. Whatever the precise meaning of μαθητής in this context, the term does not characterize Hyrcanus as a Pharisee.

[48]The latter passage is taken again from *J.W.* or its source. In *J.W.* 1.68 it is also said that he enjoyed invariable good fortune.

[49]On the peculiarity of *Ant.* in its treatment of the Pharisees see above, *Introduction* n. 53. Cf. also D.R. Schwartz, "Josephus and Nicolaus of Damascus on the Pharisees," *JSJ* 14 (1983) 157-172.

[50]*Ant.* 13.282-283; *t. Sota* 13:5; *b. Sota* 33a; *y. Sota* 9:13. In the rabbinic texts "Antiochia" must be emended to "Antiochus."

[51]*J.W.* 2.68-69; *Ant.* 23.299-300. There is, however, no evidence that Hyrcanus was considered the prophet (or, the sort of prophet) whose coming was

Josephus' generally favorable attitude towards the Hasmoneans, especially after he had discovered that he was descended from them (*Life* 4-5). This attitude leads us to assign anti-Hasmonean elements to pre-Josephan and *perhaps* more reliable sources.

Here again the viewpoint is totally different from that of the banquet story: to hold both secular and priestly office – in addition to the gift of prophecy – is a sign of distinction, even of divine favor. Josephus' source for this passage is not certain, but Nicholas of Damascus is often assumed.[52] The idea of the triple office was hellenistic, but may have been current in Jewish circles quite early, even before Philo.[53] It is in striking contrast to the suggestion that Hyrcanus should be content with secular rule.[54] Perhaps the idea of the triple office was used by the Hasmoneans to counter such a challenge.

Rabbinic Traditions About the High Priest Yohanan

Rabbinic tradition attributes several legal changes to a high priest Yohanan, commonly identified as John Hyrcanus I: (1) He did away with the declaration concerning tithe, (2) he made an end to the "Awakeners" and (3) to the "Stunners," (4) until his day the hammer used to strike in Jerusalem, and (5) in his days there was no need to inquire concerning *demai*-produce. This terse collection is found at the very end of the Mishnah tractate *Maaser Sheni* (5:15) and is repeated and discussed in other rabbinic texts.[55] These traditions are old, but we do not know how old. It is hardly necessary to doubt that they

---

expected according to 1 Macc 4:46 and 14:41. Such a prophet was expected to dispose of the stones of the defiled altar, but their storage place was still remembered in Mishnaic times (*m. Middot* 1:6). Contrast K. Fischer, *Die Herrschaft der Hasmonäer - Idee und Wirklichkeit* (diss.; Jena, 1967), p. 3. Fischer thinks that Hyrcanus was considered a messianic priestly ruler and the expected prophet, but his prophetic predictions that his two older sons would not remain in power and that Alexander Janneus, whom he disliked, would rule, do not fit such a picture (*J.W.* 2.69; *Ant.* 13.300, 322).

[52]E.g., R. Meyer, *Tradition und Neuschöpfung im antiken Judentum* (Sitzungsberichte der sächsischen Akademie der Wissenschaften zu Leipzig, Phil.-hist. Klasse 110/2; Berlin: Akademie-Verlag, 1965), pp. 45-46.

[53]Dan 3:38 (LXX) laments the absence of ruler, prophet, leader and of sacrifices, but says nothing of the high priest - perhaps because Alcimus was on hand.

[54]*Ant.* 13.291; *b. Qidd.* 66a.

[55]*m. Sota* 9:10. Cf. *b. Sota* 48a. For other rabbinic texts dealing with the same matters and for discussion see J. Neusner, *Rabbinic Traditions About the Pharisees Before 70* (3 vols.; Leiden: Brill, 1971), Part 1, pp. 160-171; S. Lieberman, *Hellenism in Jewish Palestine* (2d ed.; New York: JTSA, 1963), pp. 139-143; P. Kieval, *The Talmudic View of the Hasmonean and Early Herodian Periods in Jewish History* (diss., Brandeis, 1970), pp. 39-41.

originally referred to John Hyrcanus. They deal with tithes (nos. 1 and 5), and according to talmudic and modern interpretation with Temple ritual (nos. 2 and 3). These are primarily priestly and levitical concerns. What is meant by the striking of hammers (no. 4) is not explained in the Mishnah, but is usually interpreted as referring to work on the intermediate days of festivals. Thus, the observance of festivals was made stricter. This is in accord with the wishes of the Mishnaic authors and their interpreters.

The rabbinic view of these changes was overwhelmingly favorable. These rulings were taken as valid precedent in rabbinic circles, although it is fairly evident that if Hyrcanus initiated changes in these areas he did so *qua* high priest, not *qua* Pharisee. Another rabbinic tradition attributes to him the preparation of two red heifers (*m. Para* 3:5), and this seems to have been regarded a sign of distinction. Similarly, a comment on Prov 10:27 ("The fear of the Lord prolongs life, but the years of the wicked will be short"), attributed to Rabbah bar Bar Hana of the late 3rd century (*b. Yoma* 9a), says that Yohanan was high priest for eighty years.

In rabbinic literature almost the sole unfavorable reference to the high priest Yohanan – apart from the banquet story – is, a generation after Rabbah bar Bar Hana, in a Baraita that appears among traditions of the same Abbaye who is associated with the banquet story. It repeats Rabbah bar Bar Hana's report that "Yohanan officiated as high priest for eighty years" but then adds "and in the end he became a heretic."[56] This looks like a reflection of the tradition of the banquet story.

The rabbinic tradition does not remember that Hyrcanus was a Pharisee or sage, nor does its view of him seem to have been much affected by his alleged break with the Pharisees. Josephus calls Hyrcanus a pupil of the Pharisees who broke his ties with them because they proposed too lenient a punishment for a detractor. But this account is inconsistent with itself and is contradicted by the context. The importance of the Pharisees is stressed, but this also contradicts the context (Hyrcanus' break with them did not prevent a long and happy rule) and seems due to Josephus' concerns when he wrote *Ant.* In fact, *J.W.* knows nothing of the Pharisees at this point. *J.W.* confirms only that at some point, probably toward the end of Hyrcanus' rule, internal troubles erupted in Judea and were quashed by Hyrcanus. What

---

[56]*b. Ber.* 29a. The printed versions have "Sadducee" instead of *min* (heretic), but this may be due to Christian censors.

role, if any, the Pharisees played in this situation is impossible to ascertain from the available evidence.[57]

The position of the Sadducees is even more uncertain. Nowhere else does their name occur in connection with events of Hasmonean history and, apart from Hyrcanus, the only individual identified as a member of the sect during this period is Jonathan, Hyrcanus' close friend even before his alleged break with the Pharisees. Josephus' silence about the Sadducees might be explained by his hostility toward them, but for the Hasmonean period ignorance is an equally possible and perhaps more likely reason. While the Talmud states that Yannai (Hyrcanus?) diverged from the teaching of the sages and did not give the written and oral Torah its proper place, it does not make him a Sadducee, but says that אפיקורסות (Epicureanism, heresy) entered him. Le Moyne maintains that the rabbinic tradition generally distinguishes quite clearly between Sadducees and heretics.[58]

Thus, the meaning of the report that Hyrcanus joined the Sadducees is unclear. The report first appears in *Ant.*, and it seems contradictory to the generally laudatory Pharisaic tradition about Hyrcanus. It also contradicts the implications of Josephus' statements – if taken together – that the Pharisees controlled the people (almost certainly false) and that Hyrcanus had a long, happy and fortunate rule (in the main, true). Perhaps the banquet story was meant to explain how a high priest who was not a Pharisee could be considered good, and why Pharisaic halakah had to be (re-)introduced in the time of Salome Alexandra (*Ant.* 13.408).[59] Confidence about the role of the Pharisees and the Sadducees and their relations to Hyrcanus is unjustified.

The Coins of John Hyrcanus I

The question as to when Hasmonean coinage started has caused animated debate, because Meshorer and others argued that Alexander Janneus was the first Hasmonean ruler to issue his own coinage. The situation has been radically altered by the recent finds of "Yehohanan" coins in excavations on Mount Gerizim and in a large hoard that is being purchased by the Hebrew University. In both cases, the only Hasmonean coins are those of Yehohanan. The hoard contains

---

[57]Some scholars think that King Yannai (=Alexander Janneus) is the correct name of the Pharisees' adversary and that the attribution of the banquet story to the time of Hyrcanus is false. See Goldstein, *1 Macc.*, pp. 67-71; cf. Le Moyne, *Sadducéens*, p. 59.

[58]*Sadducéens*, pp. 97-99.

[59]Neusner suggests that the tradition about Hyrcanus' switch to the Sadducees may have its origin in the fact that he was viewed in a favorable light by the later Sadducees (*Pharisees Before 70*, Part 1, pp. 162, 173).

all major types of Yehohanan coins plus Seleucid coins of the late second century BCE. The lack of coins of Alexander Janneus and the presence of the dated Seleucid coins have led Barag as well as Meshorer to assign now *all* Hasmonean Yehohanan coins to John Hyrcanus I.[60]

Several thousand of these coins are extant, all bronze and of small denomination.[61] On the reverse most of them show a double cornucopia, a common motif on Greek coins, finding its closest stylistic parallel on Seleucid issues of the 120s B.C.E.[62] On the obverse instead they bear a Hebrew inscription which reads יהוחנן (ה)(כ)הן (ה)(ה)גדול וחבר (ה)יהודים, or similar, commonly translated "Y(eh)ohanan the high priest and the assembly (or "council") of the Jews," or similar. Thus besides Hyrcanus a communal entity is mentioned as an additional minting authority. On a smaller number of coins (Meshorer's groups R through T) ראש חבר היהודים ("head of the assembly of the Jews"?) replaces וחבר (ה)יהודים. The precise meaning of this terminology escapes us. The relationship of the "assembly" to the *Gerousia* or to the Sanhedrin is not at all clear. Also, we can not be sure how inclusive or exclusive the term יהודים is in this context.[63]

Many of Hyrcanus' coins are poorly executed and some are very difficult to read. They could not have served any propaganda purpose; they would have seemed picayune symbols of autonomy. Their lack of any representations of humans or animals, suggests that a strict interpretation of the prohibition against graven images then prevailed (Exod 20:4; Deut 4:15-18). Hyrcanus' titles on his coins demonstrate that he considered himself first and foremost high priest, not secular ruler (if this distinction be justified), and that he did not exercise his authority by himself, but in conjunction with a corporate entity, the "assembly." How much his powers were restricted by it and how much influence this entity had, we cannot ascertain, but the appearance of both authorities on the coinage is practically proof that to this extent

---

[60]These new developments were first brought to my attention in the summer of 1988 by Prof. D. Barag and were confirmed in a conversation I had with Prof. Y. Meshorer. Both authorized me to use this information, although it has not yet been published elsewhere.

[61]Meshorer (*Ancient Jewish Coins*, Vol. 1, pp. 136-155, Plates 28-53) illustrates close to 300 different types. References to Hyrcanus II should now generally be corrected to Hyrcanus I.

[62]See P. Gardner, *Syria* (British Museum Coins), p. 82 nos. 6-9 (Alexander Zabinas); p. 85 no. 1 (Cleopatra Thea, 126/5 BCE).

[63]For the range of possible meanings of the term *Ioudaios* in this period see M. Smith, "The Gentiles in Judaism 125 BCE - CE 66" in a forthcoming volume of the *Cambridge History of Judaism* .

at least they acted in concert, and that the חבר (ה)יהודים was to some extent a supporting factor in the Hasmonean state.

Conclusion

During his thirty-one year rule Hyrcanus achieved considerable successes. After narrowly escaping an attempt on his life he was able to avert a takeover by his father's murderer, his own brother-in-law Ptolemy, the son of Abubus. Later he survived a protracted siege of Jerusalem, negotiated a peace settlement with Antiochus Sidetes and after the latter's death started conquering additional territory around Judea. He swept through Idumea whose inhabitants accepted Judaism as the price for being allowed to remain in the country. He also captured the most important centers of Samaria: Shechem with Mount Gerizim and the city of Samaria. He seems to have lost Joppa and Gezer for some time, but may have regained them and even have conquered a larger section of the coastal plain between Ascalon and Straton's Tower. His alleged conquests of Medaba in Transjordan and of "Samaga" cannot be verified.

We are able to identify several groups of people that made Hyrcanus' achievements possible. At first, even before his father's death he was in charge of the Hasmonean armed forces (1 Macc 13:53). These forces remained substantially loyal to him when Ptolemy attempted a coup. Another important factor was the favorable attitude toward him in Jerusalem "on account of his father's good deeds and their hatred for Ptolemy's lawlessness" (*J.W.* 1.55; slightly different *Ant.* 13.229). Because of this he was let into the city, while Ptolemy was shut out. As we have seen, by Hyrcanus' time a large proportion of the Temple staff must have been appointed by the Hasmoneans or at least was favorable to them. Hyrcanus' power was strengthened further by mercenary troops, though we do not know how important their role was.

Outside Judea Hyrcanus presumably acquired new manpower and some supporters in the newly conquered areas. Also, he maintained friendly relations with Rome which increased his prestige and perhaps helped to regain Joppa. Hyrcanus appears to have sought friendly relations with other foreign powers too. Pergamum received a Judean embassy on its way back from Rome and stressed the friendship that existed between Jews and Pergamenians purportedly from the time of Abraham (*Ant.* 14.252-255).

About Hyrcanus' relations with Egypt we have only indirect evidence. In the complex struggles between Seleucids and Ptolemies, both John Hyrcanus and the Oniads of Egypt found themselves in opposition to Ptolemy Lathyrus.[64] Later the Oniad Ananias is said to have defended Alexander Janneus before Cleopatra.[65] This rapprochement may have begun under Hyrcanus.

The Pharisees, whose pupil Hyrcanus was said to have been, do not appear anywhere in connection with Hyrcanus except in the story about his break with them – a story which may reflect Pharisaic apologetics. Since we know nothing about their earlier activities nor hear about them again until the very end of Alexander Janneus' reign (*Ant.* 13.401), it would be rash to draw any conclusions about the importance of their support of or opposition to Hyrcanus. Furthermore, *J.W.* is ignorant of them until the time of Salome Alexandra (76-67 B.C.E.) and then states that they grew into power with her.[66] We have shown above the possibility that 2 Macc may represent a Pharisaic outlook. It is critical of Hyrcanus' father, Simon, and not interested in any member of the Hasmonean family except Judah. But whether 2 Macc was written or redacted in Hyrcanus' time is not sure, though the writing of the epitome is often connected with the letter of 124 B.C.E. now attached to it.

Our knowledge about the Sadducees is even less certain. Hyrcanus' alleged friendship with the Pharisees did not prevent his also alleged friendship with the Sadducee Jonathan – and we know nothing about the activities of other Sadducees at this time, or at any time before Herod.

Support for Hyrcanus thus came from very different segments of society. First Maccabees is the most important piece of evidence for people who associated themselves closely with the Hasmonean family and its aspirations. As has been pointed out, 1 Macc was written to show the Hasmoneans as the new leaders of all Israel in the tradition of the ancient Judges. They have been chosen to save Israel and they have been faithful to their mission. In emphasizing Hasmonean achievements, 1 Macc obviously serves also an apologetic purpose, perhaps in an attempt to gain the confidence of Torah-observing Jews.

Opposition against Hyrcanus from a variety of quarters can be identified, starting from his own brother-in-law, Ptolemy, son of Abubus, and including Judeans as well as outsiders. Of the Seleucids, only Antiochus Sidetes and to some extent Cyzicenus presented a challenge to Hyrcanus and to Judean autonomy. The other Seleucids were no threat. In the newly conquered territories the priesthood of Samaria probably showed a high degree of hostility because Hyrcanus

---

[64]*Ant.* 13.278, 285.

[65]*Ant.* 13.354-355.

[66]*J.W.* 1.110: παραφύονται δὲ αὐτῆς εἰς τὴν ἐξουσίαν Φαρισαῖοι.

apparently was harsh with them: Shechem and the temple on Mt. Gerizim were destroyed, not to be rebuilt. Even harsher was the treatment of the Samarians. The city of Samaria suffered a long siege after which, according to *J.W.*, its inhabitants were sold into slavery. These were not Israelites, nor, probably Yahwists, but Macedonians; their fate and the annihilation of their city probably improved the status of Hyrcanus in the eyes of the old Samaritans (the Shechemites) and also of most Judeans. Among the people of Idumea and of Scythopolis animosity toward Hyrcanus may have been somewhat less intense, but certainly existed.

In Judea itself, the siege of Jerusalem and its handling by Hyrcanus was not easily forgotten. It must have created friction, especially if any of the citizens were left to starve outside the city walls. Josephus says a *stasis* arose toward the end of Hyrcanus' reign. We do not have sufficient information to assess the gravity of the situation – or who led the opposition against Hyrcanus in what may have been open rebellion. The Pharisees' involvement in this is at best unclear. The opposition of the Qumran sect seems to have expressed itself in internal emigration, hostile but obscure remarks in their unpublished works, and hopes for divine punishment, not by an open challenge to the Hasmonean government.

Despite such varied opposition, Hyrcanus seems to have remained popular. After he had overcome the *stasis* he is said to have lived happily. That he was credited with prophecies is a sign of reverence. In later rabbinic literature he was usually portrayed favorably.[67]

With Hyrcanus the Hasmoneans were securely established in Jerusalem. A symbol of the long way the Hasmoneans had come since the days of Mattathias was Hyrcanus' monumental tomb, not in Modein, but right outside the gates of Jerusalem, a landmark even in Josephus' time.[68]

---

[67]Cf. also *Tg. Ps.-J.* on Deut 33:11: "May the enemies of Yohanan the high priest have no leg to stand on." Who these enemies were is open to speculation. See Geiger, *Urschrift*, p. 479. For the popularity of Hyrcanus and the later Hasmoneans see, besides Kieval (n. 55 above), G. Alon, "Did the Jewish People and Its Sages Cause the Hasmoneans to Be Forgotten?" in *Jews, Judaism and the Classical World. Studies in Jewish History in the Time of the Second Temple and Talmud* (Jerusalem: Magnes, 1977) pp. 1-17; cf. pp. 31-34.
[68]See *J.W.* 5.259, 304, and passim.

Summary Conclusions

We have traced in some detail the development of what began as a small revolutionary movement in the village of Modein and became over the course of two generations the leading power in Judea and the surrounding areas.

We have tried to define who supported and who opposed the Hasmoneans at different periods and we have seen that original support came mostly from the rural areas of southern Samaria and northwestern Judea. We have seen that almost from the beginning the Hasmonean revolt involved people from different social classes: peasants, priests, and city dwellers. It also involved people of different religious outlooks.

The coalition, if we may use this term, which supported the Hasmoneans changed considerably over the years. The first goal of the revolt was the preservation of Temple and Torah. This was essentially accomplished after the validity of Jewish law was again approved by Antiochus Epiphanes and the Temple rededicated. The accomplishment of these goals, however, did not mean the end of the Hasmonean revolt and did not cause any immediately perceptible drop in support for the continued fight by the men around Judah Maccabee. To the contrary, Judah gained more supporters when he brought a part of the Jewish population of Gilead to Judea and settled them on land perhaps formerly owned by his opponents. Judah established good relations with Rome which were kept up by each of his three immediate successors. This demonstrates the Hasmoneans' willingness to cooperate with Gentiles when that seemed to further their goals, although 1 Macc portrays the Hasmoneans and their gentile neighbors as implacable enemies. Active support for the Hasmoneans diminished drastically after Alcimus, who was acceptable to Seleucids and *Asidaioi*, became high priest. Even though Judah died abandoned by almost everyone, he later became a national hero, not only among Hasmonean supporters, but also among people indifferent or hostile toward the later Hasmoneans, as 2 Macc shows.

Judah's brother Jonathan was able to continue for several years with a small band of stalwarts. In our sources he is less prominent than either Judah or Simon, but it was Jonathan who laid the foundations for the Hasmonean state. His assumption of the high priesthood represented another turning point which on one hand gave him added responsibility and power, but also must have antagonized part of the priestly establishment. Jonathan attained partial control of Judea mostly by cooperation with Seleucid governments, not confrontation. The expeditions of his army did not result in conquests, but his military successes enhanced his prestige at home and abroad. He probably was quite popular, because Simon feared adverse popular opinion in case he failed to do everything possible to have Jonathan released by Tryphon.

Although Jonathan died as a prisoner of Tryphon, Simon was able to take over without recognizable disruption, and where Jonathan apparently had failed to be fully accepted as high priest, Simon managed to have himself gradually confirmed in office by the populace, the Seleucid authorities and, last not least, by the Jerusalem aristocracy.

While in the early years of Simon there probably was important aristocratic opposition against the high priest from Modein, no such opposition is detectable under Hyrcanus. Even after Antiochus VII had conquered Jerusalem, Hyrcanus managed to stay in or return to power, apparently without encountering strong resistance.

It is sometimes asserted that after the Hasmoneans allied themselves with the Sadducees they lost the support of the populace. As we have shown, Hyrcanus did not lose popularity after his alleged break with the Pharisees. Even Alexander Janneus who was thoroughly hated by a substantial portion of the Judean population (*Ant.* 13.372-383), had an army that included reportedly 20,000 Jews "who favored his cause" (*Ant.* 13.377). Thus it would be wrong to identify the supporters of the Hasmoneans merely as Sadducees, even at the time of Alexander Janneus.

The Hasmoneans remained popular and their popularity was still of political importance even after their downfall, as events in the reign of Herod show.

Selected Bibliography

The following is a list of works cited, generally excluding items cited only once or twice. It is not meant to be exhaustive and does not include all standard works of reference.

Abel, F.-M. *Géographie de la Palestine,* Vol. 2, 3rd. ed. Paris: Gabalda, 1967.

----, *Les Livres des Maccabées.* Paris: Gabalda, 1949.

----, and Starcky, J. *Les Livres des Maccabées.* Paris: Cerf, 1961.

Aptowitzer, V. *Parteipolitik der Hasmonäerzeit im rabbinischen und pseudoepigraphischen Schrifttum.* Vienna/New York: Kohut Foundation, 1927.

Arenhoevel, D. *Die Theokratie nach dem 1. und 2. Makkabäerbuch.* Walberberger Studien, Theologische Reihe, Bd. 3; Mainz: Grünewald, 1967.

Avi-Yonah, M. *Carta's Atlas of the Period of the Second Temple, the Mishnah and the Talmud.* Jerusalem: Carta, 1966.

----, *Gazetteer of Roman Palestine.* Qedem V. Monographs of the Institute of Archaeology. The Hebrew University of Jerusalem, 1976.

Badian, E. *Foreign Clientelae (264-70 B.C.).* Oxford: Oxford U. Pr., 1958.

Bar-Kochva, B. "Manpower, Economics, and Internal Strife in the Hasmonean State," *Colloques Nationaux du Centre National de la Recherche Scientifique,* No. 936, *Armées et fiscalité dans le monde antique.* Paris, 1977, pp. 173-185.

----, *The Seleucid Army: Organization and Tactics in the Great Campaigns.* Cambridge/New York: Cambridge Univ. Pr., 1976.

----, *The Battles of the Hasmoneans. The Times of Judas Maccabaeus.* Jerusalem: Yad Izhak Ben-Zvi Pub., 1980 (in Hebrew; English ed. announced).

Berman, D. "Hasidim in Rabbinic Traditions," in *Society of Biblical Literature 1979 Seminar Papers,* vol. 2, ed. P.J. Achtemeyer. Missoula: Scholars Press, 1979, pp. 15-33.

Bévenot, H. *Die beiden Makkabäerbücher.* Bonn, 1931.

Bi(c)kerman(n), E.J. *Chronology of the Ancient World.* 2nd ed. Ithaca: Cornell, 1980.

----, *From Ezra to the Last of the Maccabees.* New York: Schocken, 1962.

----, *Institutions des Séleucides.* Paris: Geuthner, 1938.

----, *Der Gott der Makkabäer.* Berlin: Schocken, 1937. English translation (without footnotes): *The God of the Maccabees. Studies on the Meaning and Origin of the Maccabean Revolt.* Leiden: Brill, 1979. References are to the German edition, unless otherwise noted.

----, *Studies in Jewish and Christian History.* Part 2. Leiden: Brill, 1980.

Bloch, H. *Die Quellen des Flavius Josephus in seiner Archäologie.* Leipzig, 1879; reprint Wiesbaden: Sandig, 1968.

Bringmann, K. *Hellenistische Reform und Religionsverfolgung in Judäa. Eine Untersuchung zur jüdisch-hellenistischen Geschichte (175-163 v. Chr.).* Göttingen: Vandenhoeck & Ruprecht, 1983.

Broughton, T.R.S. *The Magistrates of the Roman Republic.* 2 vols. APA, 1951-60.

Bunge, J.G. *Untersuchungen zum zweiten Makkabäerbuch. Quellenkritische, literarische, chronologische und historische Untersuchungen zum zweiten Makkabäerbuch als Quelle syrisch-palästinensischer Geschichte im 2. Jh. v. Chr.* Diss., Bonn, 1971.

----, "Zur Geschichte und Chronologie des Untergangs der Oniaden und des Aufstiegs der Hasmonäer," *JSJ* 6 (1975) 1-46.

Burgmann, H. "Das umstrittene Intersacerdotium in Jerusalem 159-152 v. Chr.," *JSJ* 11 (1980) 135-176.

Cardauns, B. "Juden und Spartaner," *Hermes* 95 (1967) 317-324.

Charlesworth, J.H. "The Origin and Subsequent History of the Authors of the Dead Sea Scrolls: Four Transitional Phases Among the Qumran Essenes," *RevQ* 10 (1980) 213-233.

Cohen, S.J.D. *Josephus in Galilee and Rome: His Vita and Development as a Historian.* Leiden: Brill, 1979.

Cross, F.M. *The Ancient Library of Qumran and Modern Biblical Studies.* Rev. ed.; Garden City: Doubleday, 1961.

Danby, J.C. *1 Maccabees. A Commentary.* Oxford: Blackwell, 1954.

Davies, P. "Hasidim in the Maccabean Period," *JJS* 28 (1977).

Doran, R. *Temple Propaganda: The Purpose and Character of 2 Maccabees.* CBQMS 12. Washington, D.C.: Catholic Biblical Association, 1981.

Efron, J. *Studies on the Hasmonean Period* SJLA 39, Leiden: Brill, 1987.

Ettelson, H.W. "The Integrity of I Maccabees," *Transactions of the Connecticut Academy of Arts and Sciences* 27 (1925) 249-384.

Feldman, L.H. *Josephus and Modern Scholarship (1937-1980)*. Berlin: De Gruyter, 1984.

----, *Josephus. A Supplementary Bibliography*. New York: Garland, 1986.

Fischer, K. *Die Herrschaft der Hasmonäer - Idee und Wirlichkeit*. Diss., Jena, 1967.

Fischer, T. *Untersuchungen zum Partherkrieg Antiochos' VII. im Rahmen der Seleukidengeschichte*. Diss., Tübingen, 1970.

----, *Seleukiden und Makkabäer*. Bochum: Brockmeyer, 1980.

Gafni, I. "On the Use of 1 Maccabees by Josephus Flavius," *Zion* 45 (1980) 81-95 (in Hebrew).

Gardner, P. *Catalogue of Greek Coins. The Seleucid Kings of Syria*. London: British Museum, 1878.

Gauger, J.D. *Beiträge zur jüdischen Apologetik*. Cologne/Bonn: Hanstein, 1977.

Geiger, A. *Urschrift und Übersetzungen der Bibel*. 2d ed.; Frankfurt/Main: Madda, 1928.

Giovannini, A. and Müller, H. "Die Beziehungen zwischen Rom und den Juden im 2. Jh. v. Chr.," *Museum Helveticum* 28 (1971) 156-171.

Goldstein, J.A. *1 Maccabees*. AB; Garden City, New York: Doubleday, 1976. Note numerous corrections in the next item!

----, *2 Maccabees*. AB; Garden City, New York: Doubleday, 1983.

----, "The Hasmoneans: The Dynasty of God's Resisters," *HTR* 68 (1975) 53-58.

----, "Tales of the Tobiads," in *Christianity, Judaism and Other Greco - Roman Cults: Studies for Morton Smith at Sixty*. Ed. J. Neusner; Leiden: Brill, 1975. 3.85-123.

Grimm, C.L.W. *Das erste Buch der Maccabäer*. Leipzig 1853.

----, *Das zweite, dritte und vierte Buch der Maccabäer*. Leipzig, 1857.

Habicht, C. "Der Stratege Hegemonides," *Historia* 1958, pp. 376-378.

----, "Royal Documents in Maccabees II," *Harvard Studies in Classical Philology* 80 (1976) 1-18.

----, *2. Makkabäerbuch*. JSHRZ 1/3; Gütersloh: Mohn, 1976.

Hengel, M. *Judaism and Hellenism*. 2 vols. Philadelphia: Fortress, 1974.

Herr, M.D. "The Problem of War on the Sabbath in the Second Temple and the Talmudic Periods," (in Hebrew) *Tarbiz* 30 (1960/61) 242-256.

Hölscher, G. *Die Hohenpriesterliste bei Josephus und die evangelische Chronologie*. Sitzungsberichte der Heidelberger Akademie der Wissenschaften. Phil.-Hist. Klasse. Band 30, 3. Abhandlung. Heidelberg: Winter, 1940.

Jacoby, F. *Fragmente der griechischen Historiker*. Berlin, 1923-.

Jeremias, G. *Der Lehrer der Gerechtigkeit.* Göttingen: Vandenhoeck & Ruprecht, 1963.

Jeremias, J. *Jerusalem in the Time of Jesus.* Philadelphia: Fortress, 1969.

Jeselsohn, D. "Hever Yehudim – A New Jewish Coin," *PEQ* 112 (1980) 11-17.

Kahana, A. *Ha-sefarim ha-hitzoniim.* Tel Aviv: Hozaat Meqorot, 1956.

Kappler, W. (ed.), *Maccabaeorum liber I.* Septuaginta: Vetus Testamentum Graecum Auctoritate Academiae Litterarum Gottingensis editum vol. IX fasc. 1, 2nd rev. ed. Göttingen: Vandenhoeck & Ruprecht, 1967.

Kappler, W., Hanhart, R. (ed.), *Maccabaeorum liber II.* Septuaginta: Vetus Testamentum Graecum Auctoritate Academiae Litterarum Gottingensis editum vol. IX fasc. 2, 2nd rev. ed. Göttingen: Vandenhoeck & Ruprecht, 1976.

Kieval, P. *The Talmudic View of the Hasmonean and Early Herodian Periods in Jewish History.* Diss., Brandeis, 1970.

Kippenberg, H.G. *Religion und Klassenbildung im antiken Judäa.* Göttingen: Vandenhoeck & Ruprecht, 1978.

Kolbe, W. *Beiträge zur syrischen u. jüdischen Geschichte.* Stuttgart, 1926.

Kreissig, H. "Der Makkabäeraufstand, zur Frage seiner sozial-ökonomischen Zusammenhänge und Wirkungen," *Studii Clasice* 4 (1962) 143-175.

Laqueur, R. *Der jüdische Historiker Flavius Josephus.* Giessen, 1920, reprinted Darmstadt: Wissenschaftliche Buchgesellschaft, 1970.

Le Moyne, J. *Les Sadducéens.* Paris: Gabalda, 1972.

Lichtenstein, H. "Die Fastenrolle. Eine Untersuchung zur jüdisch-hellenistischen Geschichte," *HUCA* 8-9 (1931-32) 257-351.

Lieberman, S. *Hellenism in Jewish Palestine.* 2d ed.; New York: JTSA, 1963.

Lindner, H. *Die Geschichtsauffassung des Flavius Josephus im Bellum Judaicum.* Leiden: Brill, 1972.

Maier, J. *Die Tempelrolle vom Toten Meer.* UTB 829; Reinhardt: Munich/Basle, 1978.

Mantel, M. *Studies in the History of the Sanhedrin.* Cambridge: Harvard Univ. Pr., 1965.

Mendels, D. *The Land of Israel as a Political Concept in Hasmonean Literature. Recourse to History in Second Century B.C. Claims to the Holy Land.* Tübingen: Mohr, 1987.

Meshorer, Y. *Ancient Jewish Coinage* Vol. 1: *Persian Period Through Hasmoneans.* Dix Hills, NY: Amphora Books, 1982.

Meyer, E. *Ursprung und Anfänge des Christentums.* Vol. 2; Stuttgart/Berlin: Cotta, 1921-1923.

Meyer, R. *Tradition und Neuschöpfung im antiken Judentum.* Sitzungsberichte der sächsischen Akademie der Wissenschaften zu Leipzig, Phil.-hist. Klasse 110/2; Berlin: Akademie-Verlag, 1965.

Mittwoch, A. "Tribute and Land Tax in Seleucid Judaea," *Biblica* 36 (1955) 352-361.

Mölleken, W. "Geschichtsklitterung im I. Makkabäerbuch (Wann wurde Alkimus Hoherpriester?)" *ZAW* 65 (1953) 208-228

Möller, C. and Schmitt, G. *Siedlungen Palästinas nach Flavius Josephus.* Wiesbaden: Reichert, 1976.

Momigliano, A. *Prime linee di storia della tradizione maccabaica.*Torino, 1931; reprinted Amsterdam: Hakkert, 1968.

Mørkholm, O. *Antiochus IV of Syria.* Classica et Mediaevalia, Dissertationes 8; Copenhagen: Gyldendal, 1966.

Murphy-O'Connor, J. "The Essenes and Their History," *RB* 81 (1974) 215-244.

Naveh, J. "Dated Coins of Alexander Janneus," *IEJ* 18 (1968) 20-26.

Neusner, J. *Rabbinic Traditions About the Pharisees Before 70.* 3 vols.; Leiden: Brill, 1971.

----, *The Idea of Purity in Ancient Judaism. The 1972-73 Haskell Lectures.* Leiden: Brill, 1973.

----, *A History of the Mishnaic Law of Purities, vol. 22: The Mishnaic System of Uncleanness: Its Context and History.* Leiden: Brill, 1977.

Niese, B. (ed.) *Flavii Iosephi Opera.* Berlin: Weidmann, 1887-1895.

----, *Kritik der beiden Makkabäerbucher.* Berlin: Weidmann, 1900.

Rappaport, U. "The Emergence of Hasmonean Coinage," *AJSreview* 1 (1976) 171-186.

Rivkin, E. *A Hidden Revolution.* Nashville: Abingdon, 1978.

Sachs, A.J. and Wiseman, D.J. "A Babylonian King List of the Hellenistic Period," *Iraq* 16 (1954) 202-211.

Safrai, S. "The Teaching of the Pietists in Mishnaic Literature," *JJS* 16 (1965) 15-33.

Schäfer, P. "The Hellenistic and Maccabean Periods," in J.H. Hayes and J.M. Miller, *Israelite and Judaean History.* Philadelphia: Westminster, 1977, pp. 539-604.

Schaumberger, J. "Die neue Seleukiden-Liste BM 35603 und die makkabäische Chronologie," *Biblica* 36 (1955) 423-435.

Schiffer, I.J. "The Men of the Great Assembly," in *Persons and Institutions in Early Rabbinic Judaism,* ed. W. S. Green. Brown Judaic Studies 3; Missoula: Scholars Pr., 1977, pp. 237-283.

Schunck, K.D. *Die Quellen des I. und II. Makkabäerbuches.* Halle: Niemeyer, 1954.

----, 1. Makkabäerbuch. JSHRZ 1/4; Gütersloh: Mohn, 1979.

Schürer, E. Geschichte des jüdischen Volkes im Zeitalter Jesu Christi. 3 vols. Leipzig, 1901-1909.

Schürer, E., Vermes, G., Millar F., et al., The History of the Jewish People in the Age of Jesus Christ. Rev. English edition. Edinburgh: Clark, 1973-87.

Sherk, R.K. Roman Documents from the Greek East. Baltimore: Johns Hopkins, 1969.

Smith, M. "Das Judentum in Palästina in der hellenistischen Zeit," in Der Hellenismus und der Aufstieg Roms. Die Mittelmeerwelt im Altertum II, ed P. Grimal. Fischer Weltgeschichte 6; Frankfurt/Main: Fischer, 1965, pp. 254-270, 382-384.

----, "Palestinian Judaism in the First Century," Israel: Its Role in Civilization. Ed. M. Davis; New York: Harper & Row, 1956, pp. 67-81.

----, Palestinian Parties and Politics That Shaped the Old Testament. New York: Columbia Univ. Pr., 1971.

----, "Rome and Maccabean Conversions: Notes on 1 Macc 8," in C.K. Barrett et al., Donum Gentilicium. Oxford: Oxford U.P., 1978, pp. 1-7.

----, "What Is Implied by the Variety of Messianic Figures?" JBL 78 (1959) 66-72.

Stegemann, H. Die Entstehung der Qumrangemeinde, Bonn (diss.), 1971.

Stern, M. The Documents on the History of the Hasmonaean Revolt. Hakibbutz Hameuchad, 2nd ed. 1972 (in Hebrew).

----, Greek and Latin Authors on Jews and Judaism. Jerusalem: Israel Academy of Sciences and Humanities, 1974-84.

Stone, M. Scriptures, Sects and Visions. Philadelphia: Fortress, 1980.

Tcherikover, V. Hellenistic Civilization and the Jews. Philadelphia: JPS, 1959.

Thackeray, H.St.J., Marcus, R., Wikgren, A., Feldman L.H., (ed.) Josephus. 9 vols. LCL Cambridge: Harvard Univ. Press, 1926-65.

VanderKam, J. Textual and Historical Studies in the Book of Jubilees. Missoula: Scholars Press, 1977.

Wacholder, B.Z. "The Calendar of Sabbatical Cycles During the Second Temple and the Early Rabbinic Period," HUCA (1973) 153-196.

----, "The Letter from Judah Maccabee to Aristobulus. Is 2 Maccabees 1:10b-2:18 Authentic?" HUCA 49 (1978) 89-133.

Welles, C.B. Royal Correspondence in the Hellenistic Period. New Haven: Yale, 1934.

Wellhausen, J. "Über den geschichtlichen Wert des zweiten Makkabäerbuches im Verhältnis zum ersten," Nachrichten von der

Gesellschaft der Wissenschaften zu Göttingen, Phil.-hist. Klasse (1905), pp. 117-163.

Will, E. *Histoire politique du monde héllenistique.* 2 vols. Nancy: Faculté des lettres et des sciences humaines de l'Université de Nancy, 1966-67.

Will, E., Orrieux, C. *Ioudaïsmos – Hellènismos.* Nancy: Presses Universitaires, 1986.

Willrich, H. *Urkundenfälschung in der hellenistisch-jüdischen Literatur.* Göttingen, 1924.

Yadin, Y. *The Temple Scroll* 3 vols. Jerusalem: Israel Exploration Society, 1977-83.

Zambelli, M. "La composizione del secondo libro dei Maccabei e la nuova cronologia di Antioco Epifane," *Miscellanea greca e romana.* Studi...Istituto Italiano per la storia antica, 16; Rome, 1965.

Zeitlin, S. *The Rise and Fall of the Judaean State.* 3 vols; Philadelphia: JPS, 1968-78.

Map of Palestine in the Hasmonean Period

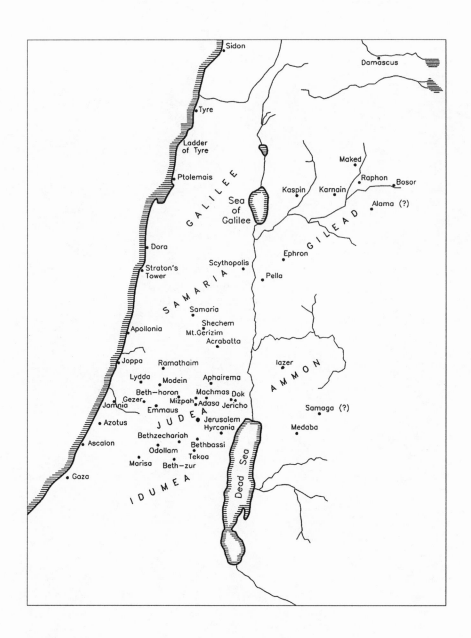

Index